Southern Parties and Elections

Southern Parties and Elections

Studies in Regional Political Change

Edited by
Robert P. Steed
Laurence W. Moreland
Tod A. Baker

The University of Alabama Press
Tuscaloosa and London

∞
The paper on which this book is printed meets the minimum requirements of
American National Standard for Information Science–Permanence of Paper for
Printed Library Materials, ANSI Z39.48–1984.

Library of Congress Cataloging-in-Publication Data

Southern parties and elections : studies in regional political change /
  edited by Robert P. Steed, Laurence W. Moreland, Tod A. Baker
    p.   cm.
  Includes bibliographical references and index.
  ISBN 0–8173–0862–8
  1. Political parties—Southern States.   2. Elections—Southern
States.   3. Southern States—Politics and government—1951–
I. Steed, Robert P.   II. Moreland, Laurence W.   III. Baker, Tod A.
JK2295.A13S66   1997
324.275—dc20   96–35563
                                                                                    CIP

British Library Cataloguing-in-Publication Data available

Contents

Part Two: Nominations, Elections, and Partisan Developments

Figures

Tables

Acknowledgments

This volume evolved from the Ninth Citadel Symposium on Southern Politics held at The Citadel in March 1994. Each of the chapters, except for the contribution by Richard Nadeau and Harold W. Stanley, was originally a paper presented at that conference. The symposium itself, directed by the editors of this volume, was facilitated by the efforts of a number of persons associated with The Citadel: Lieutenant General Claudius E. Watts III, president of the college, and Brigadier General R. Clifton Poole, vice president for academic affairs and dean of the college, both of whom have worked to promote the climate necessary for the pursuit of scholarship and professional development. We also appreciate the interest and support of the members of the Political Science Department at The Citadel, particularly its chair, Milton L. Boykin. We are especially grateful to The Citadel Development Foundation, whose financial support has been indispensable for the continuation of the symposia over almost two decades.

In relation to the development of the manuscript for *Southern Parties and Elections*, we are indebted to the discussants and other panel participants at the symposium whose comments and observations were helpful in revising the papers for inclusion in this volume. In addition, the comments and suggestions of two anonymous reviewers proved extremely helpful in developing the final manuscript. Finally, Malcolm M. MacDonald, Rick Cook, and other staff members of The University of Alabama Press worked diligently to smooth the publication process, and we wish to thank them for their invaluable assistance.

Southern Parties and Elections

Introduction

Changing Electoral and Party Politics in the South

Robert P. Steed

For approximately half a century, southern politics has been in the process of a remarkable transformation. The region emerged from World War II as solidly one-party Democratic, still devoted to racial segregation, and still largely dominated by small-town and rural areas operating through the mechanisms of malapportioned state legislatures.[1] In the intervening decades the Republican Party has become increasingly competitive, the Civil Rights movement and its legal and social successes have ended segregation and brought African-Americans into the social, economic, and political systems, and dramatic changes in constitutional law and in the region's population have diminished the power of the rural areas significantly.[2]

Within this broad framework of change, particular interest has developed regarding the changes in party and electoral patterns. For one thing, party realignments are such rare occurrences in American politics, even at the regional level, that when they do take place they generate great interest. Whether party change in the South constitutes a classic realignment is still being debated,[3] but there is little argument over whether significant party change has occurred and whether it is worthy of investigation.[4] Beyond this somewhat academic interest in realignment, there is the more immediate interest in the relationship between party change and southern electoral behavior, on the one hand, and larger patterns of national party and electoral politics, on the other. There is, for example, a strong case for the proposition that Republican successes in presidential elections since the 1960s have been greatly aided by the high levels of support rendered Republican candidates in the South.[5] Similarly, Republican gains in Congress, culminating in 1994 in control of both chambers for the first time in forty years, have been significantly bolstered by increased southern Republican support over recent decades.

The development of party competition in the South has been as slow as it has been dramatic. Although disaffection with the Democratic Party over its perceived liberal position on civil rights surfaced as early as 1948, the Republican Party was not the immediate beneficiary, as dissidents found an outlet for their unhappiness in the States' Rights Party. By 1952, however, with no viable third-party alternative, more than the usual numbers of southern voters cast their ballots for the Republican, Dwight Eisenhower, and he actually managed to carry four states (Texas, Florida, Tennessee, and Virginia). From that point onward, there developed a presidential Republicanism—sometimes interspersed with third-party and unpledged elector movements—that manifested itself with regularity through the 1950s, the 1960s, and the 1970s. From 1968 forward, the balance of power at the presidential level clearly shifted to the Republicans; Merle Black and Earl Black summarize this change by noting, "Over the past half century . . . the South has shifted [in presidential politics] from an overwhelmingly Democratic area to a region characterized initially by balanced competition between the two parties (1952–1964) and, more recently, by a distinct Republican advantage."[6] Only native southerner Jimmy Carter was able in 1976 to bring the South into the Democratic column, but even he did not carry a majority of the region's white vote.

During the 1980s the Republican success in presidential voting in the South continued as first Reagan and then Bush swept the region in 1984 and 1988. With two southerners on the ticket in 1992, the Democrats did better but still lost the region by sixty-nine electoral votes (108 to 39). Clinton and Gore carried their home states plus only two more, Georgia and Louisiana, and Clinton was only able to improve slightly on Dukakis's 1988 popular vote percentage (41.2 percent to 40.9 percent). On the other hand, the South was Bush's strongest region, giving him 108 of his 168 electoral votes.[7]

Below the presidential level, Republican growth came much more slowly, although it moved gradually in the direction of two-party competition over time.[8] Although Republicans made some gains in down-ticket elections, there was nothing to rival their gains at the presidential level. Even in the Reagan and Bush landslides in 1984 and 1988, Republican gains in state legislative elections and in other state and local elections in the region remained modest.[9] In 1992 the Republicans did make some clear gains, however, as they picked up two additional U.S. Senate seats, nine U.S. House seats, and forty-four seats in southern state legislatures (thirty-one in the state houses and thirteen in the state senates).[10]

Finally, in 1994 the slow movement toward Republican voting gained significant momentum as southern voters swarmed to the GOP in proportions unmatched since Reconstruction. Republicans gained sixteen seats in the U.S. House of Representatives and thereby became the majority in the region's collective delegations (64 of 125). Prior to 1994 Florida was the only southern state with a Republican majority in its House delegation; following the 1994 elections five southern states have Republican House delegation majorities (Florida, Georgia, Tennessee, North Carolina, and South Carolina). The GOP added enough seats in the U.S. Senate through a combination of electoral victories and party switches by incumbents (namely, Richard Shelby of Alabama) to emerge with a majority of the region's senators (twelve of twenty-two) as well. Currently, four states have two Republican senators. Republicans picked up three new governorships and now hold six of the eleven in the region (Texas, Tennessee, Alabama, South Carolina, Mississippi, and Virginia). The Republican Party made gains, albeit more modest, in state legislatures as well. The most dramatic successes took place in North Carolina, South Carolina, and Florida, where the Republicans gained majorities in one state legislative chamber for the first time in this century. Republican candidates did well in other races also, for example, in South Carolina, where the GOP captured seven of the state's nine constitutional offices, including governor, lieutenant governor, and attorney general.[11]

Whether the 1994 elections signal the long-expected party realignment in the South is not yet clear, but it is obvious that the long and gradual change in the region's party system has been significantly accelerated. And certainly continued attention to these developments is important from both regional and national political perspectives. This volume presents a series of studies that bear directly on partisan and electoral behavior in the South.

The five chapters in part 1 focus on the context of party and electoral activities. Previous research has demonstrated the importance of exploring the relationships between party and electoral activity and the external environment within which such activity occurs.[12] Indeed, in the context of southern political change, much of the transformation described above is clearly related to such things as changes in the composition of the region's population (for example, in-migration), changes in the legal system (for example, the 1965 Voting Rights Act), and party rules reforms (for example, the impact of the McGovern-Fraser Commission on delegate selection rules for the national convention).[13]

In chapter 1, Richard Scher, Jon L. Mills, and John J. Hotaling examine the evolution of the racial fairness doctrine as a part of the effort to bring minorities (especially African-Americans and Hispanics) into the political system. They give particular attention to recent court decisions relating to the creation of special majority-minority districts and to the consequences of these decisions for southern politics. Given the long battles over such central questions as access to the ballot and similar efforts to include African-Americans as active participants in southern politics, the analysis by Scher, Mills, and Hotaling goes to the heart of one of the contemporary manifestations of race and southern politics.

While Scher, Mills, and Hotaling examine the question of majority-minority districting from a legal perspective, Ronald Keith Gaddie and Charles S. Bullock III examine the question from a political perspective. That is, they explore the consequences of such redistricting for black candidate emergence and voter turnout. Utilizing data on Louisiana elections before and after redistricting in 1991, they attempt to determine whether the creation of majority-minority districts encourages more African-American candidates and greater African-American voting turnout. Clearly, understanding the actual impact of such redistricting contributes to our attempt to understand recent electoral developments in the region and helps to put the more strictly legal and philosophical concerns of Scher and his associates in proper perspective.

Majority-minority districting is a relatively recent development (although one might argue that it is little more than a modern variation of past efforts such as the gerrymander to manipulate electoral district boundaries to promote a particular outcome). The separation of presidential elections from state and local elections has a longer history in the South. Indeed, most of the southern states have undertaken to decouple these elections, most likely in the interest of moderating the impact of national electoral developments on state election outcomes. Jay Barth discusses the history of this practice and analyzes election data for the 1980s to investigate the partisan impact of this approach to scheduling elections. He is especially interested in examining the consequences of election timing for Republican growth in down-ticket elections. His chapter is a keen reminder that the rules of the electoral game help to provide a context for partisan development.

Chapters 4 and 5 switch focus from the rules of the electoral game to the nature of the electorate as a part of the context of party activity. In chapter 4, Patrick Cotter, Samuel H. Fisher III, and Felita T. Williams use National Election Studies data for the 1952–1992 period to examine selected elements of the southern electorate. Identifying some changes in the southern electorate, especially in the direction of lessened distinctiveness between the South and the non-South, Cotter, Fisher, and Williams speculate about the consequences of this for southern political change. In chapter 5 Richard Nadeau and Harold Stanley also examine National Election Studies data for the same forty-year period but focus particularly on age as a factor in party change. Their analysis of regional patterns is specially instructive in understanding the larger context of recent partisan developments in the South.

The five chapters in part 2 present discussions of selected features of nominations, elections, and partisan developments in the South. The purpose here is not to present exhaustive analyses and coverage of these topics but instead to explore some topics of particular interest in the broader effort to understand southern politics. In chapter 6, for example, David Sturrock examines one aspect of Republican growth in the region that has not received much attention: the recent surge in voter participation in southern Republican primaries. Of course, primaries have long been important features of southern electoral politics, and they have certainly come in for their share of attention. However, it has only been fairly recently that the Republican Party has gotten much into the primary business. Therefore, it would be helpful in understanding Republican growth in the region to know more about the nature of participation in Republican primaries, and Sturrock pursues this task.

Thomas Eamon examines the role of the southern states in the presidential election process in chapter 7. Recognizing the importance of the South in the electoral college, Eamon nevertheless brings into question the thesis advanced by Black and Black concerning the vital necessity of capturing the South for winning the presidency. His analysis of a group of (nonsouthern) megastates versus the southern states, he suggests, offers evidence that lessens the importance of the South in the presidential equation. Given the significant contributions of presidential politics to southern partisan change and the reciprocal relationship between southern presidential voting and presidential election outcomes, this view of the South and presidential politics is both provocative and timely.

While Eamon's analysis looks at presidential politics, Layne Hoppe explores changes in Congress as they may be related to party change in the South. Primarily utilizing data for the period since 1970, Hoppe is particularly concerned with examining possible connections between an increasingly liberal Congress and party change in the South. He extends his discussion through the 1994 elections and argues that voting patterns in Congress have come to reflect a southern party realignment along ideological lines.

The final two chapters move the discussion to the state legislatures. Clifton McCleskey presents a detailed study of changes in southern state legislatures with special attention to Virginia from roughly the 1960s forward. A case study such as this enables us to gain a rich understanding of relevant developments that, while occurring in only one state, are suggestive of similar developments beyond that state. The last chapter broadens the analysis to include data on state legislatures throughout the region. R. Bruce Anderson explores trends in such things as levels of contestation of state legislative seats and the level of electoral success in state legislative races as a means of analyzing partisan developments at this electoral level.

While the coverage of topics is not comprehensive, collectively the chapters in part 2 address points of continuing interest to students of southern partisan and electoral politics. Particularly when placed in the context provided by the chapters in part 1, they add some important pieces to the puzzle of southern politics. Together, the essays in both parts 1 and 2 should help clarify contemporary developments in the party and electoral politics of the South.

Part One
The Electoral Environment

1
Voting Rights in the South After *Shaw* and *Miller*

The End of Racial Fairness?

Richard K. Scher,
Jon L. Mills, and
John J. Hotaling

The search for voting rights goes deep into the history of the United States. The free and independent exercise of the franchise was one of the roots of the movement leading to the Revolutionary War. Issues concerning qualifications for voting were aired at the Constitutional Convention. The Fifteenth Amendment sought to extend the franchise to freed slaves.[1] The Twentieth Amendment (1920) did the same for women.[2] Twenty-four years later, the Supreme Court, in *Smith v. Allwright*,[3] affirmed that elections in party primaries could not discriminate against black voters; they were public, not private, events.

But the search for the right to vote existed outside courtrooms and on a far more immediate level than the abstractions of constitutional language. It lay at the very heart of the initial goals of the Civil Rights movement.[4] Perhaps at no time in American history has the central importance and connection of the free exercise of the franchise to the full, legitimate citizenship of African-Americans been more eloquently recognized and stated than by Martin Luther King in his famous "Give Us the Ballot" address during the 1957 Prayer Pilgrimage to Washington, D.C.:

> Give us the ballot and we will no longer have to worry the federal government about our basic rights. . . . Give us the ballot and we will no longer plead to the federal government for passage of an anti-lynching law. Give us the ballot and we will no longer plead—we will write the proper laws on the books. Give us the ballot and we will fill the legislature with men of goodwill. Give us the ballot and we will get the people judges who will "do justly and love mercy." Give us the ballot and we will quietly, lawfully, and nonviolently, without rancor or bitterness, implement the May 17, 1954, decision of the Supreme Court. . . . Give us the ballot and we will transform the salient misdeeds of bloodthirsty mobs into the calculated good deeds of orderly citizens.[5]

King's statement effectively sums up more than 150 years of American political thought: the ballot was an essential political instrument through which everyday citizens—of whatever race or color—could express their preferences about the purpose and direction of government. But even more fundamentally, King recognized that without free and independent access to and exercise of the right to vote, African-Americans (or, for that matter, any other group of people) would never be full-fledged American citizens. Possession of the right to vote freely was a fundamental indicator of political legitimacy. Its absence relegates those lacking it to second-class status or worse.

The Instrumentality of the Vote

In his speech King hinted at, but did not quite reach, another key element of voting. That is, having the right to vote, even to vote freely, is one thing. It is quite another to be certain that the vote actually counts, or that it possesses an instrumentality and a utility. This is especially a problem for minority voters surrounded by the majority community. They may very well have the right to vote and may exercise it both freely and in quantity. But if their vote is repeatedly washed out in the tide of an opposing vote of the majority, can it be said that the vote of the minority community has any real utility? Does it not therefore become merely a symbolic gesture, one devoid of any real impact on the purpose and direction of governmental activity? Does not the vote, under these conditions, ring hollow—both for the minority (which can rarely or never win) and for the majority (which can virtually always win, which can therefore manipulate election/voting rules, and which can ignore or give little heed to minority concerns as it wishes)? Is the vote not, therefore, really a cruel hoax—and the full status of first-class citizenship again denied members of the minority group?[6]

These questions lie at the very heart of the American democratic process. They are central to a consideration of the type of democratic experiment we have created in this country, to the relationship between majority and minority groups in this heterogeneous nation, and to the way in which the competing standards of equity and fairness are implemented in our political system. They point in the direction of a crucial issue associated with the instrumentality of the vote, one that the Supreme Court dealt in 1960:[7] What happens if the majority community decides to "allow" the minority community to vote but effectively blocks it from participating in elections in which it could influence the outcome?

The case arose in Tuskegee, Alabama, following a decision by officials to change the city limits from a relatively compact rectangle into a bizarrely shaped twenty-eight-sided monster. The effect of the change was to move virtually all of Tuskegee's black citizens, who formerly lived in town, outside the city limits. Thus they would not be able to vote in municipal elections. The purpose of adjusting the city limits was to ensure that blacks, whom everyone realized would eventually become a voting majority of the city, would not take over the city in an election.

Although in 1960 the Supreme Court still operated under the "political thicket" reapportionment/voting rights doctrine enunciated in *Colegrove v. Green*[8] and would wait another two years before deciding to wade in,[9] the justices held on behalf of Tuskegee's black plaintiffs, who had sued the city in federal court under the Fifteenth Amendment. In this instance the justices (including Justice Frankfurter, who had written the majority opinion in *Colegrove*) felt that Alabama had gone too far: this "was not an ordinary geographic redistricting measure even within the familiar abuses of gerrymandering."[10] The Court held that blacks had been deprived of the right to vote in municipal elections, and this act of disenfranchisement violated the Fifteenth Amendment.

Gomillion was an important decision if only because it held that blacks could not be gerrymandered in a willy-nilly fashion so as to be deprived of electoral opportunities. But the decision went even beyond this crucial step, raising the question of the utility of the vote as well as its exercise. In pushing blacks outside the city limits, Alabama officials had deprived them of the opportunity to make their votes count in city politics. This action, according to the Court, was unacceptable. Unfortunately, the Court did not enunciate in *Gomillion* any standards by which to judge the instrumentality of the vote. The Court clearly stated that Tuskegee blacks could not be victimized by actions taken by public officials *against* them. But whether the reverse was true—namely, that affirmative steps needed to be taken to ensure that the utility of the vote was preserved and enhanced—was not yet clear. It would be some time before this question was addressed.

Voting Rights and Racial Fairness

In the years following *Gomillion,* a number of key developments in voting rights took place. They cannot be detailed here.[11] Perhaps the most important, for our purposes, was the development of the racial fairness standard in voting rights.

Gomillion did more than protect African-American voters from being gerrymandered out of existence. It restated and reemphasized the idea that blacks constituted a special class of citizens. There was nothing new in this notion: blacks were conceived as a special group during the Constitutional Convention (they counted as only three-fifths of a person); the Fifteenth Amendment and the Reconstruction Acts of 1867 were predicated upon

classifying blacks differently from whites; *Plessy v. Ferguson,*[12] which legiti-
mized segregation, also treated blacks differently from whites; and the Civil
Rights Acts of 1957 and 1960 affirmed the special categorization of southern blacks.

Although specially classifying African-Americans is not new, it is no exaggeration to say that it is not a concept with which all Americans, including
black Americans, are at ease. The creation of special categories of citizens,
especially those based on race, has a long, complex, often controversial political and constitutional history. One major point about the creation of special racial categories of citizens needs to be mentioned, however. In our
democratic system, composed as it is of majority and minority populations,
it is often necessary to treat minority groups in a special manner in order
to ensure that their voice is effectively heard. In a sense, it makes the playing
field equal between minority and majority groups; otherwise, at least in electoral politics, it becomes difficult (and sometimes impossible) for the minority group to win.

These considerations lie at the heart of the concept of racial fairness in
voting rights. It presumes not just that a special category for African-American citizens can and should be created for voting but that certain affirmative steps must also be taken—the playing field made level—so that, in an
election, minority blacks can compete effectively and equally with majority
whites. More specifically, minority blacks must have an equal opportunity
with the majority white community to participate in the political process
and to elect their candidate(s) of choice to public office.

Gomillion, of course, did not go so far. It stated that certain steps could
not be taken against blacks, namely, that their vote could not be gerrymandered out of existence. But *Gomillion* did not address the question of the
affirmative steps that needed to be taken on behalf of black citizens in order
to ensure that their vote counted. It was the Voting Rights Act that began
the process of defining what obligatory measures had to be taken so that
blacks not only had free exercise of the franchise but could compete effectively and equally with the majority white community to elect their candi-
date(s) of choice to public office.

The Voting Rights Act

Much has been written about the original 1965 Voting Rights Act (VRA)
and its subsequent amendments.[13] We need not discuss its tremendous impact on southern politics.[14] We need only point out that the act was predicated, in part, on a special classification of citizens according to race. Southern blacks, in particular, had faced a long history of discrimination and
deprivation of their voting rights. The VRA established special target areas,

based on previously existing practices of discrimination against black voting rights and low minority voter turnout rates,[15] in which federal officials could force the registration of black voters, ensure their free access to the ballot, and oversee the counting of their votes. The famous (or infamous) section 5 required that any changes in election laws or practices in targeted areas be "precleared" by the U.S. attorney general or the federal district court of Washington, D.C., to ensure that they did not have the effect of perpetuating or reinstituting discriminatory practices against black voting rights.

None of this could have been accomplished were it not for the underlying assumption that affirmative steps needed to be taken by the federal government in order to ensure that blacks—at first in the South but later in other states in the North and Midwest—had full voting rights. In retrospect, the active measures taken in Washington to accomplish this purpose were fairly modest. They were, however, very controversial, especially section 5, which was regarded not just by conservative southern politicians but also by some constitutional scholars as an unwarranted intrusion by the federal government into an area traditionally left to states and local governments, namely, the establishment of voting requirements/practices and the creation of election laws. Nonetheless, the U.S. Supreme Court affirmed[16] the constitutionality of the VRA, including section 5, noting that the act did indeed provide for an "uncommon extension" of federal authority, but "exceptional conditions can justify legislative measures not otherwise appropriate."[17]

The modest steps of 1965 took a giant leap forward when the VRA—specifically section 2—was amended in 1982.[18] These changes have been well documented elsewhere[19] and require only a brief comment here. In the first place, the language of the amended section 2 specifically refers to the creation of a "protected class" of citizens based on "race or color." Clearly, it was the intent of the 1982 amendments to affirm the establishment of a category of minority citizens—namely, African-Americans—for whom special steps had to be taken in order to ensure that they had full access to voting rights. Second, section 2, in contrast to section 5, had national applicability. No target area was specified; rather, the language of the amendment says "any State or political subdivision," meaning that the act protected minority voting rights throughout the nation. Third, the new language permitted a test or standard for determining when minority voting rights had been denied, namely, if as determined on the basis of "the totality of circumstances"[20] minorities could not participate equally with the majority white community in the political process and elect their candidate(s) of choice to public office. If minority voters could demonstrate in court that this standard had not been met, and thus their voting rights were abridged, they would be entitled to relief.

The 1982 amendment to section 2 of the VRA pushed the concept of racial fairness beyond anything envisioned in *Gomillion* or, for that matter, in the 1965 act. The language of the amendment, and the accompanying report, left little doubt that voting rights for blacks were regarded in a very special way under federal law. Because of the amendments and report, black voters not only had free access to the franchise but could sue to secure their voting rights if they could present evidence that they could not compete in the electoral arena equally with whites and elect their candidate(s) of choice to public office.

Thornburg v. Gingles

The 1982 section 2 amendment to the VRA was given a major test in *Thornburg v. Gingles,*[21] a North Carolina case decided by the U.S. Supreme Court in 1986. Like the 1982 amendments, the case has received wide commentary and analysis[22] and need only concern us briefly here.

For our purposes, two major questions lay at the core of *Gingles:* specifically, are multimember legislative districts inherently violative of section 2 as amended?[23] And more generally, what are the circumstances in which a racial minority can seek a judicial remedy to protect and enhance its voting rights?

The justices in the *Gingles* majority did a better job of answering the first question than the latter. Multimember districts do not, by themselves, violate minority voting rights unless three conditions are met involving the configuration of the minority community relative to the majority and unless certain voting patterns pitting the majority and minority communities as polar opposites can be demonstrated.[24] If these conditions are met, then multimember districts will be found to violate minority voting rights under section 2, and courts can mandate a change in districting structure.

The Court was careful to point out that all three prongs of its test must be established before relief could be granted to minority plaintiffs. Nonetheless, during the districting cycle of 1991–1992, all three prongs of the test were not always met. And indeed, as districts were drawn to enhance minority representation, they often took on odd contortions and shapes in an effort to "find" minority voters in sufficient numbers to create a district that would "work," that is, would elect a minority candidate of choice.

We will return to this crucial matter shortly. For now, let us emphasize that even though some analysts regarded this part of the *Gingles* decision as a setback for minority voting rights, in fact it pushed the concept of racial fairness forward, even beyond the 1982 VRA section 2 amendments. The reason is that it specified circumstances—beyond the vague ones of the totality of circumstances—in which black voters can be granted relief and their voting rights reinforced. In other words, the Court suggested that if minority voters could enter court and argue that the three-pronged test applied to their circumstances, a district could then be designed that would enhance their voting power. Thus, the utility of the black vote was very much on the minds of the justices as they designed the three-pronged test.

In more practical terms, the *Gingles* decision permitted—but did not necessarily require—the creation of minority access and influence districts. These are relative terms, not specific ones. Access districts are those with sufficient numbers of minority voters to enhance the likelihood that the minority group will elect its candidate(s) to office on election day.[25] Influence districts do not possess sufficient numbers of minority voters to optimize this likelihood, but on the other hand the impact of the minority group on election day may well influence, and may perhaps decide, the outcome of the election; the theory is that even though the minority group may not be able to elect its candidate(s) of choice, it will be sufficiently influential to force the available candidates to attend to its needs.[26]

In more theoretical terms, *Gingles* was viewed by civil rights advocates, and those looking toward the 1991–1992 districting cycle, as a way of promoting racial fairness through the creation of access and influence districts. If the three prongs of the *Gingles* test were met, the decision could be interpreted as at least permitting those interested in fostering minority representation in legislatures to design districts that worked, that is, increased the likelihood that minority candidate(s) of choice would be elected. Whether or not this was the intent of *Gingles* is a matter for debate. Our point for the moment is to emphasize that, in both theoretical and practical terms, the pursuit of racial fairness in minority voting rights became synonymous with efforts to create minority access and influence districts, based on the rationale that many analysts read into *Gingles*.

As a result, *Gingles* opened a floodgate of efforts to create minority access and influence districts under the guise of racial fairness. The problem with the decision, however—among others—was that it failed to address other key questions: What circumstances required relief? When did minority access districts have to be created? The justices suggested what could be done but not what must be done. Moreover, they failed to resolve the question of what criteria—besides those specified by the three-pronged test—could establish a section 2 violation. They noted that establishing the existence of racially polarized voting and documenting the success rate of minority candidates were essential. But it was not clear, for black plaintiffs not living in a multimember district, what other circumstances, if any, had to be demonstrated to gain relief.

More generally, the *Gingles* decision failed to address the most fundamental questions of all: What affirmative steps *must* be taken in order to ensure minority voting rights—not what could be done but what is required? And from the opposite perspective, how much relief is necessary? What constitutes too much relief? Is there a point beyond which the assertion of minority voting rights actually discriminates against majority voting rights?

Failure to address these questions laid the groundwork for *Shaw v. Reno* and for subsequent attacks on the concept of racial fairness in voting rights. In a very real sense, the unwillingness of the *Gingles* court to move away from a narrow, fact-driven decision toward an articulation of broader standards in minority/majority voting rights provided both the impetus and the ammunition for the counterattack against racial fairness that subsequently occurred.[27]

On the other hand, the *Gingles* decision is not without major significance for minority voting rights. Seen in conjunction with the 1982 section 2 amendments to VRA, *Gingles* is another in a long series of affirmations in American democratic life that while the majority rules, minority rights must be respected and protected. In this instance, the concept extends to voting rights, specifically to the concept of racial fairness, whereby affirmative steps must be taken by government to protect not just the right to vote but also the integrity and utility of the vote. Minority voters have to be treated in a way that, despite their numerical status, allows them on election day to compete equally with the surrounding majority community to try to elect their candidate(s) of choice to public office.

Much of this, of course, was difficult for many Americans to swallow. This conception of voting rights seems, on the surface, to give advantages and privileges to minority groups not given to majority voters. It seems counter to the long-held view of everyday citizens, as well as politicians and constitutional scholars, that the Constitution—especially the Fourteenth Amendment[28]—is color blind. There have been innumerable occasions when jurists, scholars, journalists, public officials, and candidates for office have attacked the concept of using racial criteria for accomplishing certain public policy purposes.[29] Some members of minority groups, moreover, object to being singled out for special treatment as the concept of racial fairness seems to do.

On the other hand, racial fairness as articulated in the 1982 VRA Amendments and *Gingles* offers no guarantees to minority communities. It assures them of nothing except an opportunity to compete, electorally, on a level playing field with the majority white community. It does not in any way imply that the election of their candidate(s) of choice is a sure thing. Moreover, in comparison with other concepts of racial fairness, such as those articulated by Lani Guinier,[30] the standard articulated by section 2 and *Gingles* seems modest.

But what is most important about the standard of racial fairness articulated in *Gingles,* and in the 1982 VRA amendments, is how far it had evolved since *Gomillion*. As a result of these two pronouncements, it was both legitimate and necessary to take race into account in the process of drawing legislative districts. Thus race became a preeminent factor in the pursuit of minority voting rights. Rather than being ignored or left aside, racial fairness became an essential standard as public decisions about voting rights were made, including the way in which legislative representation was effectuated.

As a number of commentators have pointed out,[31] *Gingles* was stretched beyond recognition in the search for racial fairness. *Gingles* was actually a narrow decision, its three-pronged test to be applied in very specific circumstances, namely, those associated with multimember districts. But the test was applied in other, perhaps totally unrelated circumstances as well. It was assumed that *Gingles* required affirmative steps to promote racial fairness. But since the decision never said what must be done, or what could not be done, architects of plans throughout the nation took great pains to find ways to promote racial fairness. It is no exaggeration to say that the districting cycle of 1991–1992 seemed to have one goal: promoting racial fairness through the creation of minority access and influence districts.

The result was the creation of districts that looked strange and that seemed to have little basis for existence other than that they fostered racial fairness.[32] Examples were congressional districts such as the third and twenty-third in Florida, the fourth in Louisiana, the eleventh in Georgia, and the twelfth in North Carolina. There are others as well, including many state legislative and local districts.[33] All of them, but the congressional districts in particular, laid the groundwork for *Shaw* and *Miller*.

Shaw v. Reno

On June 28, 1993, the Supreme Court announced a decision[34] that questioned the validity of the racial fairness standard. Under this decision it became possible for the Court to find that at least some minority access and influence districts constitute racial gerrymanders. It also raised the possibility that creating such districts might constitute a form of reverse discrimination against white voters. Its potential importance is immense.[35]

A group of white voters in North Carolina sued the U.S. attorney general following a preclearance approval under section 5 of the Voting Rights Act of two minority access congressional districts in that state. One of the districts—the twelfth—cut diagonally across the state, following Interstate 85, and in some areas was no wider than the right-of-way. The plaintiffs argued that the district constituted a racial gerrymander and therefore violated the rights of majority white voters under the Fourteenth Amendment. Federal district court dismissed the complaint, finding that an Equal Protection claim had not been demonstrated on the basis of *United Jewish Organizations v. Carey*[36] and that the plan did not lead to proportional underrepresentation of white voters throughout the state. The Supreme Court, on a 5–4 decision, reversed and remanded the case.

Writing for the majority, Justice O'Connor was particularly concerned about the bizarre shape of District 12.[37] Her position was that the district seemed to have no rational basis apart from linking individuals solely by race. This, according to her, constituted a constitutionally invalid classification, since " '[a] racial classification, regardless of purported motivation, is presumptively invalid and can be upheld only upon an extraordinary justification.' "[38] In other words, if the district could not be justified by anything other than race, it lacked constitutional standing. In a stinging attack, she continued:

> A reapportionment plan that includes in one district individuals who belong to the same race, but who are otherwise widely separated by geographical and political boundaries, and who may have little in common with one another but the color of their skin, bears an uncomfortable resemblance to political apartheid. It reinforces the perception that members of the same racial group—regardless of their age, education, economic status, or the community in which they live—think alike, share the same political interests, and will prefer the same candidates at the polls. We have rejected such perceptions elsewhere as impermissible racial stereotypes.[39]

Shaw never reached the merits of the case, that is, whether District 12 in fact violates the rights of the white majority. It remanded the case for further hearings. But in fact it strongly pointed in the direction that O'Connor hoped judicial findings would go, namely, a ruling that the creation of odd-shaped districts based solely on race is constitutionally invalid.

A major ambiguity in *Shaw* requires comment. O'Connor was especially concerned about the seemingly artificial construction of congressional minority access districts—that is, those with tortuous (bizarre) shapes that link minority populations across wide geographic areas. She did not discuss, however, criteria that define a bizarre shape. True, she points out that such districts violate other standards of districting—compactness, contiguity, respect for political boundaries, and protection of communities of interest.[40] But while these may on occasion be useful standards, when viewed closely and analytically, they invariably fail to provide helpful guidelines.[41] Different tests for compactness, for example, invariably lead to varying conclusions about the compactness of specific districts. Moreover, other case law and constitutional requirements—especially equal population standards stemming from the one person–one vote rule in *Reynolds v. Sims*—often demand that these other standards be honored more in the breach than in practice.

The matter goes deeper, however, even beyond the vague classification of districts as bizarre in shape. The decision raised the possibility that virtually all minority access districts may be subject to constitutional attack. In other words, even ones that presumably satisfy the three-pronged *Gingles* test, as well as others that may not satisfy all three prongs but were created out of the aggregation of minority groups sufficiently numerous to compose a majority-minority district, or close to it, will inherently be based on racial classifications. Do these violate the standards laid down by O'Connor in *Shaw*? If they do not, then what is the real difference between these districts and those about which she complains in the opinion? If there is a difference, then some can stand and some will have to be dismantled; but where is the break point? If there is no difference, then presumably all minority access districts will have to be disassembled; if this happens, what are the appropriate standards for treating minority populations during districting, and what happens to minority voting rights—especially racial fairness—generally?

The issues raised by O'Connor in *Shaw* ran very deep. In summary form, we can list them as follows:

- Do congressional majority-minority districts constitute a racial gerrymander, thereby violating majority white voting rights?

- Is the primary issue the artificial linking of widely separated minority population concentrations—thereby creating bizarre districts—or is the issue more fundamental: Is it unconstitutional to take affirmative steps, however small and of whatever kind, to permit members of minority groups to participate equally with the majority white community in the political process and to elect its candidate(s) of choice to public office (the current standard for racial fairness)?

- Is it possible to create minority access or influence districts that satisfy constitutional requirements? If so, how is it to be done? What arguments or data can be advanced to satisfy courts that they are legitimate?

- If majority-minority congressional districts are suspect, are state legislative districts created by the same legal principles of racial fairness also suspect? If so, does this rule apply only when congressional/legislative districts are nested, or does it apply if they are independently drawn and situated?

- If *Gingles* is modified substantially by *Shaw* or other cases, what legal standards will govern racial fairness in future drawing of congressional and state legislative district lines?

- If *Gingles* is overturned, and the 1982 amendments to the Voting Rights Act are held unconstitutional, will there be any remaining legal standards other than the Fourteenth and Fifteenth Amendments governing minority voting rights? What will they be? How will they be used during districting and supervised by the Court?

- If racial fairness loses its preeminent position as a districting criterion, what standards will replace it: compactness? preservation of communities of interest? respect for political boundaries? maintenance of existing district cores? If these criteria achieve a legal renaissance, how will they be utilized in the districting process? What conceptual and technical problems need to be faced and solved so that they become useful?[42]

Legal Developments After *Shaw*

Developments after *Shaw* have answered some, but not all, of the questions. The first major legal effort to clarify the issues in *Shaw* came in *Hays v. Louisiana*[43] and the second in *Miller v. Johnson*.[44] *Hays* has not, as of this writing, been heard on its merits by the U.S. Supreme Court, although lower federal courts have issued pointed opinions.[45]

Hays v. Louisiana

In Louisiana white plaintiffs sued to overturn Congressional District 4 on the ground that it constituted a racial gerrymander. A federal district court in December 1993 declared Louisiana's Congressional District 4—indeed, the entire legislative act creating it—unconstitutional.[46] The district had been called the "Zorro" district because it resembled the signature mark of the fabled swordsman.[47] The case proceeded in two stages, the first taking place prior to the Supreme Court's decision in *Shaw* and the second occurring after *Shaw*, when the federal district court in Louisiana asked for further hearings and argument in light of *Shaw*.

After sifting the evidence, the court concluded that there was both inferential and direct evidence that the intent[48] of District 4 was to create a district based solely on race.[49] The decision cited evidence both from architects and from critics of the plan that race was the single factor that created the district;[50] that plan architects disregarded the traditional districting criteria of compactness, contiguity, respect for political boundaries, and preservation of communities of interest in creating the district;[51] and that defenders of the plan could not demonstrate that any other factors, such as partisanship or protection of incumbents, played any "cognizable" role whatsoever in construction of the district.[52] Thus although the court recognized that plaintiffs carried the burden of proof to document that the creation of District 4—indeed, the entire congressional districting plan—was "motivated by racial considerations," it concluded that "the plaintiffs have met that burden—comfortably."[53] Thus, the Court asserted, the districting plan, and District 4 in particular, constituted a racial gerrymander—that is, "the intentional, not the accidental, segregation of voters on the basis of race."[54]

This conclusion forced the application of strict scrutiny.[55] "The bedrock principle underlying the Court's decision in *Shaw* is that racially gerrymandered redistricting plans are subject to the same strict scrutiny that applies to other state legislation classifying citizens on the basis of race. As such, racially gerrymandered plans violate the Equal Protection Clause of the Fourteenth Amendment unless they are narrowly tailored to further a compelling governmental interest."[56]

The state argued that creation of a minority access district satisfied strict scrutiny standards on the basis of five assertions: District 2 satisfied section 2 of the Voting Rights Act as amended in 1982; it conformed to the requirements of section 5 of the Voting Rights Act;[57] it promoted the proportional representation of African-Americans in the U.S. House of Representatives; it addressed the effects of past forms of discrimination against Louisiana blacks;[58] and it promoted racial fairness and other types of fairness.[59]

The district court took a swipe at these factors and appeared essentially to dismiss them. Importantly, it chose not even to evaluate them but was willing to assume that one or more might actually constitute a valid state interest. Instead, it chose to focus on the "narrowly tailored" test of strict scrutiny—that is, did the creation of District 4 go beyond a *de minimis* approach in creating a scheme based on race?

The court held that the plan violated the narrowly tailored test. It argued that the plan actually created more segregation than was necessary; that it packed blacks unnecessarily into District 4; and that in the process a number of third-party interests were violated because alternative plans could have been created that were more compact, respected political boundaries, and preserved communities of interest more fully than did the plan passed by the legislature.[60] Thus the court concluded,

> In summary, we hold that the Plan is not narrowly tailored, either relatively or absolutely. This is so because it embraces considerably more racial gerrymandering—and thus more segregation—than is needed to satisfy any advanced state interest, and because the Plan unnecessarily violates a host of historically important redistricting principles, thereby adversely affecting countless third party interests. These several and varied interests—some constitutionally protected and others merely important—may not be callously sacrificed on the altar of political expediency, particularly when less broadly tailored plans are conceivable.[61]

Hays did not address all of the issues raised in *Shaw*. It is clear, however, that the judges of the district court seized upon *Shaw* to attack perceived excesses of districting that had been brought on by the zeal in the last round of congressional districting to foster minority representation. Moreover, while the point is not totally clear, it seems likely that the judges did not think highly of the concept of racial fairness—taking affirmative steps to ensure both the integrity and efficacy of the black vote—as a mechanism for ensuring minority voting rights.[62]

Miller v. Johnson

On June 29, 1995, the U.S. Supreme Court announced a major reapportionment decision called *Miller v. Johnson,* which declared unconstitutional Georgia's Congressional District 11.[63] But the decision has far broader implications, because it spoke to a number of issues raised in both *Gingles* and especially *Shaw.* It did not do so definitively, however, and while it is a very important decision, it may indeed have served to muddy further already murky waters.

To state the facts briefly, Georgia's congressional districts were reapportioned by the legislature in a special session meeting in August 1991. The resulting plan, which provided for one influence and two majority-minority or access districts, was submitted to the Department of Justice (DOJ) for preclearance under section 5, as the entire state is a covered jurisdiction. DOJ rejected the plan and a subsequent one on the grounds that the state "failed to explain adequately"[64] why it did not create a third majority-minority district. Finally, the state drew a plan originally proposed by the American Civil Liberties Union (called the "max-black" plan)[65] that did construct by connecting black residents in Atlanta and Savannah, some 260 miles apart.[66] It was this district that both a federal district court and the U.S. Supreme Court found unconstitutional.

Miller follows directly from a question raised in both *Shaw* and *Hays,* namely, can race be used as a valid criterion in constructing congressional districts? It answers both *Shaw* and *Hays* in two ways. First, it indicates that race can be a criterion in congressional districting but only under conditions of strict scrutiny. Furthermore, the decision goes beyond either of the other cases in stating that even if race as a criterion satisfies strict scrutiny, race nonetheless cannot be the "overriding and predominant force" driving the districting process.[67]

This last consideration pushes *Miller* potentially into the realm of watershed Supreme Court cases. By severely limiting the conditions under which race can be used as a districting criterion, the Court substantially altered the entire approach taken to congressional (and possibly state and local) districting in the 1991–1992 cycle. Moreover, it brought to a halt thirty-five years of attempting to enhance minority representation in legislatures through special attention to race during the districting process and by directly recognizing race as a major principle of redistricting. While the racial fairness standard may not be completely dead, as a practical matter it will not again have nearly the impact on southern districting that it had in the 1980s and early 1990s unless the Court, or the U.S. Congress, chooses to return it to its previous status. Neither seems likely to do so in the near future. As a result of *Miller,* the whole tenor of legislative districting has been altered. Its impact on southern politics is likely to be considerable. Let us take a close look at the decision and then at its likely implications.

Justice Kennedy, writing for the 5–4 majority in *Miller,* made it abundantly clear that using race as a primary criterion in districting immediately triggers the strict scrutiny standard: "We recognized in *Shaw* that . . . statutes are subject to strict scrutiny under the Equal Protection Clause not just when they contain express racial classifications, but also when . . . they are motivated by a racial purpose or object."[68] In the instance of Georgia's Congressional District 11, the Court found, both the purpose of the district and its classification were based on race: the entire rationale behind District 11 was to create a minority access district.

Such purposes and classifications are probably unconstitutional, and assuredly suspect, according to the majority decision. "Just as the State may not, absent ordinary justification, segregate citizens on the basis of race in its public parks, . . . golf courses, . . . beaches, . . . and schools, . . . so did we recognize in Shaw that it may not separate its citizens on the basis of race."[69]

Kennedy continued,

> The idea is a simple one: At the heart of the Constitution's guarantee of equal protection lies the simple command that the Government must treat citizens as individuals, not as "simply components of a racial, religious, sexual or national class." . . . When the State assigns voters on the basis of race, it engages in the offensive and demeaning assumption that voters of a particular race, because of their race, "think alike, share the same political interests, and will prefer the same candidates at the polls." . . . Race-based assignments "embody stereotypes that treat individuals as the product of their race, evaluating their thoughts and efforts—their very worth as citizens—according to a criterion barred to the Government by history and the Constitution." . . . "Racial classifications with respect to voting carry particular dangers." Racial gerrymandering, even for remedial purposes, may balkanize us into competing racial factions; it threatens to carry us further from the goal of a political system in which race no longer matters—a goal that the Fourteenth and Fifteenth Amendments embody, and to which the Nation continues to aspire. It is for these reasons that race-based districting by our state legislatures demands close judicial scrutiny.[70]

Having unequivocally placed race-based districting under the aegis of strict scrutiny, Kennedy found that in applying it to District 11, the district was found wanting on grounds that it was not narrowly tailored. He conceded that efforts to overcome past discrimination might well constitute "a significant state interest."[71] But "whether or not in some cases compliance with the Voting Rights Act, standing alone, can provide a compelling interest independent of any interest in remedying past discrimination, it cannot do so here."[72] The reason is that the Department of Justice exceeded its authority, as well as acted counter to the wishes of both Congress and the Supreme Court, in demanding a max-black approach to districting under section 5.[73] Indeed, Kennedy suggested that the original plan proposed by the Georgia legislature, which contained one influence and two majority-minority districts and was clearly both nonretrogressive and ameliorative,[74] was all that was required under section 5. Forcing a third majority-minority district not only caused race to become the "overriding and predominant factor" in drawing the district but also caused the plan to fail the narrowly tailored test of strict scrutiny because the Voting Rights Act did not require the additional step of creating it: "The Government's position is insupportable. [A]meliorative changes, even if they fall short of what might be accomplished in terms of increasing minority representation, cannot be found to violate section 5 unless they so discriminate on the basis of race or color as to violate the Constitution."[75]

However, while the majority were clearly uncomfortable with race-based districting, Justice Kennedy did not go so far as to reject it as unconstitutional on its face. Indeed, the role to be played by race goes to the heart of the decision and raises the most troubling questions possible. As we already noted, Kennedy stated that overcoming past racial discrimination might be a valid state objective, one that could (if narrowly tailored) satisfy a compelling state interest, pass the rigorous test of strict scrutiny, and be found acceptable by courts.[76] But Kennedy went beyond this limited formulation. Race, he stated, will inevitably and naturally be a consideration during districting: "It is true that redistricting in most cases will implicate a political calculus in which various interests compete for recognition. . . . Redistricting legislatures will, for example, almost always be aware of racial demographics."[77]

This line of reasoning leaves the door open for a legitimate argument that racial awareness can be a part of the politics and legalistics of redistricting. It rejects, at least for the moment, the notion that a fully color-blind approach to districting is required. Both *Shaw* and *Hays,* as we noted, suggest also that race-based districting, governed by strict scrutiny, may be permissible.

But *Miller* goes beyond either of these earlier cases by imposing a crucial additional burden. Race can be used, but it cannot be the "overriding, predominant factor"[78] or force in making decisions about districts, as the Court found it was in Georgia's District 11. Rather, race must be subordinate to "race neutral considerations"[79] such as "compactness, contiguity, respect for political subdivisions or communities defined by actual shared interests,"[80] and possibly others. How this is to happen is decidedly unclear. The decision suggests that race can be a part of the mix, or "calculus," of districting, but where it fits on the list of other districting criteria is left unsaid. Kennedy did distinguish between awareness of "racial considerations" in districting (presumably a legitimate part of the process) and "being motivated by them" (which is not), although he conceded that it is a difficult distinction to make.[81] He offered no guidance for doing so. He further recognized that race may constitute grounds for identifying a community of interest: "A State is free to recognize communities that have a particular racial makeup, provided its action is directed toward some common thread of relevant interests."[82] But he then muddied the waters by stating "where the State assumes from a group of voters' race that they 'think alike, share the same political interests, and will prefer the same candidates at the polls,' it engages in racial stereotyping at odds with equal protection mandates."[83] Thus while racial communities of interest can abstractly be said to exist, in practice it may be difficult to define them.

The central ambiguity leads to a number of consequences and implications that we shall discuss below. Before addressing them, however, let us turn to another key theme of *Miller:* the matter of district shape. It is one part of the decision that is relatively free of ambiguity.

Readers will recall that *Shaw* raised a question about the bizarre shape which some minority access districts had achieved. Not only were they artificial constructs, in Justice O'Connor's view, but their weird shape may have been evidence that they constituted a racial gerrymander. Thus, according to *Shaw,* it is possible that an inquiry into possible Equal Protection violations against white voters might have required an examination into the actual shape of legislative districts.

Kennedy clarified and simplified this possibility in *Miller.* He indicated that it was not the Court's intention in *Shaw* to hold that a district must have a weird shape before it constituted a racial gerrymander: "Our observation in *Shaw* of the consequences of racial stereotyping was not meant to suggest that a district must be bizarre on its face before there is a constitutional violation."[84] Nor is it necessary that plaintiffs demonstrate a threshold level of bizarreness[85] before they can allege an Equal Protection violation. Rather, shape is relevant only because it might be suggestive of something deeper, namely, that a district was designed with race as the overriding and predominant factor above and beyond all other districting principles. In a sense, it is indirect evidence of a wrong: "Shape is relevant not because bizarreness is a necessary element of the constitutional wrong or a threshold requirement of proof, but because it may be persuasive circumstantial evidence that race for its own sake, and not other districting principles, was the legislature's dominant and controlling rationale in drawing district lines."[86]

The matter extends further. According to Kennedy's view, district shape may be relevant to a constitutional inquiry. But it is not essential. It is possible that an Equal Protection violation may take place even when a district does not have a weird or bizarre shape. Thus other presumably more direct and empirically based avenues are open to plaintiffs alleging that their constitutional rights have been violated. Kennedy points out that other courts have held that "parties may rely on evidence other than bizarreness to establish race-based districting" and concludes, "evidence other than a district's bizarre shape can be used to support the claim."[87]

Miller thus simplifies plaintiffs' task. In a sense, two possibilities exist for them to demonstrate the existence of race-based districting. In some instances the shape of the district alone will be "persuasive circumstantial evidence" that it exists. But plaintiffs need not rely solely on this approach, nor need they demonstrate a certain threshold level of bizarre shape to get a court to listen to them. In instances where shape is not an issue, they can still marshal other evidence as part of their argument that a districting system was based on race predominantly and thus is unconstitutional. It follows that plaintiffs alleging an Equal Protection wrong have two avenues open to them in establishing their case—one based on the "persuasive circumstantial evidence" of district shape and the second on other forms of evidence, such as empirically based facts, legislative history (the situation in *Miller*), or something else. Moreover, they can be used separately or, when appropriate, in combination. Thus the Court went out of its way in *Miller* to assist plaintiffs attacking race-based districting in structuring their voting rights violation cases. This feature of the decision alone indicates how much the Court has shifted in its voting rights attitudes since *Gingles*.

Two other major themes in *Miller* are worthy of our attention here. The first was the way the Court took the Department of Justice to task for its max-black policy in section 5 cases. Whereas in *South Carolina v. Katzenbach*[88] the Court went out of its way to defend vigorously the assertive position taken by DOJ to overcome discrimination in southern voting rights, in *Miller* the court is openly hostile to the manner in which DOJ did so in Georgia. This too represents a major change in the position of the Court on voting rights. Finally, *Miller* not only declined to follow up on the invitation offered in *Shaw* to attack the constitutionality of the Voting Rights Act but specifically reaffirmed the importance of the act, particularly section 5: "The Voting Rights Act, and its grant of authority to uncover official efforts to abridge minorities' right to vote, has been of vital importance in eradicating invidious discrimination from the electoral process and enhancing the legitimacy of our political institutions."[89]

This last point is curious. It would have been a relatively easy step for Kennedy to limit the applicability of the VRA significantly, but in no place does he do so. He chose instead to criticize DOJ for its implementation of the act. But his unwillingness to attack VRA suggests something of his purpose in writing the majority opinion in *Miller* and can perhaps help us understand the decision more fully. Taken together, *Shaw* and *Miller* clearly signal a change in Court attitude toward voting rights. In the past, the Court has been largely sympathetic toward the claims and problems of minority voters. But these two cases suggest that the Court feels that we may have gone too far in our efforts to enhance minority voting rights, especially in promoting minority representation. *Shaw* at least raises the question that we may have done so; *Miller* takes the additional step of saying that, in Georgia's case, the state assuredly did.

On the other hand, *Miller* should not be read as a draconian decision. It is not an open invitation to turn the clock back to a Jim Crow era, nor does it signal the end of minority voting rights.[90] Rather, *Miller* is best read as a compromise decision between parts of the Supreme Court wishing to move toward an exclusively color-blind approach to the Constitution and parts wanting to maintain the *Gingles* approach. It is an assertion that the Court wishes to downplay race on the American political and legal agenda but probably not eliminate it altogether. In a sense, Kennedy sought to walk a tightrope between competing factions on the Court; readers may remember that in the same term when *Miller* was handed down, the Court also announced decisions drawing back the federal government's role in promoting affirmative action, minority scholarships, and school desegregation. The direction in which *Miller* points, and the language and tenor of the decision, are consonant with these other cases. Clearly there are new winds blowing on the Court concerning the role of race in American public life, and Kennedy was very conscious of needing to take cognizance of them. But at the same time he did not want to move so far away from precedent that the Court could be accused of becoming either insensitive to minority rights or of turning back the clock on them.

Perhaps more fundamentally, *Miller* needs to be understood as seeking a return to an earlier style of districting, pre-1982 (when section 2 of the Voting Rights Act was amended). This earlier approach can perhaps best be called "accommodationist" because it rested primarily on a clash ("calculus," to use Kennedy's term) of a variety of political interests—partisan, governmental, regional, economic, religious and ethnic, ideological, cultural, and so forth. Race was present but was not predominant; it was merely a part of the mix. Following 1982 and especially the *Gingles* decision of 1986, as we have seen, our whole approach to districting changed. It became what we might call "polarized" rather than accommodationist. Districts, especially in the South, were frequently designed, after satisfying equal population requirements, heavily on the basis of race: African-Americans got theirs, and white Americans got theirs. The *Shaw* and *Miller* Court's view was that we had created two separate, nonintersecting worlds of legislative districts. This approach clearly stuck in the craw of a majority of the Supreme Court beginning in 1993. It was not a style of districting with which five justices, at least, felt comfortable. Perhaps they saw it as counter to the grand political tradition of this country and as potentially injurious to our political institutions; certainly there is language in both *Shaw* and *Miller* to suggest that they felt this danger was real. In any case, and regardless of the reasons, in both cases a majority of the Court felt we had moved too far in using race as a districting principle, and they wanted to reduce it to a much lower priority—but not remove it altogether so as not to be seen as totally reversing fields—in the future. In the end, it is likely that their goal has been to eliminate the "polar" approach to districting, and *Miller* must be read in this sense.

Nonetheless, *Miller* raises more questions than it answers.[91] The case leaves us with some serious difficulties. We can categorize most of them in four distinct but related groups. The first problem concerns the relative position that race is to occupy in future districting decisions, especially but not exclusively in the South. *Miller* states categorically that it cannot be the "overriding and predominant" factor. It must, rather, give way before traditional, race-neutral districting principles including, among others, contiguity, compactness, preservation of communities of interest, and respect for political boundaries.[92] But the *Miller* formulation is not helpful to legislators, courts, consultants, journalists, citizens' groups, or anyone else involved in the districting process. The reason is that while the Court has indicated what is not possible—namely, to use race as a primary consideration—it does not then indicate what is either possible or necessary. In other words, the Court, in providing essentially negative guidance, does not give any indication as to how race should or can be a part of the mix of districting principles. In designing districts, for example, does the legislature adopt the other, race-neutral principles as first priority and then race secondarily? Are racial issues to be addressed specifically, or merely as a by-product or result of decisions made about these other principles? If they are to be addressed specifically, when and under what circumstances? If not, what is to prevent the political interests of minority groups (which *Miller* recognizes as legitimate) from being ignored or paid only the most minimal attention?

This latter point leads to a major internal ambiguity and tension in the decision. As we noted earlier, on the one hand, the majority opinion clearly stated[93] that there is a continuing state interest in overcoming past voting rights discrimination; indeed, at the end of the majority opinion, Justice Kennedy reaffirmed the role of the Voting Rights Act in doing so.[94] But how is this to be done, if racial considerations are to be subordinated to a host of other, race-neutral districting principles? In other words, is there not the possibility that the promise held out by the Court is really an empty one, since racial considerations in districting cannot be placed front and center during districting deliberations? How is it possible to overcome discrimination without addressing it directly and preeminently? Does the Court really think that residual discrimination and racism in the South and elsewhere can be overcome as a by-product of decisions made on the basis of equal population, contiguity, compactness, and so forth?

These are hard questions to answer. They are just as difficult to ask, because they force discomfiting issues onto the table. Sooner or later, however, they must be faced, especially as we move toward the next districting cycle later in the 1990s. Moreover, they loom even more ominously because the so-called race-neutral principles on which Kennedy relies so heavily are not easily workable and are often unreliable as mechanisms for creating legislative districts.

These considerations and questions lead to the second issue: the meaning of "race" for the purposes of districting and protecting minority voting rights; or, put another way, which components or aspects of race are acceptable during the districting process (including courtrooms), and which are not? "Race" is not a simple term. It can refer to many different things, conjure up many different images, and evoke a variety of meanings, thoughts, and emotions. *Miller* is not specific on how "race" is meant to be interpreted in the districting context.

Indeed, the matter is not as abstract as these statements suggest, and in fact another internal tension within the decision concerning the meaning and impact of race cries out for resolution. As we noted, race cannot be a predominant factor in districting. The decision recognizes a distinction between "awareness" of race and "being motivated" by it.[95] But the majority opinion also notes the legitimate distinction between "assignment of voters on the basis of race" and hearing "a vote dilution claim."[96] The former is not permissible, but the latter may well be grounds for a valid complaint. The former would seem to be based on the very fact of racial identity, even skin color, while the latter rests primarily on a concern with the utility or instrumentality of the vote.[97]

The tension within *Miller* lies in that at some point the set of distinctions attempted by the majority decision cannot be made, at least in practice. Most fundamentally, claims of minority vote dilution are not simply based on awareness, which is legitimate, but in fact must be motivated by race, which is not. How are the courts to decide when awareness becomes motivation in a vote dilution case? How are legislators to design districts that do not dilute minority votes without being motivated by a concern for the worth or instrumentality of the minority vote? What does race really mean as a factor in the districting mix?

Indeed, we can raise these issues to an even more fundamental level, one causing such difficulties that it is hard to see, at the moment, how any of them can be resolved. The matter is easily put but requires a bit of explanation. In brief, as a result of this Court decision, white voters bringing racial gerrymandering suits can conceivably win under *Miller* but lose under section 2 of the Voting Rights Act, especially if the defense can effectively show that a change in districts will result in minority vote dilution. The reason is that nothing in *Miller* attacks section 2, which, as we have seen, makes racial considerations in voting rights (including being motivated by them) legitimate, even top priority. Thus, an effective defense against racial gerrymandering claims can conceivably be based on avoidance of vote dilution under section 2. But black plaintiffs also face a difficult burden. They could win a section 2 case by showing vote dilution but lose a *Miller* case because a district has been constructed predominantly on the basis of race.

In other words, at this point there is a colossal tension between section 2 of the Voting Rights Act (at least, in its vote dilution dimensions) and *Miller*. Plaintiffs and defendants, regardless of their interest, standing, or race, must walk a very fine line between these two contrasting legal forces. Too much emphasis on race might trigger a *Miller* response from a court; but to argue solely on the basis of *Miller* leaves the case open to attack from section 2. Legislators trying to design districts face the problem up front. Somehow they have to balance the demands of section 2 with the requirements of *Miller*. At least plaintiffs and defendants, planning cases, have a set of facts and legislative history with which to work. For legislators facing the next districting cycle, unless the Supreme Court or Congress clarifies some of this tension, it will be a little like flying completely blind in a fog, close to the ground. A thundering crash is virtually inevitable, for there are no firm guidelines, at this point, to help them proceed. And whatever plan is adopted can be attacked, from either the *Miller* side or the section 2 side, and undoubtedly will be.

A third problem that *Miller* raises concerns its relationship to *Gingles*. At no point does *Miller* attempt to overturn *Gingles*. Indeed, at least on one level it affirms the purpose of section 5, which lies at the heart of the *Gingles* case; on another level it modifies how far section 5 actually extends. Indeed, this last point raises a crucial issue left untouched in *Miller*. A major difficulty in *Gingles*, readers will recall, is that it failed to address the problem of how far governments must go to enhance minority voting rights. It is clear from both section 5 and especially section 2 that government has an affirmative duty to try to increase minority representation. But guidelines or benchmarks for doing so are sparse. *Miller* is only of limited additional help. Justice Kennedy recognized the affirmative role for government to play but put a fence around it: he noted that Georgia created an "ameliorative" congressional districting plan by creating a second access and an influence district; according to him, this was enough. But what is the standard by which to judge when "enough is enough" or "enough is too much"? His statement that "increasing the number of majority-minority districts . . . cannot violate §5 unless the new apportionment itself so discriminates on the basis of race or color as to violate the Constitution"[98] begs the question: What is the standard for determining when the Constitution has been violated? As a result of this important omission in the decision, governments are no further along in knowing what is their affirmative duty to enhance minority voting rights than they were under *Gingles*. They only know that, as a result of *Miller,* they probably have to do less than they thought they did before, but how much less is unknown, and merely because they have to do less does not mean they do not have to do something. What is their duty?

Miller raises at least one more major issue. Intentionally or unwittingly, the Court may have opened up some heavily white districts to attack under the standards it enunciated. The reason is that in the districting cycle of 1991–1992, as minority access and influence districts were created, at the same time a number of very white districts were also formed, especially in the South. In a way, they were by-products of the implementation of the racial fairness standard; designing minority districts of necessity "bleached" many districts of minority voters and allowed residual white districts to become even whiter because members of the majority population were picked up to keep population levels equitable.

As a result of this phenomenon, it is entirely conceivable to argue, under *Miller,* that these "superwhite" districts were drawn with race as an "overriding, predominant factor." The argument can be made two ways. First, there was a deliberate, overriding concern to push minority voters out. Second, there was a deliberate, overriding concern to pull white voters into these districts. Either way, or in combination, following the reasoning in *Miller* these districts may constitute a racial gerrymander. They were based on racial considerations primarily; and the legislative history will undoubtedly show, at least in some instances (perhaps many or all), that these considerations displaced traditional, race-neutral districting principles, or at least made them a low priority. *Miller* makes clear that this outcome is not acceptable. Whether or not the majority in *Miller* intended for cases of this sort to be tested remains to be seen. The line of reasoning to construct them, however, is clearly suggested by the case. It is of interest that one possible consequence of a finding that these superwhite districts constitute a racial gerrymander might be injurious to the Republican Party, since, as election results in 1992 and 1994 show, Republicans did especially well in these new, heavily white districts.

One other matter in *Miller* requires discussion here: its relationship to a key issue raised in *Shaw*. The latter case, it will be recalled, implied that race-based districts not only are unconstitutional but might even result in reverse discrimination against white voters. In a sense, *Miller* makes the last point unnecessary. The reason is that under the *Miller* standard, white plaintiffs need not demonstrate harm, that is, that they are discriminated against because of racially drawn districts. *Miller* clearly states that "race for its own sake"[99] creates a harm if used as the predominant factor in districting and/or if its use fails the strict scrutiny test. White voters thus need not demonstrate additional harm/discrimination they may have suffered as a result of a racially drawn district. In a way, then, *Miller* simplifies the task that white plaintiffs face as a result of the possibilities opened up by *Shaw*.

Voting Rights and Districting: New Directions, New Ambiguities

Law and politics intertwine in voting rights in a way unusual for both the study of law and academic political science. The sometimes obscure concepts of constitutional law have a direct and immediate impact in determining electoral laws and governing. The interpretations of courts on voting rights issues will have a monumental impact on which individuals serve in office, the nature of their constituencies, and which parties and policies prevail in American government during the next ten years. Perhaps nowhere is this more true than in the South, where districting issues involving race not only strike resonant historical chords but immediately influence the rapidly evolving political dynamic of the region.

Since these issues are so momentous, projections and speculations are inevitable. What will the courts do with the twin obstacles to districting plans in the next four years? The immediate speculation must center on current plans being challenged or susceptible to challenge after *Shaw* and *Miller*. Many of these challenges, and assuredly the major ones, are in the South.

Race as a Predominant Factor

How much racial consideration constitutes a "predominant" consideration? We know that a bizarre district, as in *Shaw*, will raise the inference that race is overriding, and we know that unequivocal responses to Justice Department mandates to emphasize race, as in *Miller*, will trigger the strict scrutiny test.

If a jurisdiction has attempted to comply with voting rights principles in anticipation of challenges, the question it must face is, were its districts drawn for predominantly racial purposes? Only factual considerations can help a court reach this conclusion. And the question itself remains fuzzy. It seems the best way to show that race was not the predominant factor would be to demonstrate that other standards were equally important, perhaps even more so.

The Court in *Miller* pointed out that specific expressions of intent are not necessary to prove predominance, because circumstantial as well as direct evidence can be considered. Circumstantial evidence could include an oddly shaped district that did not follow political or geographic boundaries. In other words, the district lines were drawn to encompass numbers for racial purposes in derogation of the principles of compactness and respect for political boundaries. On the threshold question of predominance of race, a district that includes a supermajority of a racial group and violates traditional principles of compactness is likely to trigger strict scrutiny.

It is important to reiterate that no damage need be shown to raise an Equal Protection issue. Plaintiffs need only show that race was the predominant factor. Consequently, plaintiffs need not be white or belong to any particular race. *Hays* tells us only that the plaintiff must live in the district. Could a black plaintiff sue to declare a predominantly white district drawn for predominantly racial reasons a violation of Equal Protection? Why not? If the case showed there was no compelling state interest and the plan was not the least intrusive, then the district might well be invalid regardless of harm to plaintiffs and regardless of their race.

Strict Scrutiny: Compelling Interest

Neither *Shaw* nor *Miller* tells us precisely what will constitute a compelling state interest. Justice Kennedy in the latter case opines that historic discrimination might be so construed. From the standpoint of lower courts, *Shaw II* provides a comprehensive view of historic and current discrimination. In some recent cases involving affirmative action the Court also addressed the question of state interest; in them, the standard would seem to require more than simply a history of discrimination. The Court, in particular Justice O'Connor, expects to see continuing harm to be remedied. In cases of violation of the Voting Rights Act, discrimination was found to be continuing in that bloc voting was operating so as to prevent election of minority candidate(s) of choice.

The kind of evidence that was used in *Shaw II* is not dissimilar to the type of evidence developed in the three-pronged *Gingles* test or from the "Senate factors"—the totality of circumstances. After all, the goal is basically the same: to determine discrimination. In the *Miller* circumstance the existence of discrimination or a history of discrimination is an element of proof establishing compelling state interest that may justify the use of race as a predominant factor. But beyond these rather vague formulations, the Supreme

Court has not yet identified the specific components of a compelling state interest.

Strict Scrutiny: Least Intrusive Means

The final hurdle for a plan that has been identified as racially based is whether the plan, in furtherance of the state's compelling interest, has accomplished that purpose in the least intrusive way (that is, whether the plan is narrowly tailored). Obviously, the nature of the compelling interest will affect directly how the remedy can be implemented in the least intrusive way. In a case involving minority scholarships, providing them exclusively for African-American students was not considered the least intrusive means.[100] In *Miller,* the plan demanded by the Department of Justice was not found to be narrowly tailored. Clearly, a court may find a compelling interest but may also find that a plan fails to be least intrusive.

It is at this point that the 1980s VRA reasoning and the Equal Protection cases relating to race-based districts may reach an irreconcilable conflict. In the reasoning of VRA cases, scholars and legislators believed that districts had to surmount certain *numerical* hurdles to pass the test of sections 2 and 5. In other words, to meet the standard of providing a fair opportunity for minority voters, a demographic and electoral analysis had to show an opportunity to obtain 50 percent plus one vote to select a minority candidate of choice.

These statistical analyses generated districts with racial majorities ranging from about 50 percent to upward of 65 percent. The reasoning was that districts must provide these numbers for fair access with little regard for shape and with the intent to make race a predominant factor in the creation of the district. Now that the shape and predominance of race subject the district to strict scrutiny, the question for courts is whether or not the plan is the least intrusive method available for alleviating discrimination. To complicate matters, some have even argued that the very act of using race to create new legislative districts actually exacerbates racial prejudice.

If the wrong to be addressed is the lack of minority representation in elected office, then demographics and numerical analysis would be needed. Is the least intrusive test going to demand that the district chosen be less extreme in terms of the number or percentage of the racial majority? Probably. The signal from *Miller* was that the maximum available remedy was not acceptable.

Are there keys for demonstrating what is least intrusive? The following short list might serve for starters:

- districts must be more compact than before, honor political boundaries, and respect communities of interest;

- a minimum majority of the minority group (and, in some cases, less than a majority) must be used to demonstrate the least intrusive, narrowly tailored plan;

- perhaps other means can be used to show that a plan is in fact narrowly tailored, such as relying on voter registration as opposed to voting age population.

What Have We Wrought?

Courts are still refining the final results of the watershed cases of *Shaw* and *Miller*. At a minimum, racial districting as done in the 1980s is history. American government will have a chance to display itself at all levels on this issue. From the courthouse to Congress and even the White House, the effects of these cases will be felt. Candidates will lose and win elections based on the interpretation of these cases. How courts handle the complex issues raised by these cases will affect every citizen.

There is an opportunity to continue to solve problems of racial discrimination in critical areas of voting and representation. However, the remedies will require a rare intermingling of law, political science, and raw partisan politics.[101] The likelihood that racial tensions will be sustained and increased is almost 100 percent. The challenge to forge new alliances is daunting. While retreat has begun full scale on affirmative action, there is cause to treat voting rights differently from affirmative action in education and contracting. Ultimately, voting is more fundamental and more important. Therefore, a compelling state interest should be met when historic discrimination exists and the current will of minority voters is frustrated. At the same time, we acknowledge that minority districts should not necessarily be considered a permanent remedy for dealing with racial issues. At some point, they can and should fade away. However, they should do so on the basis of absence of discrimination, not on the basis of an arbitrary time limit.

We advocate continuing race-based districting where circumstances justify it. Why? For the foreseeable future, political districts will be designed on the basis of geographic boundaries. While some observers talk of communities of interest that span state borders and others talk of political communities existing in cyberspace, in the immediate years ahead we must use social science rather than science fiction to design political districts.

To take the next step we must acknowledge that the Constitution and circumstances, acting in tandem, have made it impossible for us to go backward. This statement is true in two separate senses. First, we cannot go back to the race-based districting of the 1980s without extreme justification. The kind of racial access districts we have seen will diminish or disappear. Second, and more important, we cannot retreat from the progress we have made in racial fairness. We have come far in the South during the last forty years in terms of black-white relations. Yet, as Justice Kennedy correctly said in *Miller,* racism still exists in America today. We cannot ignore that fact. It is essential that these decisions not be seen as a signal to slip back into the abyss of racism.

2

Voter Turnout and Candidate Participation

Effects of Affirmative Action Districting

Ronald Keith Gaddie and
Charles S. Bullock III

This chapter examines the impact of the 1991 redistricting in Louisiana to determine the influence of creating African-American districts "wherever possible" on black candidate emergence and voter participation. The number of African-American candidates in the postredistricting election is compared with the preredistricting 1987 election, controlling for incumbency status. The rates of African-American and white turnout are examined. Our analysis indicates that the creation of majority black districts substantially increased participation of black candidates in Louisiana elections, although most of that increase is confined to open seats. There is no evidence of increased black voter participation due to the creation of black districts. White turnout, particularly in the House, was sensitive to the racial composition of legislative districts.

Redistricting in the South has contributed to the promotion of descriptive representation for minorities.[1] Creation of majority-minority and minority-access districts intended to increase the opportunities for the election of African-Americans has often increased Republican representation[2] and may impact candidate emergence and voter participation.[3] The 1991–1992 round of redistricting was impacted by the influence of amended section 2 of the 1982 Voting Rights Act. This legislation was interpreted by the U.S. Department of Justice as requiring that majority-minority districts be created whenever possible. States subject to section 5 preclearance were compelled to redraw districting plans until the number of minority districts had been substantially increased, if not maximized. The need to increase majority black legislative districts in Louisiana was underscored when the Justice Department rejected a reapportionment plan for the Board of Elementary and Secondary Education because it failed to increase the number of majority black districts from one to two even as the board was reduced from eight to seven members.

In this chapter, we examine legislative elections prior to and following the 1991 redistricting in Louisiana to determine the consequences of creating black districts "wherever possible" on candidate emergence and voter participation. Conditions associated with the massive juggling of legislative district lines are expected to encourage candidacies. Experienced politicians display progressive ambitions when conditions are promising, and even ambitious amateurs are most likely to run when they perceive chances for success to be greatest.[4] Redistricting created a large number of open seats likely to result in active contestation. While any new district will release pent-up ambitions, the creation of a number of new majority black districts is expected to produce an especially high incidence of candidacies. African-Americans who have heretofore seen little prospect for winning a legislative seat may be expected to file for candidacy in these new majority black districts. The combination of an open seat plus the prospect that the individual elected in 1991 might hold the seat indefinitely should provide an added impetus for candidacy.

The creation of minority legislative districts to enhance descriptive representation may promote internal political efficacy among minority voters. Black voters who abstained when only whites ran for office may be attracted to the polls when they have the option of supporting an African-American candidate. In contests featuring viable black and white candidates, voters of both races may have an incentive to participate, leading to higher overall turnout.[5] When it is perceived that only a minority candidate is competitive in a district, white voters may participate at lower rates.[6]

The redistricting done prior to Louisiana's 1991 elections may depress participation in the short run. In the more creatively gerrymandered districts designed to bring together small, geographically dispersed black communities, confusion over what district a voter resides in and which candidates are on the ballot could discourage participation.[7]

Literature

Candidate Emergence

Changing districting schemes has a variety of consequences for legislative representation, one of which is candidate emergence. Competition in a given seat may be more likely in some group of single-member districts (SMDs) than if the same seats were combined as multimember districts (MMDs).[8] However, Standing and Robinson found a higher degree of contestation for MMDs than SMDs.[9] Altering district lines may unleash rampant ambition by creating open seats. Or strong challengers may be emboldened to take on incumbents who have been dealt less secure districts by having supporters removed and/or new voters added. Assuming that black candidates perceive success to be tied to the percentage of blacks in the constituency, strategic African-American politicians should emerge in more heavily black districts.[10] Creation of additional black majority constituencies should contribute to black candidate emergence and success. The presence of an incumbent of either race can scare off other aspirants. Features that may encourage African-American candidacies (a new majority black district and high percentages of black registrants) are expected to discourage white candidates.[11]

Voter Participation

Voter turnout is a neglected aspect of state legislative elections. Austin et al. find turnout patterns for state legislative races similar to trends in turnout for higher-level offices, although the level of participation in legislative elections was lower. Bullock and Gaddie find that contestation of state legislative elections contributes to overall voter turnout in Democratic primaries and in general elections in Florida, although this relationship weakens substantially after eliminating MMDs.[12]

Voter participation is usually higher in general elections than in party primaries, although this was not always true in the one-party South.[13] Louisiana has historically enjoyed unusually high levels of voter participation in off-off-year gubernatorial contests, and turnout is generally higher among Caucasians than among African-Americans. However, blacks are known to vote in greater numbers when an African-American is on the ballot[14] or when a racist Caucasian candidate such as David Duke emerges.[15] Under other circumstances African-American participation is lower than Caucasian participation,[16] although the effect may not be racial in origin but may instead result from socioeconomic deprivation.[17]

Contests involving incumbents may lower turnout if the presence of an incumbent discourages opposition. State legislators who seek reelection have consistently enjoyed a high degree of reelection for over two decades, a finding in keeping with the assumption that incumbents suppress competition and discourage voter participation.[18]

The Political Context

Prior to the 1975 elections, Louisiana eliminated partisan primaries, forcing all candidates to compete in a nonpartisan contest. If no candidate receives a majority of the vote, then a second (runoff) election is held between the top two finishers, unless the second-place finisher declines.[19]

The elections we study were the last under the districting plan based on the 1980 census and the first following adjustments to reflect population shifts of the 1980s. From 1980 to 1990 Louisiana's population moved away from the inner-city districts of Baton Rouge and New Orleans and toward the suburban and exurban River Parishes and the "Florida Parishes" around Lake Pontchartrain and the Mississippi River. Louisiana is subject to the pre-

clearance provision of the Voting Rights Act, and the Justice Department
pressured the legislature to create majority-minority districts wherever possible while also responding to the shift of population to new suburbs.[20] The
plan ultimately approved by the Justice Department was dubbed "black
max" in light of the numbers of new majority black districts that it created.
According to the 1992–1996 edition of the *Grassroots Guide to the Louisiana
Legislature,* thirty-four house and senate districts underwent substantial re-
structuring to create majority black districts. Black majority house districts
increased from 15 to 25 of the 105 seats, and the number of majority black
senate seats rose from 5 to 9 in the 39-member upper chamber.

The creation of majority black districts resulted in several contorted legislative districts that used many of the classic features of gerrymandering
such as stretches, bottlenecks, bacon strips, and wraps.[21] According to Assistant Clerk of the Louisiana House Kathleen Randall, the state legislature
had to "create some very contorted districts to satisfy the Justice Department."[22] Designing additional majority black districts resulted in the creation of overwhelmingly white districts on the fringe of the Black Belt, and
large numbers of heavily white districts in suburban New Orleans, East Baton Rouge Parish, Caddo Parish (Shreveport), and in central Louisiana surrounding Rapides Parish (Alexandria) were also created. The number of
senate districts with less than 20 percent black population increased from
thirteen in 1987 to eighteen in 1991. The number of house districts less
than 20 percent black increased only from fifty to fifty-two; however, the
number of seats less than 10 percent black increased from twenty-three to
twenty-nine, and the number of house districts between 30 and 50 percent
black decreased from nineteen in 1987 to seven in 1991. The initial electoral
impact of these districts is readily apparent. In 1991 with the black max plan
in place, black representatives grew from fifteen to twenty-three, and black
senators from five to eight. All African-American legislators were elected
from legislative districts having a black majority among registered voters.

Data and Sources

The Louisiana State Office of Elections and Registration maintains voter
turnout and registration data by race. Candidate race was identified from
various editions of *The National Roster of Black Elected Officials,* newspapers
such as the *Morning Advocate,* the *New Orleans Times-Picayune,* the *Shreveport
Times,* the *Alexandria Town Talk,* and the *Baton Rouge Register,* and from interviews with observers of black politics. Information on incumbency came
from 1988–1992 and 1992–1996 editions of the *Grassroots Guide to Louisiana
Politics.*

We examine the first primaries in 1987 and 1991. The first primaries in both years were held under similar electoral conditions, with large candidate fields and unpopular governors seeking reelection. Runoff turnout is not examined because not all legislative districts have runoffs. No gubernatorial runoff was held in 1987, while a hotly contested battle between Edwin Edwards and David Duke in 1991 stimulated turnout.[23]

Findings

The analysis is divided into two sections. First, we assess the impact of creating majority black districts on black and white candidate emergence. Creating minority districts is expected to increase overall black candidate emergence across the state, since few black candidates competed in majority white districts previously. White candidates are expected to be less common in districts having racial characteristics associated with more black candidates. Second, we discuss the impact of creating majority black districts on voter turnout in legislative constituencies. This analysis is conducted at the district level to determine whether black and white turnout is related to the presence of substantial minority populations, especially in newly created black districts.

Candidate Emergence

The institution of the new legislative map had a substantial impact on the emergence of candidates, although in the house this impact was limited to open seats. The total number of senate candidates—including incumbents—increased from 89 in 1987 to 116 in 1991. House candidates decreased from 295 to 284, although the average number of candidates for an open seat in the house of representatives increased by almost one, from 4.5 candidates per seat in 1987 to 5.4 candidates in 1991. In open senate contests, the number of candidates increased from an average of 2.75 in 1987 to 4.22 in 1991 (see table 2.1).

There was no change in the average number of opponents faced by house incumbents from 1987 to 1991, when the race of the incumbent is considered (a change from 1.77 to 1.70 opponents for black incumbents and from 1.46 to 1.47 for white incumbents; see table 2.2). White senate incumbents faced .2 more opponents, on average, in 1991 than in 1987 (an increase from 1.40 to 1.60). Of the ten black senators seeking reelection in 1987 and 1991, only one had an opponent.

The nature of the shift in candidate emergence and contestation becomes clearer when the racial characteristics of all candidates are considered (see table 2.3). Nineteen house and six senate districts were contested by blacks in 1987; in 1991, the number of seats contested by black candidates jumped to thirty in the house and twelve in the senate. The mean

Table 2.1. Open Seats in the Louisiana Legislature in 1987 and 1991

Open seats	Number of candidates				Mean	Districts with Black	Districts with White	Black M	White M
	N	2	3	4+					
House, 1987	16	2	4	10	4.50	2	15	0.37	4.13
House, 1991	19	1	4	14	5.42	12	14	2.47	2.95
Senate, 1987	4	3	0	1	2.75	0	4	0	2.75
Senate, 1991	9	1	1	7	4.22	4	9	1.00	3.22

Source: Compiled from election documents and newspaper campaign/election reports for 1987–1991.

Table 2.2. Candidate Emergence in Louisiana in 1987 and 1991

Candidate/year	N	M	Opponent			Black M	White M
			None	Black	White		
Black incumbents							
House, 1987	13	1.77	3	10	3	1.46	0.31
House, 1991	10	1.70	2	7	1	1.40	0.30
Senate, 1987	5	0.20	4	1	0	0.20	0
Senate, 1991	5	0	5	0	0	0	0
White incumbents							
House, 1987	76	1.46	19	4	57	0.07	1.39
House, 1991	76	1.47	20	8	53	0.30	1.17
Senate, 1987	30	1.40	8	1	22	0.03	1.37
Senate, 1991	25	1.60	9	3	18	0.24	1.36

Source: Compiled from election documents and newspaper campaign/election reports for 1987–1991.

number of black house challengers to white incumbents increased from .07 candidates/district in 1987 to .30 per district in 1991 and from .03 per district in the senate in 1987 to .24 per district in 1991. The mean number of white opponents remained essentially unchanged. In open seats, the average number of black candidates increased from .37 in 1987 to 2.4 in 1991 in the house, while an average of 1.4 black candidates appeared in each 1991 open senate seat, up from zero four years earlier. White candidates for open house seats declined from 1987 to 1991 by an average of 1.2 per seat, while the average number of white senate contestants increased by .5.

As noted above, the total number of senate candidates increased by 30 percent, while house candidates actually decreased slightly from 1987 to 1991. However, both chambers experienced a substantial increase in black candidates. African-American candidates made up only 7.9 percent of senate candidates and 14.6 percent of house candidates in 1987 (see table 2.3). By 1991, blacks constituted approximately a quarter of all candidates for both chambers—an increase largely due to the black max plan. In table 2.3, the rate of black and white candidate emergence is examined, controlling for district composition and chamber. Competition is polarized by race, with black candidates predominating in the majority black districts and white candidates emerging in majority white districts. It is interesting that the polarization is most extreme in the Louisiana Senate in 1987, while in both years the house had white contestants in even some of the most heavily black districts.

The descriptive analysis indicates that a variety of incumbency and constituency factors are affecting candidate emergence. To test these influences simultaneously, we specified a simple regression equation of black and white candidate emergence, based on the literature and descriptive evidence presented above. For 1987:

$$Y = b_1 \text{BLACKREG} + b_2 \text{BLACKINC} + b_3 \text{WHITEINC} + e \text{ [1]}$$

where Y = number of candidates; BLACKREG = the percentage of registered voters who were black; BLACKINC = 1 if there is a black incumbent, 0 otherwise; and WHITEINC = 1 if there is a white incumbent running, 0 otherwise. For 1991, we specify the following:

$$Y = b_1 \text{BLACKREG} + b_2 \text{BLACKINC} + b_3 \text{WHITEINC} + b_4 \text{NEWBLACK} + e \text{ [2]}$$

where NEWBLACK is a dummy variable indicating that the district was redrawn to be majority black for 1991, and all other variables are the same as in Equation 1.

The results of the analysis for black candidate emergence appear in table 2.4. The equation explains at least two-thirds of the variance in black can-

Table 2.3. The Emergence of Black Candidates in Louisiana in 1987 and 1991

Black population (%)	1987 Districts	Total candidates	Candidates per district	Black candidates (%)	1991 Districts	Total candidates	Candidates per district	Black candidates (%)
Senate								
0–10	5	16	3.2	0.0	6	14	2.3	0.0
10–20	8	18	2.3	0.0	12	40	3.3	2.5
20–30	15	38	2.5	2.7	8	20	2.5	0.0
30–40	5	9	1.8	0.0	3	7	2.3	14.3
40–50	1	2	2.0	0.0	1	6	6	33.3
50–60	1	1	1.0	100.0	4	14	3.5	71.4
60+	4	5	1.3	100.0	5	15	3.0	100.0
Total	39	89	2.3	7.9	39	116	3.0	25.0
House								
0–10	22	70	3.2	0.0	30	63	2.1	0.0
10–20	28	78	2.8	0.0	22	67	3.0	1.5
20–30	20	45	2.3	0.0	19	47	2.5	0.0
30–40	14	39	2.8	5.1	7	15	2.1	0.0
40–50	6	22	3.7	22.7	2	14	7.0	35.0
50–60	1	6	6.0	66.7	8	35	4.6	68.6
60+	14	35	2.5	91.4	17	43	2.5	81.4
Total	105	295	2.8	14.6	105	284	2.7	22.9

Source: Compiled from election documents and newspaper campaign/election reports for 1987–1991.

didate emergence for each chamber. The results are remarkably consistent within each chamber, although differences in black candidate emergence for the house and senate are apparent. Black population is significantly related to black candidate emergence in 1987 and 1991 in both chambers. The slope is steeper in the house for both years than in the senate, indicating that black candidacy rates are more responsive to the racial composition of the less populous house districts. Since house districts are less populous, they will generally have fewer economic bases of support than do senate districts, so that racial composition is more salient in elections for the lower chamber.[24]

Of greatest interest to us is the impact of changing district boundaries to maximize black voting strength. New black senate districts averaged about 1.25 more black candidates than other districts, and new majority black house districts averaged .75 additional black candidates. Even with controls for the impact of black registration, drawing districts with black majorities was an incentive for black candidacies. The larger coefficient in the senate than the house is probably due to greater opportunities for candidacy afforded by the larger senate districts. Senate districts are more likely to have distinctive economic or geographical subgroups that could provide the financial and voter bases for a campaign.

Incumbents, as expected, generally suppress competition. Districts where black incumbents sought reelection had fewer black candidates than other districts. For both chambers, the coefficient for black incumbents was steeper in 1987 than in 1991, and the decrease in the size of the coefficient was most substantial in the senate. That the presence of a black incumbent had less of a retarding effect on candidacies in 1991 is not surprising. Changes in district boundaries encouraged more challengers than did the stasis of 1987. White incumbents significantly reduce black candidate emergence in the house but had no significant impact on black senate challenger emergence. Once racial composition of the district was taken into consideration, white incumbents in smaller, more homogeneous house districts more readily discouraged black challengers than in the larger, more heterogeneous senate districts. In analyses for both chambers, the presence of a black incumbent was a more substantial impediment than was a white incumbent to candidate emergence. This finding was not unexpected, given the racial makeup of districts that have elected blacks and whites in the past. If black legislators who were elected in 1991 seek reelection, black candidacy rates should tumble in 1995.

For comparative purposes, the emergence of white candidates in 1987 and 1991 was also analyzed (see table 2.5). The equation is less successful in explaining white candidate emergence. While all of the hypothesized predictors are statistically significant (except for black registration in 1991

Table 2.4. Regression Estimates of Black Legislative Candidate Emergence in Louisiana in 1987 and 1991

Variable	Senate		House	
	1987[a]	1991[a]	1987[a]	1991[a]
Black registration	.048	.031	.068	.060
t	7.819**	4.588**	12.190**	8.910**
Black incumbent	−1.602	−.774	−2.343	−1.822
t	−4.371**	−2.022*	−5.645**	−3.660**
White incumbent	−.244	−.246	−.653	−.581
t	−1.103	−1.302	−2.385**	−2.128*
New black district	—	1.239	—	.747
t		3.752**		1.846**
Constant	−.499	−.257	−.328	−.300
R^2	.691	.782	.717	.726
Adjusted R^2	.665	.756	.708	.715
N	39	39	105	105
F	26.294	30.507	85.250	66.318

Note: All F values are significant at .01.
[a]The dependent variable is the number of black candidates seeking election.
* $p < .05$, one-tailed test.   ** $p < .01$, one-tailed test.

senate districts), the equation explains only between 25 and 50 percent of the variance in white candidate emergence.

The effect of black registration on white candidate emergence is apparent in the senate in 1987 and in the house in 1987 and 1991. Fewer white candidates come forward as black registration increases. Incumbency demonstrates the same effect on white candidates as on blacks. Black incumbents are much less likely to have white opponents, especially after redistricting, when the coefficient increases by almost one over 1987 in both chambers. The effects of white incumbents on white candidate emergence are virtually unchanged from 1987 to 1991, and except in the house in 1987, white incumbency is less discouraging than black incumbency. Creating new black districts significantly reduces white candidate emergence, as expected.

Louisiana's black max plan resulted in more African-American candidates and fewer white opponents in new majority black districts. However, in the wake of competitive elections for black open seats, challengers of

**Table 2.5. Regression Estimates of White Legislative Candidate
Emergence in Louisiana in 1987 and 1991**

Variable	Senate		House	
	1987[a]	1991[a]	1987[a]	1991[a]
Black registration	−.036	.013	−.034	−.023
t	−2.622**	.754	−4.034**	−2.185*
Black incumbent	−2.029	−3.174	−1.493	−2.325
t	−2.493**	−3.334**	−2.340**	−3.043**
White incumbent	−1.246	−1.243	−1.549	−1.662
t	−2.529**	−2.642**	−3.683**	−3.966**
New black district	—	−1.711	—	−1.192
t		−2.085*		−1.921*
Constant	4.338	4.004	4.372	−.300
R^2	.463	.542	.273	.299
Adjusted R^2	.417	.468	.252	.271
N	39	39	105	105
F	10.058	9.353	12.670	10.679

Note: All F values are significant at .01.
[a]The dependent variable is the number of white candidates seeking election.
* $p < .05$, one-tailed test. ** $p < .01$, one-tailed test.

either race rarely opposed black incumbents, indicating that these seats may become relatively uncompetitive after the initial election of a black. The initial increase in competitiveness observed is not very different from what occurred in the 1980s in Florida, Georgia, and South Carolina following redistricting.[25] In the Louisiana house, competition in terms of candidates did not increase substantially; instead, the composition of the candidate fields was transformed. As a result of the creation of numerous majority black open seats, 39.7 percent of all open-seat candidates were black.

Voter Participation

Voter turnout data are available at the district level for both 1987 and 1991; however, racial turnout data are available only for 1991. In 1991, white voter turnout was 74.8 percent of those registered, while black voter turnout was only 65.2 percent, for a statewide figure of 72.1 percent. Greater white voter turnout than black is common in white-white contests in the South. However, as we noted above, a variety of factors may influence voter turnout, especially among black voters. Voter turnout often increases when black candidates are on the ballot and was evident at the congressional district level in Louisiana in 1988.[26] Incumbency effects are also evident in participation, as voters perceive incumbent elections to be forgone conclusions, an attitude that depresses turnout.

If the effect of affirmative action gerrymandering is to increase black voter efficacy, we expect that black candidates, concentrations of black voters, and newly created opportunities to elect "one of our own" should increase black turnout. In order to test for multiple effects on voter turnout, we specify a regression equation to capture not only voter registration effects but also the effects of black and white candidate presence and the impact of creating new black districts. The equation specified is:

$$Y = b_1 \text{BLACKREG} + b_2 \text{WHITECAND} + b_3 \text{BLACKCAND} + b_4 \text{NEWBLACK} + e \ [3]$$

where BLACKREG = the percent black voter registration; WHITECAND = the number of white candidates running; BLACKCAND = the number of black candidates running; and NEWBLACK = 1 if the district was a newly created black majority district, 0 otherwise.

The results in table 2.6 do not support the increased-efficacy argument of black turnout. Even with the introduction of controls for candidate field composition and redistricting effects, the equations explain virtually none of the variance in black voter turnout. Significance tests may be confounded by multicollinearity between black registration and the black candidate field, although the low R^2 renders such speculation moot. Nor were alternative models more successful. Inclusion of terms to capture biracial contestation, polynomials for black registration and the presence of an incumbent, failed to improve our ability to explain variations in African-American participation levels.

Some variation in white voter turnout is explained by the model. In house elections, white turnout is significantly and positively related to the presence of multiple white candidates, indicating that the presence of white competition brings white voters to the polls. A second significant relationship—and this one holds in both chambers—is a negative one with black registration. The implication may be that concentrations of African-Americans discourage whites from voting who have little expectation of electing their candidate of choice in a heavily black district. Whites who live in legislative districts in which they are a minority may see little chance of electing a white and may have little interest in choosing from among competing blacks. An alternative explanation is that white voters in predominantly black districts may face socioeconomic obstacles to participation.[27] In Louisiana, however, and particularly in New Orleans, patterns of gentrification and neighbor-

Table 2.6. Regression Estimates of Black and White Voter Turnout in Louisiana in 1987 and 1991

Variable	Senate		House	
	Black turnout[a]	White turnout[b]	Black turnout[a]	White turnout[b]
White candidates	.648	.031	.448	.527
t	.865	.080	1.272	1.770*
Black candidates	−.306	−.848	.483	−.359
t	−.146	−.791	.872	−.768
Black registration	−.049	−.078	−.029	−.087
t	−.607	−1.884*	−.558	−2.743**
New black district	4.157	6.595	−2.004	2.629
t	.863	2.677**	−.926	1.437
Constant	64.485	76.182	64.596	75.086
R^2	.094	.342	.033	.273
Adjusted R^2	−.013	.265	−.006	.244
N	39	39	105	105
F	.882	4.226	.842	9.375

[a]The dependent variable is the percent black voter turnout at the district level.
[b]The dependent variable is the percent white voter turnout at the district level.
* $p < .05$, one-tailed test.   ** $p < .01$, one-tailed test.

hood integration frequently place affluent white neighborhoods in districts with majority black populations.

The final statistically significant relationship in table 2.6 is for the new black district variable in the senate model. White turnout is 6.6 percentage points higher in newly created black senate districts. This relationship probably arises from the mobilization effort of successful white senate candidates in several newly black districts in Baton Rouge and the Delta.[28]

Conclusions

The rationale for creating majority-minority districts "whenever possible" has rested on assumptions that: (1) minority voters prefer members of their own racial group who cannot be elected in districts where they are the minority; (2) creating conditions to promote the emergence of minority candidates will increase the likelihood that the expressed minority preference will be elected; (3) increasing the likelihood of descriptive outcomes increases the efficacy of minority voters. This study indicates that changes in districting schemes increased the number of minority legislative candidates—an increase more than offset by the decrease in white candidates. The effect of affirmative action gerrymandering stopped at encouraging black candidate emergence and creating descriptive outcomes. Despite several racial incentives, black voters were no more likely to go to the polls in heavily black districts, new or otherwise, than in any other constituencies. Instead, black voters may not have been motivated to turn out in black constituencies precisely because the result is foreordained. Given that an African-American will win, black voters and community leaders may not work as hard at increasing turnout. The benefits derived from mobilization are "guaranteed," and therefore any uncertainty over what may be seen by some as the detrimental outcome of a white victory is eliminated.

The failure of the incidence of black candidacy to be related to African-American turnout parallels findings for South Carolina and Florida. Bullock and Gaddie found that contestation in legislative districts—as opposed to numbers of candidates, the predictor used in this chapter—was infrequently related to turnout once MMDs were replaced with SMDs in the 1980s.[29] When most Florida legislators represented MMDs, counties having more contested house elections usually had higher turnout. The Louisiana research adds creation of new majority black districts to the set of predictors that seem not to have a consistent impact on black voter participation.

The failure of variables in table 2.6 to explain variation in African-American turnout does not mean that fluctuations in black participation rates are unrelated to political context. Bullock, Gaddie, and Kuzenski have shown that increased black turnout in response to the David Duke challenge in the 1991 gubernatorial runoff was greatest in parishes experiencing larger increases in black registration.[30] Bullock and colleagues also observed that white turnout in the 1991 runoff was related to heightened black registration. Obviously the finding is the opposite of that for the primary as reported in table 2.6. Why the difference?

We speculate that in the first round of 1991 elections, white participation was depressed in heavily black house and senate districts because whites had little interest in the outcome of a contest destined to be won by a black. Without a white candidate, some white voters may have felt that they "had no dog in the fight" and rolled off. (Interestingly, in New Orleans councilmanic elections the presence of an all-black slate is related to higher white turnout.)[31] In the statewide gubernatorial runoff the likely outcome was not as obvious. Massive publicity supporting Edwin Edwards over Duke encouraged people to "Vote for the crook; it's important." In the runoff, whites voted in larger numbers in parishes where black registration grew most, perhaps a continuation of the pattern observed by Key in which whites in heavily black areas were the most hostile to African-Americans.[32]

Efforts to model candidate emergence were more successful. Concentrations of blacks prompted African-Americans to seek office and dissuaded whites. Above and beyond the racial composition of the district, the creation of a new majority black district added to the likelihood that black candidates would run and that whites would not. The presence of incumbents of either race generally discouraged challenges, with this factor being particularly strong when the incumbent was black.

3

The Impact of Election Timing on Republican Trickle-Down in the South

Jay Barth

While the Republican gains at all levels in the southern states in 1994 were impressive, they should not be overstated, particularly in races for statewide executive office. The GOP does now hold governorships in six of the eleven southern states, but the majority of subgubernatorial offices are held by Democrats in almost all of the southern states.[1] This composition contrasts dramatically with the GOP dominance at the presidential level.

Why does Republican electoral success in the eleven southern states in subpresidential, and particularly subgubernatorial, races remain so inconsistent, when GOP success at the presidential level has become quite steady over the past two decades? Four decades after Dwight Eisenhower made the first lasting Republican inroads into the South at the presidential level, and more than twenty years after Richard Nixon swept the region, the top-to-bottom realignment of the region's politics predicted at the time by observers such as Kevin Phillips, has not occurred.[2] This chapter examines one of the potential barriers to the trickle-down theory of Republicanism from the presidential level to lower levels of southern state politics: the scheduling of almost all state elections in the South in nonpresidential years, a decoupling of presidential and state elections that has been part of a national trend over the past several decades.[3]

While some southern states began holding state elections outside of presidential years as early as the turn of the century, such separation has occurred in almost all of the southern states over the years, with a number of southern states moving state races out of presidential years since the GOP began to make significant inroads into the region at the presidential level. Some of these separations have come about as states (Tennessee in the early 1950s, Texas in the early 1970s, and finally Arkansas in the 1980s) shifted from two-year to four-year terms for state officials. In all three cases these new four-year terms were placed in a nonpresidential election cycle.

Three southern states hold state elections in odd-numbered years, separated even from elections for the U.S. Senate and House of Representatives. Table 3.1 shows the current scheduling of state elections in the southern states. As can be seen, North Carolina is now the only state that holds its regular election for statewide offices in presidential years.

A detailed examination of the process through which the timing of state elections was changed in the Democratic-dominated state of Arkansas (as part of a move to four-year terms)—too lengthy to be covered here—presents no evidence that the move had a partisan purpose. In Arkansas, the last of the southern states to make such a move, the constitutional amendment seems to have been a legitimate "good government" measure that had bipartisan support.[4] A different story is seen in North Carolina, the lone state not to move its statewide executive branch elections out of presidential years. Two recent attempts to alter the election calendar in that state have been extremely partisan at every stage. Unanimous Republican opposition to the movement of gubernatorial and Council of State elections has been essential to blocking these attempts.[5]

It is clear that the timing of state elections has a marked impact on the *turnout* in them. Jewell and Olson show that, when elections for governor and other state officials are held in nonpresidential years, turnout is significantly lower.[6] This finding is unsurprising, in view of the long debate over the phenomenon of "surge and decline" in congressional elections.[7] The more crucial issue is whether the altered timing of elections changes the dynamics of the process at the state level to the benefit of candidates of a particular party.

V. O. Key argued that holding statewide elections in presidential election years can hasten the success for a traditional minority party. As Key stated: "If the governor is chosen in presidential years, the minority, despite the weakness of local forces, gains advantage from the fact that in these years the voters are aroused by the issues and events of the national campaign."[8] Conversely, it would be expected that separation of state elections from presidential elections might retard the trickling down of a realignment from the presidential level to state elections.

Key supported his theory with election data indicating that indeed off-year elections had insulated local majority parties against inroads by minority parties that were stronger at the national level. Austin Ranney replicated Key's study for the 1952-to-1970 period, again finding support for the thesis that state election timing affects the potential impact of national forces on lower-level politics.[9]

Examining the election results since 1900 from the four states that held onto two-year terms into the 1980s, Russell Benjamin found a significantly stronger relationship between party presidential vote in the state and that party's gubernatorial candidate in presidential years than in nonpresiden-

Table 3.1. Timing of State Elections in the Eleven Southern States as of 1995

State	Presidential year	Off year	Odd year
North Carolina	x	—	—
Alabama	—	x	—
Arkansas	—	x	—
Florida	—	x	—
Georgia	—	x	—
South Carolina	—	x	—
Tennessee	—	x	—
Texas	—	x	—
Louisiana	—	—	x
Mississippi	—	—	x
Virginia	—	—	x

Source: Compiled from data presented in *The Book of the States, 1994–1995* (Lexington, Ky.: Council of State Governments, 1995), 209–212.

tial years.[10] As a whole these findings indicate that the gradual shift of almost all state elections in the South to nonpresidential years indeed could be inhibiting the success of the GOP, the new majority party at the presidential level in the region, in state elections.

The Impact of Timing on Southern Elections

Many scholars rely heavily upon survey data measuring the electorate's psychological affiliation with the parties when considering the realignment issue. For instance, relying upon such survey data, Harold W. Stanley notes that while southern white Republican Party identifiers are more loyal to their presidential candidates than are white Democratic partisans, these Democratic partisans are consistently more loyal than are Republicans in voting for the U.S. Congress.[11]

It is safe to say that *voting behavior* is at least as good a way, if not a better way, to evaluate the extent or the existence of a realignment. The typical problem with using voting behavior is that the degree to which partisanship has influenced the voters' decisions is neither readily apparent nor easily measurable. Other factors obviously enter into voters' minds when they consider how to vote. Incumbency, name recognition, candidate appeal, campaign spending, and the "coattail effect" are all factors that have been shown to impact voting decisions for particular offices. These other factors play significant and decisive roles for many voters in high-profile races, like those for president, U.S. Senate, and governor. The difficulties in ferreting out the impact exerted by party affiliation on a particular voter, either in the aggregate or in individual cases, are therefore considerable.

Importantly, though, races for low-profile offices in southern state politics—specifically those for lieutenant governor, secretary of state, attorney general, state treasurer, and state auditor or comptroller—naturally control for many of these factors that typically mitigate voting behavior. For instance, candidates for these offices are typically not well known, and usually much less money is spent in their campaigns. So voters in these races are much more likely to cast votes based on their perceptions of the parties rather than on their perceptions of particular candidates. In this respect, these races offer advantages over analyses of state legislative voting, races that are "further down the ballot," in that voters are much more likely to be familiar with the personalities of these candidates for local offices.

Data and Analysis

The primary data for this analysis consist of county-level election returns for president in 1980, 1984, and 1988 and for contested races for the statewide elected offices of lieutenant governor, secretary of state, attorney general, state treasurer, state auditor, and state comptroller in ten of the eleven states of the Confederacy since 1980.[12] Tennessee, the eleventh state, has no statewide elected executive positions below the office of governor. In the past, county-by-county election returns for these low-profile races have been difficult to obtain. They are particularly valuable data because the large number of cases permits detailed analysis of political behavior.[13]

The data are separated into three waves, corresponding to each of the three presidential elections.[14] Down-ticket race voting results are grouped with the votes from the previous, or accompanying, presidential election. So, for example, the 1980 presidential results are grouped with down-ticket races from 1980 through 1983. In the 1980 cycle, nineteen contested down-ticket races are available for analysis. For the 1984 cycle, twenty-three contested lower-level races are analyzed. And in the third, 1988 cycle, twenty-six such races are available for analysis.

The data are then separated into three categories for purposes of determining the impact of timing of down-ticket elections on the degree to which trickle-down has occurred: presidential year elections; off-year elections, meaning those held in even-numbered nonpresidential years; and odd-year elections, meaning those held either the year immediately before or after a presidential election. So, for example, in the 1980 cycle, presidential year down-ticket races would be those elections from 1980; off-year elections would be those from 1982; and odd-year elections would be those from 1981 and 1983. The fact that since 1980 southern states have held a good number of elections in each of the three types of election years offers an opportunity to compare the relationship between presidential level and state-level voting in all three settings.[15]

These odd-year elections are even more isolated from politics at the national level because they coincide with neither presidential nor congressional elections. In his work comparing presidential and gubernatorial voting patterns in the off-year state of Louisiana, John Wildgen termed the voting cycle adopted by three southern states a "double filter" against national political trends affecting state politics.[16]

I hypothesize that, while GOP presidential vote in the counties in the accompanying or preceding election should be positively related to down-ticket vote in all three categories, the degree to which presidential vote is explaining down-ticket should vary according to the timing of the elections. The appropriate statistical measure to determine the variable's explanatory power is the adjusted R^2.[17] Specifically, adjusted R^2 scores should typically be highest in presidential years, lower in off years, and lowest in odd years. Rather than pooling all of the data from the three election cycles, the separation of the data into the 1980, 1984, and 1988 cycles allows for an examination of whether trends regarding the timing of elections have been consistent over the years. This is made feasible by the large number of cases that county-by-county returns from these elections produce. Pooling the data presents the danger that one particular election cycle might drive the findings for the period as a whole.

Results

The results of regression analyses for the three sets of election types in the three cycles are shown in tables 3.2, 3.3, and 3.4. As can be seen, in all cases, the positive relationship between presidential vote and the vote for down-ticket offices is highly significant.

More crucially, the hypotheses regarding the differing degrees to which presidential vote explains down-ticket vote, based on the timing of elections, are also upheld by the analyses. The adjusted R^2 scores for each of the three cycles are shown in figures 3.1, 3.2, and 3.3, respectively. Most important, in all three cycles, the adjusted R^2 scores for down-ticket races held in presidential years are considerably higher than for other years. In the 1980 cycle, the adjusted R^2 for presidential years is .713. While slightly lower, the adjusted R^2 of .603 for the 1984 cycle is strong, considering that Reagan's landslide intruded into traditionally strong Democratic counties in the region. In the third cycle, the adjusted R^2 for presidential year down-

Table 3.2. Parameter Coefficients for the Model of the Percentage of Republican Vote in Down-Ticket Races Held in Presidential Years in Ten Southern States, 1980–1988

Item	1980 Cycle	1984 Cycle	1988 Cycle
PRES%	1.074**	1.142**	1.032**
Standard error	0.025	0.043	0.022
Constant	−0.127**	−0.288**	−0.128**
N	175	475	467
R^2	.715	.604	.819
Adjusted R^2	.713	.603	.819
F	433.877**	720.739**	2106.372**

** $p < .0001$.

Table 3.3. Parameter Coefficients for the Model of the Percentage of Republican Vote in Down-Ticket Races Held in Off Years in Ten Southern States, 1980–1988

Item	1980 Cycle	1984 Cycle	1988 Cycle
PRES%	0.825**	0.658**	0.700**
Standard error	0.016	0.025	0.012
Constant	−0.124**	−0.059*	−0.005
N	1,861	1,077	2,007
R^2	.601	.391	.370
Adjusted R^2	.601	.391	.370
F	2804.692**	690.941**	1177.050**

* $p < .0005$. ** $p < .0001$.

ticket elections is .819. All the scores are considerably higher than those for off-year or odd-year elections in the same cycle. This finding indicates that the common separation of state elections in the South from presidential elections presents a powerful barrier to the trickling down of Republican success to lower-level races.

In the 1980 and 1984 cycles, the adjusted R^2 score for off-year elections is considerably larger than that for odd-year elections, as hypothesized. For the 1980 cycle, the adjusted R^2 for off-year elections is .601, and that for odd-year races is .392. A similar explanatory gap is found between the two

Table 3.4. Parameter Coefficients for the Model of the Percentage of Republican Vote in Down-Ticket Races Held in Odd Years in Ten Southern States, 1980–1988

Item	1980 Cycle	1984 Cycle	1988 Cycle
PRES%	1.041**	0.528**	0.713**
Standard error	0.062	0.054	0.048
Constant	–0.159**	0.004	0.016
N	436	664	354
R^2	.394	.126	.384
Adjusted R^2	.392	.125	.382
F	281.751**	95.756**	219.383**

** $p < .0001$.

types of elections in the 1984 cycle: for off-year races, the adjusted R^2 is .391; for odd-year elections, a minuscule .125. However, in the third cycle, the adjusted R^2 scores for the two types of elections are essentially the same, with the adjusted R^2 for odd-year elections of .382 slightly higher than the .370 for off-year races. So, while holding elections in odd years may further separate state elections from the realigning forces of national politics, the data seem to indicate that the separation of state elections from the presidential year, whether in off or odd years, is the key to limiting GOP trickle-down.

Discussion and Conclusion

While—as mentioned earlier in the chapter—it is not clear that Democratic elites in the southern states were strategic actors in moving state elections out of presidential election cycles, it is clear that the decoupling of statewide elections in the region has worked to limit the trickle-down of Republicanism from the presidential level into southern state politics. This purely structural barrier that is apparently mitigating lower-level Republican success must be added to other factors that previous research has identified as pieces of the puzzle explaining the inconsistency of down-ticket Republicanism in the South: the ideological tightrope that southern state Democrats regularly walk to keep biracial coalitions vibrant and the continued difference in the quality of the candidates of the two parties in the region.[18] Previous research has shown that one traditional explanation for the divergence between GOP presidential and state success in the region,

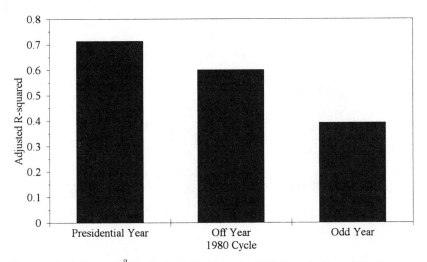

Figure 3.1. Adjusted R^2 for the Basic Model in the 1980 Cycle, by Year of Election. *Source:* Compiled from voting data supplied by national party headquarters.

dual partisanship at the mass level, is no longer a significant factor in the politics of the southern states.[19]

It appears that a phenomenon essentially the same as the surge and decline that has been shown to exist in congressional voting is present in these non-presidential-year elections. Unfortunately, we still lack a clear understanding of exactly how that phenomenon operates. Angus Campbell argued that independents are more likely to turn out in high-stimulus presidential elections, a time when these peripheral voters also generally support congressional candidates of the president's party. Because these voters then typically do not vote in off-year congressional elections, the party of the president is comparatively disadvantaged and regularly loses seats.[20] James Campbell has pointed out that while aggregate data support the original surge and decline theory, that theory is not supported by individual level data.[21] Campbell presented a revised theory, arguing that high-stimulus elections prompt independents not to turn out but instead to vote for the winning presidential candidate and his/her party's congressional candidate. These independents replace *weak* partisans of the losing presidential party, who are *less* likely to turn out when their candidate is going to be a clear loser. This revision was tested with aggregated individual-level data. While an improvement over Angus Campbell's data, the theory still needs to be tested with *true* individual-level data to determine better how the shifts in turnout impact not just congressional elections but also elections like those examined in this analysis.

Since this rule of the game in southern politics has had a clear impact in

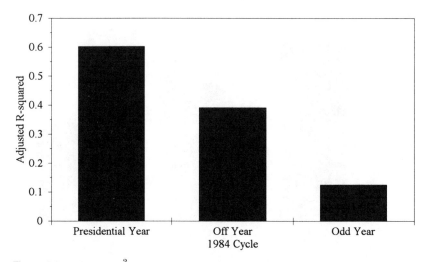

Figure 3.2.   Adjusted R^2 for the Basic Model in the 1984 Cycle, by Year of Election.
Source: Compiled from voting data supplied by national party headquarters.

limiting Republican success in lower-level races in the region, it would also be worthwhile to consider other, similar election rules that could be affecting the two parties' success rates in subpresidential elections. For instance, the potential impact of the runoff elections, an election rule now unique to southern states, has been analyzed, with conflicting interpretations, by Black and Black and Bullock and Johnson. Black and Black contend that "the dual primary system strengthens the electoral chance of Democratic nominees in general elections by providing a mechanism for eliminating many weak frontrunners."[22] Bullock and Johnson focus on the downside of runoffs for Democrats: "The end result is, arguably, the nomination of a weakened Democrat who limps into battle against a well-rested Republican."[23] On the basis of the data they employ, both sets of authors present sound arguments for their case.

Another rule that has insulated Democrats from Republican threats in the region are succession laws, usually limited for the governor's office but typically unlimited for lower-level executive positions. An examination of the effect of incumbency on the races included in this study indicated that incumbency does not have a direct impact on voting patterns in these down-ticket races, but by discouraging strong opposition, incumbency could have a significant *indirect* stifling effect on Republicanism. However, this "rule" may soon be significantly altered by term limit mechanisms, which have already been approved in some southern states, in that incumbency will no longer mean what it has in the past.[24] It would be beneficial to examine systematically the consequences of these and other election laws—and the in-

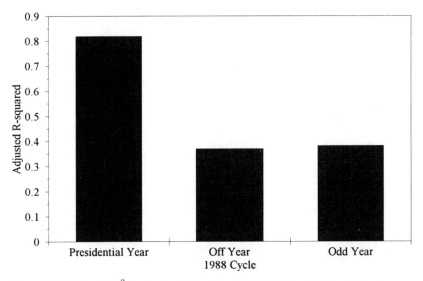

Figure 3.3. Adjusted R^2 for the Basic Model in the 1988 Cycle, by Year of Election.
Source: Compiled from voting data supplied by national party headquarters.

teraction of these rules—that conceivably could be altering the success rates of the two parties' candidates in state elections in the South.

Despite the attempts of its Democratic legislators, North Carolina is the lone southern state not to move its statewide executive branch elections out of presidential years. The most recent 1994 elections in the South indicate that, contrary to the arguments made in this chapter about electoral trends in the post-Reagan South, North Carolina Democrats were likely very lucky that their party's efforts have failed. Major shifts occurred at every level of that state's politics in races that were up for election in 1994, including dramatic transitions in the state legislature. However, the Democratic governor and Council of State officers did not have to face the voters. Democratic candidates in similar positions in most other southern states were not as lucky; while the Democrats retained most statewide executive offices, the GOP won a number of statewide positions that they had not won since Reconstruction.

The findings of this chapter indicate that strong Republican presidential candidates have aided candidates in lower-level statewide races who are also on the ticket, compared with similar GOP candidates in elections held in nonpresidential years. However, when national electoral tides impact congressional elections in a way that favors the Republican Party, disadvantages the Democrats, or—as in 1994—does both, races further down the ticket can be affected. The year 1994 could mark the beginning of a new trend in the South, where such nationalization occurs in the even-numbered nonpresidential years when most southern states hold their statewide elections. The more likely scenario, considering the unique nature of the 1994 Republican landslide, is that the decoupling of state elections from presidential elections will, in the South, continue to serve as a barrier to realigning trends.

4
Changes in the Composition of Political Activists, 1952–1992

Patrick R. Cotter,
Samuel H. Fisher III, and
Felita T. Williams

In studying political participation, political scientists have focused much of their attention on the questions of (1) how much participation occurs, (2) what types of citizens participate, and (3) what impact participation has on the political process. With regard to the impact of participation, researchers have particularly examined the issue of bias. That is, they have sought to determine the extent to which the views and concerns of political activists represent or correspond to those of politically inactive citizens.[1]

The issue of bias in political participation is the focus of this paper. We examine this issue with regard to the American South. The reason we examine the South is that for the first half of this century the region was characterized by a distinctively low level of political participation.[2] A relatively poor and uneducated public, one-party electoral politics, and, most important, a system of restrictive election laws meant that most residents of the region lacked the resources, incentives, and opportunity to participate. Evidence suggests that those few who were active in the region's politics were quite unrepresentative of the southern population as a whole.[3]

Since midcentury, political participation rates have increased substantially in the South. In his analysis of the Solid South, V. O. Key found that presidential election turnout in the region was roughly half that found nationally.[4] Now voting levels in the South almost equal those found nationally. For example, in the 1992 presidential election, the eleven southern states had an average turnout rate of 51.6 percent, compared with 55.2 percent nationally.[5]

Much of the increase in participation rates in the South is attributable to changes in election laws that have made registering and voting much easier for all citizens. The increase is also the result of rising income and education levels and the development of a competitive party system within the region.[6]

In this study, we examine how the composition of southern political activists has changed since midcentury. The results of this examination will indicate (1) the extent to which the level of bias, with regard to political participation, has changed in the region during the last forty years and (2) the amount and type of participation bias that currently exists within the South. Also, by comparing regions, our examination will show the degree to which the level of participation bias in the South differs from that in the remainder of the country.

Citizens can participate in politics in a variety of ways. They can vote, talk about politics with their friends and acquaintances, work in political campaigns, be active in community organizations, or hold formal party or government positions. Obviously, the different forms of participation vary in the demands they place on potential participants, the types of citizens they ultimately attract, and, perhaps most important, the amount of information they convey to leaders.[7]

We are interested in examining the amount and type of bias associated with different forms of participation. Thus in this study we will examine two forms of political participation: voting and campaigning. These two types of activities differ in the resources they require from citizens and the amount of pressure they potentially place on political leaders. Specifically, campaigning requires more time and effort from citizens than does voting, but it has greater potential for conveying information to leaders about an individual's preferences and concerns.

It is possible to examine bias with regard to a number of socioeconomic characteristics. Race, class, and gender are the characteristics we have chosen to study. Race and class are investigated because these two variables are central topics in the study of both political participation and electoral and party politics in the South.[8]

As compared with race and class, the relationship between gender and political participation has not received as much research attention. However, in recent years several studies have examined the amount and cause of different participation rates among men and women.[9] Also, according to some research, one area of southern distinctiveness is the low level of political participation found among southern females.[10] Given this increased research attention, and the possibility of interesting or important findings, it is worthwhile to examine the amount and type of participation bias regarding gender in the South.

As stated previously, research into participation bias is important because it shows whether some concerns or viewpoints are better represented in the political arena than are others. We, and others, have chosen to study the existence of participation bias by examining the relationship between political activity levels and individual characteristics such as race, class, and gender. These variables are selected for study because they stand as surrogates for an individual's issue preferences or priorities.

An important and obvious limitation to this approach is that the relation-ships existing between an individual's issue preferences or priorities and his/her race, class, or gender are far from perfect. In the present study we try to overcome this shortcoming by conducting a limited analysis of par-ticipation bias with regard to actual policy opinions. Our approach is lim-ited because we examine only two of the many issue areas potentially inves-tigated. The two are, however, among the most important in American politics. Specifically, we will examine participation bias with regard to opin-ions about racial and social service issues.[11]

Method

The data used in this study come from the 1952–1992 presidential elec-tion surveys conducted by the National Election Study.[12] With these data, southerners are operationalized as respondents residing in one of the for-mer Confederate states at the time they were interviewed.

Respondents are classified as voters if they report that they voted in that presidential year's general election, even if they did not cast a ballot for president.[13] Campaigners are respondents who, during the election year, en-gaged in at least one of the following activities: (1) attended a political meet-ing, rally, speech, or dinner, (2) worked for a party or candidate, or (3) con-tributed money to a political candidate or party.[14]

The indicator of social class used here is a respondent's education.[15] Specifically, respondents with a high school education or less are classified as less educated. Those with more than a high school education are in-cluded in the more educated group.

In examining race, class, and gender, we have chosen to measure partici-pation bias in a simple and direct fashion. Specifically, our measure is the percentage of "dominant" group members (that is, whites, upper class, men) saying that they participated in some activity (that is, voting, cam-paigning) minus the percentage of "subordinate" group members (that is, blacks, lower class, women) saying that they participated in this same activ-ity. This measure will equal to zero, indicating that no participation bias exists, if the dominant and subordinate groups are equally active. Positive scores on the measure indicate that bias exists in the direction of the domi-nant group. Conversely, negative scores indicate that bias exists in the direc-tion of the subordinate group. The more the score differs from zero, the greater the amount of bias.[16]

An understandable lack of consistency in questions asked and question wording makes it impossible, with the National Election Survey data, to con-struct measures of racial or social service issue opinions that are strictly comparable across time. We have sought to minimize this problem by employing similar methods and procedures in constructing separate opinion scales for each election survey.

Specifically, in constructing a measure of racial opinions, we first identified the items included in each election survey that asked about racial issues. Second, the identified items were recoded so that responses ran in the same "direction" and had the same range. Third, the items were summed. Finally, to take into account the fact that the number of racial issue items asked varies from year to year, the scale scores were adjusted so that the values ranged between zero and one.[17] Similar procedures were used to construct the social service issue measure.[18] The items used in constructing the racial and social service issue measures are listed in the appendix (table 4.A1).[19]

In examining racial and social service opinions scales, our interest is not in how liberal or conservative activists or nonactivists are but rather in the size (and direction) of the difference, or bias, in issue opinions that exists between these groups. We will measure the magnitude and direction of issue bias by calculating the difference between activists and nonactivists in mean scores on the racial and social service scales. The greater the opinion difference, the greater the level of bias.

Results

Socioeconomic Characteristics

Race. Figure 4.1 shows the participation bias measure for black and white southerners in the area of voting. The figure shows, as expected, that the amount of racial bias in the South has undergone considerable change since midcentury. This change occurred in three stages. First, between 1952 and 1960, voting was heavily biased in the direction of white southerners. During this time, reported turnout among southern whites was about 50 percent higher than among southern blacks. Second, in 1964, the amount of participation bias decreased by about half. In this election year, southern whites were about 22 percent more likely than southern blacks to say that they had voted. Finally, since 1968 the amount of racially based participation bias in the area of voting has been relatively small in the South. Reported turnout rates among white southerners are now only slightly higher than among southern blacks. It is interesting to note, however, that the amount of bias found in the 1988 and 1992 studies is somewhat greater than that found for the 1980 and 1984 elections.

Roughly similar results are found with regard to campaigning among southern whites and blacks (figure 4.2). In the 1956 and 1960 elections there was a substantial bias toward whites with regard to campaigning. Since then the amount of bias has been smaller. Also, the amount and direction of race-based campaign bias has fluctuated from year to year. As with regard to voting, the amount of bias in 1992 is somewhat higher than was found

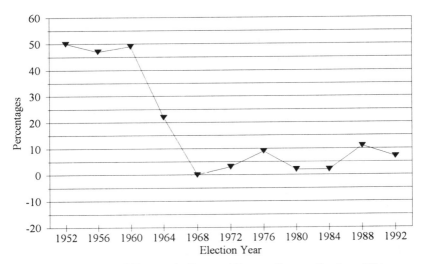

Figure 4.1. Percentage Difference in Reported Turnout Between Southern Whites and Blacks: 1952–1992. *Source:* The American National Election Studies, 1952–1992, conducted by the Center for Political Studies at the University of Michigan.

during the 1970s and 1980s. Overall, however, blacks and whites in the South are now about equally likely to participate in campaign activities.

Class. Throughout the period under study, a substantial amount of social-class-based participation bias has existed in the South. Figure 4.3 shows that between 1952 and 1960, reported voting turnout among more educated southerners was about 30 percent higher than among less educated southerners. Between 1964 and 1984 the amount of class-based participation bias became smaller. Even in this period, however, reported turnout rates were about 20 percent higher among more educated than less educated southerners. In the two most recent presidential elections, class-based differences in reported turnout increased to a level about equal to that found in the 1952–1960 period. In 1992, for example, reported voting turnout was 34 percent higher among more educated than less educated southerners.

Bias is also found when the campaign activity levels of more and less educated southerners are examined (figure 4.4). Compared with voting, the amount of class-based bias in the area of campaigning has remained more stable over time. Still, as in the case of voting, a rough U-shaped pattern is observed when the amount of class-based campaign bias is examined. In particular, the amount of class bias in campaigning was high at the beginning of the period under study, became somewhat smaller between 1964 and 1984, and then rose in the 1988 and 1992 contests. As a result, in the area of campaigning, the amount of class bias in the South in the last two presidential elections is about equal to that found thirty to forty years earlier.

Gender. In the area of voting, the amount of gender-based bias has gen-

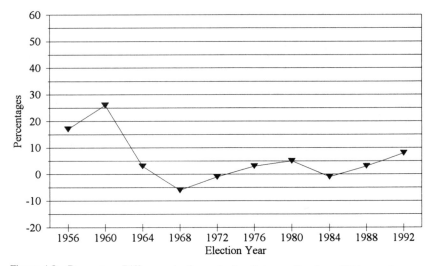

Figure 4.2. Percentage Difference in Campaigning Between Southern Whites and Blacks: 1956–1992. *Source:* The American National Election Studies, 1956–1992, conducted by the Center for Political Studies at the University of Michigan.

erally diminished over time (figure 4.5). Through 1960 the reported turnout rate among southern males was about 20 percent higher than among southern females. This difference diminished in 1964, increased in 1968 (to a 20 percent difference in reported turnout), and then declined again. In three of the last four presidential elections, the reported turnout rates of southern men and southern women have been about equal. Indeed, in 1980, southern women were 2 percent more likely to say that they voted than were southern men.

With regard to campaigning, the amount of gender-based participation bias in the South has remained relatively small and roughly stable across time (figure 4.6). In 1964, men were about 12 percent more likely than women to engage in campaign activities. In 1976, campaign participation was about 7 percent higher among women than men. In general, however, southern men are only slightly more likely to engage in campaign activities than are southern women.

Issue Opinions

Racial issues. The first section of table 4.1 shows the results of calculating the difference in mean racial issue opinion scale scores between southern political activists and nonactivists. Overall these results parallel those found earlier when participation bias with regard to race was examined. In particular, early in the time period under study, a considerable amount of participation bias existed in the region. In 1956 and 1960, and to a lesser extent

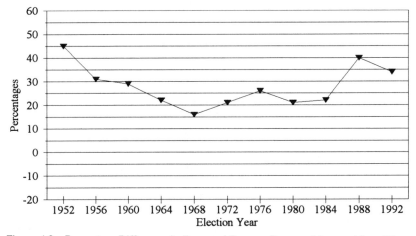

Figure 4.3. Percentage Difference in Reported Turnout Between More and Less Educated Southerners: 1952–1992. *Source:* The American National Election Studies, 1952–1992, conducted by the Center for Political Studies at the University of Michigan.

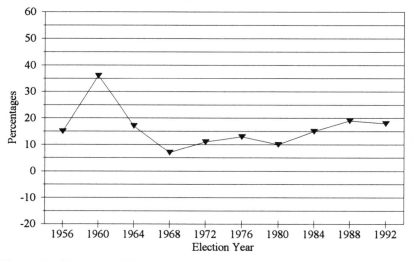

Figure 4.4. Percentage Difference in Campaigning Between More and Less Educated Southerners: 1956–1992. *Source:* The American National Election Studies, 1956–1992, conducted by the Center for Political Studies at the University of Michigan.

in 1964, southern voters were significantly more conservative in their racial issue opinions than were nonvoters. Since then the amount of participation bias has declined. No statistically significant differences are found in racial issue opinions between southern voters and nonvoters between 1968 and 1984. However, somewhat higher levels of participation bias regarding racial issue opinions are found in the last two election years examined. Still, the

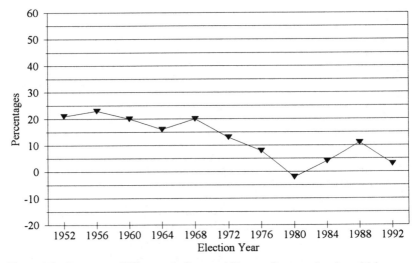

Figure 4.5. Percentage Difference in Reported Turnout Between Southern Males and Females: 1952–1992. *Source:* The American National Election Studies, 1952–1992, conducted by the Center for Political Studies at the University of Michigan.

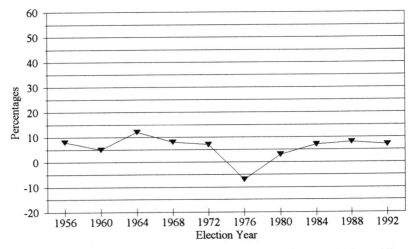

Figure 4.6. Percentage Difference in Campaigning Between Southern Males and Females: 1956–1992. *Source:* The American National Election Studies, 1956–1992, conducted by the Center for Political Studies at the University of Michigan.

differences found between voters and nonvoters in 1988 and 1992 are smaller than those existing in either 1956 or 1960.

With regard to campaigning, in 1952 activists were more conservative in their racial issue opinions than were nonactivists. Since then, no significant differences appear in racial issues opinions between the two groups.

Table 4.1. Differences in Mean Racial and Social Service Issue Scale Scores Between Southern Political Activists and Nonactivists, 1956–1992

Issue	Voters and nonvoters	Campaigners and noncampaigners
Racial		
1956	0.11[a]	0.09[a]
1960	0.21[a]	0.00
1964	0.07[a]	0.03
1968	−0.04	−0.04
1972	0.01	−0.07
1976	0.04	−0.06
1980	0.00	−0.03
1984	0.02	0.00
1988	0.07	0.03
1992	0.05	0.01
Social service		
1956	0.14[a]	0.15[a]
1960	0.14[a]	0.22[a]
1964	0.18[a]	0.14[a]
1968	0.11[a]	−0.01
1972	0.05	0.00
1976	0.11[a]	0.04
1980	0.01	0.05
1984	0.12[a]	0.03
1988	0.08[a]	0.05
1992	0.04	0.03

Note: Scores greater than zero indicate that the average score of voters or campaigners is more conservative than the average score of nonvoters or noncampaigners. Scores less than zero indicate that nonactivists are more conservative than activists.

[a]The difference between voters and nonvoters, or campaigners and noncampaigners, is significant at the .05 level.

Source: The American National Elections Studies, 1956–1992, conducted by the Center for Political Studies at the University of Michigan.

Social service issues. The second section of table 4.1 shows that between 1956 and 1968 southern voters were significantly more conservative in their opinions regarding social service policies than were nonvoting southerners. Since then, similar (though slightly smaller) differences have occurred in 1976, 1984, and 1988. In 1972, 1980, and 1992, however, no significant differences in social service issue opinions are found between southern voters and nonvoters. When campaigning is examined, the results show that since 1960 no significant differences in social service opinions have occurred between southern campaigners and noncampaigners.

In sum, the results shown in table 4.1 indicate that in recent years southern voters have occasionally had different views on racial and social service issues than have nonvoters. When this bias has occurred, it has always been the result of voters' being more conservative than nonvoters. Similar differences have not occurred between campaigners and noncampaigners.

Regional Differences

Socioeconomic characteristics. To determine whether the South has a distinctively high or low level of participation bias we must first repeat the analysis involving race, class, and gender among nonsoutherners and then compare the findings for the two regions.[20] Table 4.2 shows that through 1960 (and to a lesser extent in 1964 with regard to voting) there was a higher level of participation bias regarding race in the South than in the non-South. For example, in 1952 southern whites were 50 percent more likely to vote than were southern blacks. Outside the South in 1952, the voting rates of whites and blacks differed by "only" 19 percent. Since 1960 the amount of participation bias regarding race has been about the same in each region. Indeed, in recent years, the level of racial participation bias has often been higher in the non-South than in the South. For example, in 1984 the difference in reported voting rates between whites and blacks was 11 percent in the non-South compared with 2 percent in the South.

With regard to class the results consistently show that in each region more educated citizens are more politically active than are less educated citizens. However, with the exception of 1960, relatively small differences are found between the regions with regard to participation bias in the area of campaigning. Similarly, in the area of voting, relatively small regional differences are found during the 1960–1984 period. However, at both the beginning and end of the time period under study, substantially more class-based participation bias is found in the South than elsewhere in the country. For example, in 1992, the reported voting rate among more educated southerners was 34 percent higher than that of less educated southerners. Outside the South in 1992, there was an 18 percent difference in voting rates between these two groups of citizens.

Regional differences in gender bias in the area of voting have also diminished over time. In 1952 there was a 21 percent gap in voting rates between southern males and females, compared with a 5 percent difference among nonsoutherners. In 1992, however, the difference in reported voting rates between males and females was 3 percent in the South and 2 percent elsewhere in the country. With regard to campaigning, the regions have generally never experienced large differences in the amount of gender bias.

Table 4.2. Race, Class, and Gender Participation Bias Between Southerners and Nonsoutherners, 1952–1992

Year	Participation bias					
	Race		Class		Gender	
	South	Non-South	South	Non-South	South	Non-South
Voting						
1952	50	19	45	19	21	5
1956	47	22	31	15	23	8
1960	49	10	19	11	20	5
1964	22	-2	22	11	16	1
1968	0	13	16	14	20	-1
1972	3	6	21	17	13	4
1976	9	3	26	16	8	10
1980	2	8	21	23	-2	6
1984	2	11	22	20	4	-2
1988	11	4	40	20	11	1
1992	7	0	34	18	3	2
Campaigning						
1956	17	7	15	17	8	7
1960	26	5	36	13	5	-3
1964	3	-6	17	18	12	0
1968	-6	-5	7	12	8	0
1972	-1	-8	11	19	7	3
1976	3	-7	13	14	-7	2
1980	5	8	10	11	3	3
1984	-1	5	15	15	7	3
1988	3	-4	19	15	8	3
1992	8	1	8	9	7	4

Note: Scores represent difference in the percentage of "dominant" group members (i.e., whites, upper class, men) saying that they voted or campaigned minus the percentage of "subordinate" group members (i.e., blacks, lower class, women) saying that they participated in the same activity.

Source: The American National Elections Studies, 1956–1992, conducted by the Center for Political Studies at the University of Michigan.

Issue opinions. Table 4.3 presents the difference between southern and nonsouthern activists and nonactivists in mean racial policy and social service scale scores. Through 1960 greater differences in racial issue opinions were found between southern voters and nonvoters than between their nonsouthern counterparts. The size of this regional difference has generally

Table 4.3. Participation Bias Regarding Racial and Social Service Issue Opinions Among Southerners and Nonsoutherners

Issue	Difference, voters and nonvoters		Difference, campaigners and noncampaigners	
	South	Non-South	South	Non-South
Racial				
1956	0.11	0.01	0.09	0.03
1960	0.21	−0.01	0.00	0.00
1964	0.07	0.01	0.03	−0.01
1968	−0.04	0.03	−0.04	−0.06
1972	0.01	−0.01	−0.07	−0.06
1976	0.04	0.01	−0.06	−0.03
1980	0.00	−0.01	−0.03	−0.01
1984	0.02	0.01	0.00	−0.02
1988	0.07	0.00	0.03	−0.06
1992	0.05	0.01	0.01	−0.01
Social service				
1956	0.14	0.07	0.15	0.03
1960	0.14	0.18	0.22	0.04
1964	0.18	0.14	0.14	0.10
1968	0.11	0.17	−0.01	−0.01
1972	0.05	0.02	0.00	0.03
1976	0.11	0.06	0.04	0.07
1980	0.01	0.08	0.05	0.05
1984	0.12	0.06	0.03	0.01
1988	0.08	0.10	0.05	0.04
1992	0.04	0.07	0.03	−0.01

Note: Scores represent differences in mean opinion scale scores between activists and nonactivists. Scores greater than zero indicate that the average score of voters or campaigners is more conservative than average score of nonvoters or noncampaigners. Scores less than zero indicate that nonactivists are more conservative than activists.
Source: The American National Elections Studies, 1956–1992, conducted by the Center for Political Studies at the University of Michigan.

diminished over time, though it did increase somewhat in 1988 and 1992. Overall, in recent years the amount of bias with regard to voting and racial issues has been about the same in the North and the South.

None of the regions consistently showed the largest difference in racial policy opinions between campaigners and noncampaigners. For example, in 1956 there was more bias in the South (.09) than in the non-South (.03). In 1988 there were more differences between campaigners and noncampaigners in the non-South (-.06) than in the South (.03). Overall, however, neither region has experienced much bias with regard to campaigning and racial issue opinions.

Between 1956 and 1964, differences in social service issue opinions between voters and nonvoters, or between campaigners and noncampaigners, were generally larger in the South than in the non-South. Beginning in 1968, none of the regions consistently or clearly exhibited the largest opinion difference between activists and nonactivists. Overall, the amount of participation bias in the area of social service issue opinions has been about the same in both regions.

Summary and Conclusions

In this study we have examined the amount and type of participation bias existing in the South. The results show that the level of racial or gender-based participation bias occurring within the region has generally diminished over time. As a result, in the South, whites and blacks and males and females now vote and campaign at nearly the same rates. The amount of class-based participation, however, has not disappeared to the same extent. Indeed, the amount of class bias in the two most recent presidential elections is about equal to that found forty years earlier.

Our analysis also found that since the mid-1960s activists and nonactivists have generally held similar opinions regarding racial issues. Differences, particularly between voters and nonvoters, are somewhat more likely to occur with regard to social service issues.

Finally, the analysis shows that during the early years of the period under study, there was a higher level of participation bias in the South than in the rest of the country. Now, however, relatively little regional difference in participation bias exists. The one important exception to this pattern involves class and voting. In 1988 and 1992, the South experienced more class bias in voting than did the non-South.

Overall, our results reveal a South that is generally becoming both less and less biased in its politics and more and more like the rest of the country. On the basis of these findings, the next research step is to examine how the changes in participation bias have affected southern state governments. Specifically, have the changes in participation resulted in increasingly "modern" and responsive state governments?

Our impression is that this change in southern state governments has not occurred. If this impression is correct, then research efforts should be directed at examining how the apparent backwardness and unresponsiveness of southern state governments continue in spite of the relatively low level of participation bias now existing in the region.

Appendix

Table 4.A1. Items Used in Forming Measures of Racial and Social Service Issue Scales

	1956	1960	1964	1968	1972	1976	1980	1984	1988	1992
Racial										
Job-housing discrimination	44	62	—	—	—	—	—	—	—	—
School integration	75	70	144	75	106	3,211	—	—	—	5,932
Job discrimination	—	—	143	73	104	—	—	—	865	5,938
Housing discrimination	—	—	145	—	115	—	—	—	—	—
Segregation	—	—	127	88	118	3,217	—	—	—	—
Public accommodations	—	—	408	78	110	—	—	—	—	—
Busing	—	—	—	—	202	3,257	1,133	—	—	—
Aid to Blacks	—	—	—	—	629	3,264	1,062	382	—	3,724
Blacks get less than deserve	—	—	—	—	—	—	—	—	962	6,127
Spending blacks	—	—	—	—	—	—	—	—	381	5,936
Affirmative action	—	—	—	—	—	—	—	—	856	3,729
College quotas	—	—	—	—	—	—	—	—	869	5,948
Social service										
Jobs	32	54	93	66	172	3,241	1,110	414	323	3,718
Health care	38	66	92	64	208	3,273	—	—	318	3,716
Aid to education	53	58	90	60	—	—	—	—	—	—
Gov't. services	—	—	—	—	—	—	291	375	302	3,701

Note: Entries refer to variable numbers used for the items in the election surveys codebooks. In conducting the analysis for the 1964 survey, a summary measure was constructed by combining the item that asked about the direction of the respondent's feelings about open accommondations (V408) with one that asked how strongly he/she felt about the issue (V409).

Table 4.A2. Participation Among Southerners and Nonsoutherners, 1952–1992 (percent)

	1952	1956	1960	1964	1968	1972	1976	1980	1984	1988	1992
					VOTING						
South											
White	61	62	74	68	68	62	66	70	67	61	67
Black	11	15	25	46	68	59	57	68	65	50	60
Male	61	66	79	72	79	69	68	68	68	63	67
Female	40	43	59	56	59	56	60	70	64	52	64
More educated	84	76	86	79	78	75	79	78	77	82	85
Less educated	39	45	57	57	62	54	53	57	55	42	51
Non-South											
White	83	81	85	83	80	77	74	73	78	76	80
Black	64	59	75	85	67	71	71	65	67	72	80
Male	84	84	86	83	78	79	80	76	76	76	81
Female	79	76	81	82	79	75	70	70	78	75	79
More educated	90	90	91	90	87	86	82	82	84	86	89
Less educated	79	75	80	79	73	69	66	59	64	66	71
					CAMPAIGNING						
South											
White	—	19	26	27	20	17	13	16	19	15	22
Black	—	2	0	24	26	18	10	11	20	12	14
Male	—	20	26	33	26	21	8	17	23	18	23
Female	—	12	21	21	18	14	15	14	16	10	16
More educated	—	27	47	39	26	24	20	20	27	26	30
Less educated	—	12	11	22	19	13	7	10	12	7	12
Non-South											
White	—	27	29	25	20	25	19	18	24	20	20
Black	—	20	24	31	25	33	26	10	19	24	19
Male	—	30	27	25	20	27	20	19	25	22	22
Female	—	23	30	25	20	24	18	16	22	19	18
More educated	—	39	36	36	27	36	26	22	29	28	24
Less educated	—	22	26	18	15	17	12	11	14	13	15

5

Age and Partisanship, 1952–1992

Richard Nadeau and
Harold W. Stanley

This chapter reexamines the changing patterns between age and partisanship for whites in the United States, paying particular attention to the issue of periodization and differences between the South and the non-South. Warren Miller's discussion to the contrary, competing notions of partisanship—"standing decision" or "running tally"—are not resolved by conventional cohort analysis. Examination of the partisan changes among cohorts of native whites in the South leads us to question the "steady-state equilibrium" description of American white partisanship for 1952–1964, to reassess the relative contribution of generational replacement and period effects to partisan changes, and to suggest that the young, specifically the post-1960 voters, have, until recently, "stabilized" the Democratic edge over the Republicans. We qualify speculation about the more recent trend of the young toward the Republicans, noting the perils of projecting future partisan balances from cohort data.

Enduring controversies and elements of consensus have emerged from studies of age and partisanship in the United States over the past few decades.[1] The problem of estimating life-cycle gains in partisanship and the importance of these gains relative to partisan gains from other sources such as generational replacement and period effects have been at the core of the Converse-Abramson controversy.[2] Controversy exists, but consensus has also arisen. For instance, most scholars have stressed generational replacement as a central explanation of partisan changes—the decrease in the level of partisanship in the South and in the nation[3] and the narrowing of the Democratic pluralities in the South and in the nation.[4] Moreover, the conventional wisdom about studying age and partisanship links in the United States calls for separate analyses of blacks and whites.[5] And studies typically agree about the general periods in the partisanship of whites: a steady-state equilibrium period, a shock, and a "return to a kind of normalcy."[6]

Warren Miller recently stressed that a more accurate analysis of age and partisanship over the last forty years should include a previously neglected distinction: nonsouthern and southern whites must be studied separately, he contended, because "in the South, the story was dramatically different."[7] Following Miller, we exploit the contrast between whites in the South and the non-South to gain new insights into the relationships between age and partisanship since 1952.

Although we capitalize on Miller's suggested contrast, we depart from Miller's approach in four respects: we do not focus the analysis on voters, we do restrict the analysis to native southern whites and native nonsouthern whites, we adopt a different periodization, and we do not believe that cohort analysis contributes solidly to the debate over whether partisan attitudes are a running tally or a standing decision. The reasons for each we discuss below; the principal findings we reach are these: the phrase "steady-state equilibrium" does not accurately describe native southern white partisanship for 1952–1964; period effects on partisanship have mainly characterized native southern whites rather than all whites; and the young have, until recently, stabilized the Democratic edge over the Republicans, suggesting that the long-term implications of the recent attraction of youth to the Republicans may have been overemphasized. Though cohort analysis provides suggestive data on party identification, such analyses cannot discriminate between competing notions of partisanship—whether partisanship is a standing decision or a running tally.

The Approach

The primary dependent variable for an analysis of age and partisanship, following the conventional practice, is the percentage of partisans, partisans being defined as weak or strong Democrats or Republicans.[8] We go beyond the percentage of partisans to discuss also the relationships between age and the direction of partisanship.

Some readers might see such stress on partisanship as misplaced. After all, partisan voting defection and the growth of independents mean that election outcomes have hinged on far more than mobilizing the party faithful. White southern Democrats voting Republican, particularly for president, have been prominent features of the southern political landscape.[9] Be that as it may, partisanship has been and remains a very strong indicator of the vote.[10] This statement holds true across age cohorts and regions. Particular elections—the Wallace candidacy in 1968 and the McGovern candidacy in 1972—strain the linkage of party ties and the vote, but even among native southern whites, two-thirds or more of the Democratic identifiers typically vote Democratic for president.

Why not restrict the analysis, as Miller does, to voters?[11] Doing so inflates the level of partisanship, since partisans are more likely to vote than independents. Moreover, since the strength of the relationship between partisanship and voting changes over time,[12] this change introduces further distortions. Who votes has also undergone change, particularly in the South, among whites as well as blacks.[13] Moreover, focusing only on voters would exacerbate the problem of small sample size and limit the comparability of these findings, since most previous literature includes all respondents.[14] Miller's basic concern about limiting the analysis to voters involves partisan direction during presidential years.[15] Since none of the substantive conclusions in the study about the strength or direction of partisanship was altered when the analysis was restricted to voters, we decided on both theoretical and empirical grounds to base this chapter on voters and nonvoters.

Why restrict the analysis to native southern or native nonsouthern whites?[16] Cohort analysis of the South/non-South contrast should control for the interregional migration patterns, whose most notable feature has been the influx of nonsouthern whites into the South.[17] Our attempt to observe more closely than did Miller the closed-population requirement in cohort analysis,[18] by contrasting native nonsouthern and native southern whites, avoids the problem posed by in-migrants to either region, a problem particularly serious for the South.[19] In 1952 migrant whites made up 7 percent of southern whites, in 1964 20 percent. This growing proportion of less Democratic, migrant whites produced partisan change in the region, a complication in region-based attempts to sort out the relationships between age and partisanship.[20]

"One problem which has created substantial mischief in past cohort analyses of party identification . . . is a lack of sensitivity to the issue of periodization, in nearly an historiographic sense."[21] Following Converse's admonition, efforts to exploit the South/non-South contrast require careful consideration of the issue of periodization for at least two reasons. First, periodization offers a sound basis for pooling similar years, thus relieving the problem of having a small n—inadequate sample size—that has inhibited cohort analysis of southern partisanship for single survey years. Second, and perhaps more important, periodization is an integral part of the message conveyed by cohort analysis. Periodization consists in establishing a chronology, a calendar of sets of circumstances presumed to have durably shaped the partisan profile of extended segments of the electorate. Periodization is more than mere time marks categorizing movements in the dependent variable; periodization seeks to cluster similar years, whether of political quiescence or of turmoil and in so doing imposes an interpretation on the phenomena under study. In this sense periodization should constitute a major step toward explanation.

For our purposes, we propose the following seven periods for considering strength of partisanship: 1952–1958, 1960–1964, 1966, 1968–1970, 1972–1980, 1982–1990, and 1992. For considering the direction of partisanship we propose the same periods but combine the last four into three: 1968–1982, 1984–1990, and 1992 to capture better the reduction of the Democratic plurality typifying the 1980s.

The periods proposed are not the ones conventionally adopted in studies of age and partisanship, but we contend that they fit the facts, particularly in light of the regional contrast between the South and the non-South. Moreover, the literature on partisan change offers support for the periods we advance. A brief political history of the last four decades will have to suffice.

The first period begins in 1952 with Eisenhower's election and continues through 1958. The year before the 1958 elections, southern images of the parties on civil rights were reaffirmed: "When Eisenhower sent federal troops in Little Rock in September, 1957, to protect school desegregation efforts just after a Republican administration had succeeded in passing the first civil rights act since Reconstruction over a Southern Democratic filibuster, there was considerable readiness in both black and white communities to believe that the battle had been joined between the party of Lincoln and the lily-white Democrats."[22] Religion rather than race marked the 1960 election as different. For native white southerners, predominantly Protestant, somewhat conservative, Kennedy's Catholicism in 1960—like Goldwater's conservative Republicanism in 1964—presented cross-pressures that strained Democratic ties.[23] As Miller put it, "A realignment of southern voters had begun with the Kennedy election of 1960."[24] That 1966, marked in part by an upturn in those considering themselves independent, was a turning point for partisanship has been previously noted.[25] The political shocks of the late 1960s (such as the Wallace candidacy, Nixon's southern strategy, and Vietnam) further strained partisan ties, particularly Democratic ones. The span 1968–1970 is treated as a distinct period. Watergate and the Ford and Carter presidencies dominated partisan patterns in the 1972–1980 period. During the 1980s Reagan's legacy to party politics figured prominently.[26] Bush may not have built on that legacy to the degree some Republicans would have liked, but the partisan patterns, discussed later, show that Reagan's legacy was not reversed. The low level of overall partisanship in the 1970s followed by a partial recovery in the 1980s[27] and an apparent further reduction in 1992 justifies treating 1972–1980, 1982–1990, and 1992 as distinct periods.

The periods demarcating partisan direction for recent years (1972–1982, 1984–1990, and 1992) differ slightly from those for level of partisanship because of the substantial reduction of the Democratic plurality among whites in 1984 and later. The historical low water mark for the Democratic plurality among native southern whites in 1992 supports setting aside the most recent election year as a distinct period.

Results

Periodization

Perhaps with periodization as with pudding, the proof is in the eating. If so, a discussion of the perspectives resulting from this periodization will help us judge the merits of these periods. What tastes of age and partisanship linkages do these periods present? Table 5.1 provides an overview of the levels of partisanship; table 5.3 reports the partisan balance between Democrats and Republicans.

Consider the regional contrasts. The most marked southern distinctiveness characterized the first period, 1952–1958, whether we measure that distinctiveness in terms of the partisan level or the partisan balance. Among native southern whites 84 percent were partisans, and Democrats enjoyed a comfortable 62 point lead over the Republicans. In the non-South, partisans made up only 73 percent and Democrats had a single-digit lead of only five percentage points. Initial signs of dealignment first appeared in the South, as the overall percentage of partisans slipped by four percentage points during 1960–1964. The slippage was more marked among the youngest (those under thirty-five). In the non-South, the percentage of partisans remained essentially the same, with only a minor rise. The subsequent period, a single year (1966), saw dealignment accelerate in the South as it was first appearing in the non-South. In 1966 the two regions converged, with 71 percent of native whites in each claiming partisan ties. Convergence receded in 1968–1970, with partisanship dropping another ten percentage points in the South but only three percentage points in the non-South. By 1968–1970 the South was no longer eleven percentage points more partisan than the non-South (as it had been in 1952–1958) but trailed the non-South by seven percentage points—a dramatic reversal in such a brief span. In the two decades after 1970 the regions have again virtually converged in terms of the proportion of partisans. But the level exhibited between 1982 and 1990 in the South represented a relative stability in the proportion of partisans. In the non-South 64 percent partisan in 1982–1990 signaled a slight recovery after bottoming out at 60 percent in 1972–1980. However, the level of partisanship among whites declined in 1992—perhaps as a temporary reflection of the Perot presidential candidacy, perhaps as an initial indication of even lower levels in the years ahead.

Table 5.3 reveals convergence in the party balance between nonsouthern and southern native whites, although far more movement is registered by

Table 5.1. Level of Partisanship Among Native Southern Whites and Native Nonsouthern Whites by Period and Age Group

Group/age	1952–1958	1960–1964	1966	1968–1970	1972–1980	1982–1990	1992
Native southern whites							
Overall	84	80	71	61	63	62	60
18–35	76	70	55	44	52	57	52
36+	87	84	76	68	71	66	65
Native nonsouthern whites							
Overall	73	75	71	68	60	64	60
18–35	67	71	66	57	49	56	55
36+	76	77	73	73	68	69	63

Note: In this and subsequent tables, partisans include only strong and weak identifiers. The 1952–1958 period does not contain the 1954 survey, since it lacks a state variable, nor the 1962 survey, since for that survey the lack of a variable indicating the state in which the respondent grew up precludes determination of native status.
Source: National Election Studies data.

the southerners. As Democrats lost favor with native southern whites over the 1960–1982 period, nonsouthern whites initially moved toward the Democrats, then reverted to their previous party balance. In 1984 and later, Democrats continued to lose ground among both southern and nonsouthern native whites. The permanence of this conspicuous regional convergence is an open question.

Steady State? But Not in the South

We contest the notion that 1952–1964 was a steady-state period in party loyalties for all U.S. whites. Abramson took Converse to task for generalizing the steady-state period to all adults: "Converse . . . fails to mention that the 'steady-state' period in American party loyalties was a period of stability only for whites. For blacks, this was a period of dramatic change."[28] Abramson's point is appropriate but incomplete: all whites did not experience a steady-state period in partisanship. We contend that native southern whites also underwent dramatic change during this period previously presumed quiescent. The 1952–1964 span did contain a quieter partisan segment, 1952–1958, followed by politically more tumultuous years during which blacks mobilized in the South and native southern whites drifted away from the strong party ties they had previously held. Other scholars have noticed partisan changes in the early 1960s among southern whites: Wolfinger and Arseneau concluded that the "unmistakable . . . decrease in Democratic identification . . . began in 1962," and Beck placed the rising level of independence among native southern whites well before the third-party activity of the 1960s—in 1964, if not even earlier.[29]

Steady-state partisanship did not characterize the native southern white during the 1952–1964 span. The partisan change that would become more pronounced later was already perceptible from 1960 to 1964. Lest one think a drop of a few percentage points is a quirky result from the 1960 and 1964 National Election Studies (NES) surveys, corroborating evidence is available from other surveys:[30] reanalysis of a survey from the spring of 1961 showed the overall partisanship of native southern whites (n = 551) to be 79 percent, a drop of five percentage points compared with the 1952–1958 period.[31] Beyond this drop of four or five percentage points in partisanship (table 5.1), did other manifestations of partisan change appear?[32] First, the share of independents increased among native southern whites from 12 percent in 1952–1958 to 18 percent in 1960–1964 (while remaining at 25 and 24 percent, respectively, for native nonsouthern whites).[33] Second, the inverse class polarization in partisanship characterizing native southern whites prior to 1964 changed in that year.[34] Moreover, the subregional patterns of Democratic domination in the 1950s (Deep South, Black Belt, and Bible Belt) had been altered by 1960 and 1964.[35] The initial indications of major changes that would alter the southern political landscape included the mobilization of southern black voters, notable prior to 1964,[36] and the fielding of competitive Republican candidates below the presidential level that began in earnest in the early 1960s in some areas. Such changes left imprints on southern partisanship, imprints whose existence cannot be dismissed by the relatively larger partisan changes occurring later. The 1952–1964 period was not a steady-state equilibrium for white partisanship; native southern whites registered change that would accelerate in the years to follow.

Generational and Period Effects

Partisan changes in the South have been principally discussed in "generational" terms.[37] Whether partisan changes appear only for entering voters or for all age groups is at the core of the distinction between generational and period effects.[38] The study of partisan changes among all American whites has not produced such a clear-cut consensus, fueling many debates about the relative contributions of generational and period effects in explaining partisan changes.[39]

The state of the literature is surprising, since the compelling evidence for a period effect is in the South (table 5.2). Consider, in particular, the contrasts between the periods 1968–1970 and 1952–1958. Drops of fourteen and twenty percentage points distinguish the southern generations, while no change characterizes the nonsouthern ones. Moreover, the younger native southern whites, those entering the electorate after 1960, exhibit more depressed mobilization into partisanship than do their nonsouthern counterparts during 1968–1970. The native southern white seems a textbook example of period effects. The decrease in the level of partisanship has been widespread, sudden, and—in contrast to the North—evident even among the older voters.

The evidence for a period effect in the non-South is later and much more limited. Contrasting 1972–1980 with 1952–1958, we note a four-percentage-point drop in partisanship among the nonsouthern generations—hardly an indication of a compelling period effect.

The perspective of table 5.2 can help explain the opposite conclusions reached by some scholars. Older voters in the non-South modestly "dealigned" in the 1970s. A study comparing the early 1970s (1972 to 1976, for instance) to the late 1960s will conclude that generational replacement falls short as an explanation of the decrease in the level of partisanship.[40] With the passage of time, one can take a longer perspective, noting that older nonsouthern native whites recovered the partisan levels comparable to those of the steady-state period. Given the growing weight of the post-1960 cohort, one would conclude, with Miller,[41] that generational replacement best explains the overall drop in level of partisanship.

Evidence of a period effect is weak outside the South; in the South even the older cohorts underwent substantial dealignment. As a result of this contrast, combining the two regions produces a distorted picture of the timing and the extent of the dealignment: in the years 1966–1970, the depth of the dealignment was far more modest among nonsoutherners, virtually nonexistent among the older cohorts; in 1972–1980 the older southern cohorts were recovering slightly toward previous levels of partisanship while their nonsouthern counterparts were dealigning. Even so, the magnitude of the dealignments, when contrasted with the 1952–1958 period, were far greater among the older southern cohorts.

Partisan Direction

To complement consideration of the relationships between age and level of partisanship, we turn to a discussion of the party balance, measured here as the percentage of Democrats minus the percentage of Republicans. Overall, among native southern whites, Democrats retain a lead, but the size of that lead dropped from sixty-two percentage points to six (table 5.3). Smaller changes were evident among native nonsouthern whites. After an early partisan change favoring the Democrats, the Democratic lead has virtually vanished since 1982. The party balances in the South and non-South have converged although native southern whites retained through 1990 a pro-Democratic edge larger than native northern whites ever displayed. In

**Table 5.2. Level of Partisanship Among Generations of
Native Southern Whites and Native Nonsouthern Whites by Period**

Group/generation	1952–1958	1960–1964	1966	1968–1970	1972–1980	1982–1990	1992	(1952–58)–(1982–90)
Native southern whites								
Solid South	85	85	76	71	75	74	70	−11
Post–World War II	78	70	66	58	64	66	67	−12
Post-1960	—	—	50	38	53	57	56	—
Native nonsouthern whites								
Pre–World War II	76	77	74	76	72	77	72	1
Post–World War II	66	72	69	66	62	68	66	2
Post-1960	—	—	63	51	49	58	56	—

Note: For this table, generations are defined by the year when the individual entered the electorate. The Solid South generation had birth years of 1923 or before and the post–World War II generation was born in 1924–1939. The post-1960 generation was born after 1939.
Source: National Election Studies data.

this context, the historically low level of the Democratic plurality among native southern whites in 1992 takes on added significance. Twenty years ago southern and nonsouthern native whites converged in levels of partisanship, and results from 1992 suggest a convergence in direction of partisanship as well. Time will tell, but if trends continue, in the years ahead native southern whites may become more Republican than nonsouthern native whites.

What connections did age have with this Democratic decline? Presumably, youth show little attachment and great volatility in partisan commitment, and the elderly exhibit stronger and more stable partisan ties. Contrasting native whites in the South and non-South offers interesting, counterintuitive insights into the behavior of older and younger voters, here demarcated as those who were eligible to vote in 1960 or before and those who were able to vote after 1960 (born in 1939 or before versus those born in 1940 and later). These definitions of cohorts (table 5.4) are based on previous scholarship on age and the direction of partisanship.[42] The 1892–1907 cohort clearly belongs to the pre–New Deal era. The 1908–1939 cohort corresponds to the New Deal/Fair Deal period of Democratic dominance. The 1940–1963 and post-1963 cohorts reflect the Republican attraction among the younger respondents in the 1980s. Analyses based on these cohorts demonstrate that younger cohorts provided stability, and older cohorts instability, in the direction of partisanship.

First, focus on the 1952–1958 and 1968–1982 periods, contrasting the South and non-South. There has been significant change in the party bal-

**Table 5.3. Party Balance for Native Southern Whites and
Native Nonsouthern Whites by Period**

Period	Native southern whites	Native nonsouthern whites	Difference
1952–1958	62	5	57
1960–1964	57	10	47
1966	49	10	39
1968–1982	34	8	26
1984–1990	18	1	17
1992	6	2	4

Note: "Party balance" is the percentage of Democrats (strong and weak) minus the percentage of Republicans. Weighting properly the southern subregions in 1964 (Deep South, Rim South), reduces the party balance by more than three points for 1964 and would decrease the balance for 1960–1964 to 55 and the difference to 45.
Source: National Election Studies data.

ance among the older cohorts in the South: the oldest sliced fifteen percentage points off the Democratic edge over four decades, the next oldest nineteen. Even in the non-South among presumably die-hard Democratic cohorts, net shifts to the disadvantage of the Democrats appeared (for instance, 1908–1939, 42 percent Democratic to 28 percent Republican, or +14, in 1952–1964, 38 to 30, or +8, in 1968–1982). Such change among the older cohorts is striking. Generational replacement also lowered the Democratic edge in the party balance in the South because younger voters were not as disproportionately Democratic as the older. In the non-South, the story is different: the more Democratic group is found among the younger cohorts, whose Democratic tendencies have offset the movement of the older cohorts away from the Democrats. Prior to 1984, the younger, entering cohorts helped to stabilize the overall party balance in the non-South. The stabilizing effects of the entering voters during the turbulent years, which contrasted with the erosion of Democratic strength among older and presumably immune cohorts, is worth noting in view of the destabilizing influence on partisanship and turnout attributed to the post-1960 voters.[43]

In 1984 and later, these trends changed. Just as the die-hard Democratic cohorts had moved toward the Republicans during the 1968–1982 period, younger voters moved toward the Republican fold after 1982. At the height of this process, a 3 to 2 pro-Republican ratio characterized the post-1963 cohort among native nonsouthern whites in 1984–1990, displaying a more even division between the parties in 1992. Among native southern whites, the post-1963 cohort divided equally between the parties in 1984–1990, moving toward a 3 to 2 pro-Republican ratio in 1992.

Republican success among the young has fueled speculations about the

Table 5.4. Democratic and Republican Identification Among Birth-Year Cohorts of Native Southern and Nonsouthern Whites for Selected Periods

Group/period	1952–58		1960–64		1966		1968–82		1984–90		1992	
	D	R	D	R	D	R	D	R	D	R	D	R
Native southern whites												
1892–1907	74	12	76	10	61	17	63	16	61	16	—	—
1908–1939	72	9	65	13	69	12	56	12	49	17	45	22
1940–1963	—	—	—	—	—	—	34	16	34	22	31	28
Post-1963	—	—	—	—	—	—	—	—	29	29	21	29
Native nonsouthern whites												
1892–1907	36	41	39	42	32	45	34	42	39	41	—	—
1908–1939	42	28	44	28	43	34	38	30	39	33	38	31
1940–1963	—	—	—	—	—	—	32	19	30	30	29	28
Post-1963	—	—	—	—	—	—	—	—	19	29	26	25

Note: D = Democrat. R = Republican.
Source: National Election Studies data.

possibility of realignment "underway and here to stay."[44] Our findings suggest that the argument of youth's conversion to Republicanism paving the way to a long-awaited realignment has been overstated. Even as the Republican attraction peaked among younger cohorts, the ideological mismatch between the GOP and younger voters was evident.[45] The closeness of younger voters to the Democrats in terms of policy preferences led Geer to note that "it would be difficult to argue that the newest members of the electorate will provide a foothold for the GOP as it strives to become the majority party."[46] The 1992 election results confirm prior evidence that Republican success may have been more a short story than a long-running epic.[47] However, for more than a decade the Democrats have not recovered their previous 2 to 1 margin among younger voters, and in this sense 1992 manifested more continuity than evidence of Republican decline. Moreover, in 1992 the younger cohorts split their allegiance between the major parties. But Republican hopes are not pinned on youth alone. The partisan malleability of older cohorts—older cohorts moving in a pro-Republican direction—raises questions about the stability of party identification and the predictability of the party balance.

Trivial though it may seem, a basic point is worth noting. Cohort analysis has more usefulness as a diagnostic tool than as a forecasting tool. Projection of political trends from cohort analysis is a risky enterprise always at the mercy of unpredictable shocks and countervailing trends. New period ef-

fects may loom ahead.[48] Consider the South. The previous shocks that
shook this region, from *Brown* to Wallace, were unpredictable, as was their
impact on the various cohorts of southerners. Unstable periods may be
highly unpredictable. For that matter, periods of stability are probably
equally unpredictable. Take the level of partisanship among native southern whites. It has been virtually stable between 1968 and 1982, an outcome
hardly foreseeable, given the continuous growth of the entering, less partisan (and less Democratic) cohorts. What happened? Table 5.2 shows that
older voters partially remobilized as partisans in the 1970s. In doing so, they
formed a countervailing force that stabilized the overall level of partisanship for fifteen years. (But in partisan terms, the events of the 1980s dented
the partisan ties, even of the older cohorts—table 5.4.)

The case of nonsouthern native whites is also revealing. Considering the
party balance among the different cohorts, one would have predicted an
increased plurality for the Democrats in the 1970s. What happened? The
party balance stayed the same through 1982 as a mix of predictable and
unpredictable trends: the fading out of a Republican cohort, the slow erosion of Democratic pluralities in the New Deal and post–World War II cohorts, and the good showing of the Democrats in the post-1960 cohorts.
Then came 1984 with its mix of young Republicans and old Democrats turning Republican.

Enticing though it is, such considerations caution against hazarding pre-
dictions about future partisan equilibria on the basis of cohort analysis.

Standing Decision or Running Tally?

Examining the relationships between age and partisanship across regions among whites provides a perspective from which to comment on theoretically contrasting notions of partisanship—partisanship as a running
tally or as a standing decision. Working with cohort data rather than panel
data means that even aggregate stability cannot be taken as confirmation
of the enduring nature of party identification as a political attitude. A cohort's stability in the aggregate, even over several decades, could mask substantial but offsetting individual-level changes within that cohort.

With this critical qualification in mind, the evidence presented offers
support for both concepts of partisanship. For instance, we have found impressive aggregate stability (in terms of both strength and direction) in the
northern 1892–1907 cohort. Also revealing is the relative stability of the
partisan mobilization rate of the northern New Deal cohort (1908–1939)
during the turbulent 1960s and 1970s. That the oldest cohorts of native
southern whites still exhibit a pro-Democratic tendency can also be seen as
a tribute to the robustness of this attitude, given the circumstances of the
1960s.

Yet we also noted extensive partisan malleability in our data. The halving of the Democratic lead among the die-hard 1908–1939 cohort, the shift of the 1940–1963 cohort toward the Republicans (equaling the shift of the 1908–1939 cohort among native southern whites and surpassing the comparable shift among native northern whites), and the continued erosion of Democratic loyalties among southerners long after the turbulent 1960s could be interpreted as evidence for the short-term responsiveness of party identification. We thus contend, after reviewing the relationships between age and partisanship over four decades, that these "large pieces of temporal evidence pertaining to stability and change"[49] cannot convincingly discriminate among competing notions of partisanship.

Conclusion

This chapter reexamined the shifting patterns between age and partisanship, paying particular attention to periodization and the South/non-South contrast. The aggregate nature of cohort analyses, suggestive though they are for comprehending the dynamics of partisan change, cannot definitively discriminate between competing notions of partisanship. Whether partisanship is a standing decision or a running tally will have to be decided by other means on other grounds.

Studying birth-year cohorts of native southern and nonsouthern whites, we found that the long-recognized "dealignment" in the nation concealed important regional differences—the decline in the levels of partisanship occurred earlier, developed faster, and went deeper in the South than in the non-South. These distinctive regional patterns call into question the labeling of the 1952–1964 period as a steady-state equilibrium in the partisanship of native southern whites.

Several implications flow from noting that the compelling evidence of period effects are found among native southern whites. First, this finding underscores an irony: partisan change in the South has been mainly discussed in generational terms. Second, this finding clarifies some aspects of the debate on the relative contributions of generational and period effects in explaining partisan change in the nation. Third, this finding argues against the practice of merging all American whites to understand the dynamics of partisanship in previous decades.

Perhaps most aggregates could be subdivided into groups for which significant relationships differed. One could quibble that questioning the steady-state partisan period label by distinguishing southern and nonsouthern native whites merely illustrates this point, thus minimizing the significance of the regional contrasts. Yet the 1952–1964 period was not a quiescent one for black partisanship. The suspicion is strong that black mobilization into Democratic partisanship affected the partisan loyalties of native southern whites,[50] who compose about one-quarter of all U.S. whites. To dismiss such partisan change and stick with the steady-state label for 1952–1964 is definitely misleading.

A conspicuous feature of cohort analysis is the pivotal role attributed to younger voters in the explanation of partisan changes. The case of American whites is no exception to this pattern as the younger voters have been seen as leading the way not only in a dealignment process nationwide[51] but also in the Republican growth in the South[52] and in the nation.[53] Implicit in such readings is the notion that older voters resist change, helping stabilize partisanship. When we contrast the South and non-South, we see that noticeable partisan changes occurred among older voters. Outside the South the party balance[54] found a crucial pillar in the stabilizing influence of the younger voters, who were pro-Democratic as entering cohorts (until the early 1980s).

A regional contrast also shows that since the mid-1980s the age and partisanship relationship has never been so flat in the non-South, whereas it has never been so steep in the South. Presumably this finding makes safer the prediction that generational replacement will lead to further Republican growth in the South, though the pace of the GOP advance is unpredictable. The sizable reduction of the Democratic plurality among native southern whites in 1992 illustrates Republican growth but further, future gains are not fixed. In the non-South, the decline of the Democratic pluralities among the presumably older cohorts more resistant to change; the stabilizing pro-Democratic tendencies of the post-1960 voters until 1982; and younger voters trending Republican more recently—these pieces form the puzzle whose complexity and unpredictability call for caution in making projections from cohort data in general and in predicting an emergent Republican majority in particular. Obviously, cohort analysis has been, and will continue to be, more useful as a diagnostic tool than as a forecasting technique.

Part Two
Nominations, Elections, and
Partisan Developments

6

Out of the Phone Booths

Republican Primaries in the Deep South

David E. Sturrock

In no region of the country did the 1994 Republican sweep cut more deeply, nor defy more history, than in the South. For the first time since Reconstruction, Republicans now hold a majority of southern governorships, places in the U.S. Senate, and House seats. Nor was the GOP landslide confined to high-visibility contests or to races decided on national issues. Republicans also won 46 percent of statewide executive and judicial races, 36 percent of the region's state legislative seats, and county courthouses from Texas to North Carolina.

Although the sheer scale of this landslide is impressive, no one should be surprised by the advent of a broadly based Republican majority in the South. (Indeed, many observers have long wondered why the Republicans were taking so long to translate their presidential majorities into dominance in other races.) Certainly, the emergence of two-party competition in the South has received considerable scrutiny from scholars, in terms of both its political dynamics[1] and the broader socioeconomic and cultural trends that have shaped it.[2]

This study addresses one aspect of that Republican growth that has not drawn much attention, the recent surge in voter participation in southern Republican primaries. There are two basic tasks here: to document and analyze the increase and to test some possible explanations for it. More specifically, I will analyze the effect of certain demographic variables on county-level trends in Republican primary turnout between the late 1970s and the early 1990s.

Why is a sharp increase in Republican primary turnout important? Several implications for the larger world of southern politics can be suggested. First, the candidates who win these primaries are increasingly likely to win in the general election. Second, the dramatic shift in the Democratic-to-Republican ratio of southern primary voters suggests increasing voter interest in the Republican Party and its candidates and a transformation in the internal composition of the Democratic primary electorate.[3] Finally, analyzing the sources of new GOP primary voters should tell us something about the composition of Republican support in the modern South and perhaps about the party's prospects for maintaining or expanding this support in the future.

The Southern Republican Primary in Historical Context

The direct primary election has a long and colorful history in southern politics; indeed, by 1915 every state in the region had adopted some type of primary for nominating statewide candidates.[4] The Republican Party had ceased to be a serious political force in most of the South by this time, so winning the Democratic primary was quickly recognized as tantamount to election for almost all offices. By contrast, the southern Republican primary was an infrequent and nearly invisible ritual. Most GOP nominees were "selected informally and declared nominated without opposition, or, if legally necessary, placed on the primary ballot as a matter of form."[5] This general practice prevailed even in the six states that had enacted mandatory primary laws. Only occasionally were contested statewide Republican primaries held in Florida, North Carolina, Tennessee, and Virginia, and they seemed to account for only 3–5 percent of the total two-party primary turnout.[6] Local Republican primaries were likely "only in areas in which Republicans ha[d] local majorities," which meant eastern Tennessee, western North Carolina, and scattered upland counties in Alabama, Arkansas, Georgia, and Virginia.[7]

Republican primaries came into regular use when the party began to mount serious statewide campaigns in the 1960s, although some state parties did not adopt primaries for major offices until the early 1970s. The single exception to this practice is found in Virginia, where commonwealth election law still allows for party option. While Virginia's Republicans and Democrats often held primaries in the past, most recent statewide candidates have been chosen by party conventions.

In some southern states, the adoption (and maintenance) of Republican primaries has been complicated by election laws that place the major responsibility for organizing and conducting primaries upon the parties themselves. This remains the case, though in varying degrees, in Mississippi, South Carolina, and Texas. Often, limited resources require the party to consolidate primary polls at a small number of sites within a county, and at least as recently as 1987, Mississippi Republicans were struggling to establish even one primary poll in each of the state's eighty-two counties. Not surprisingly, party officials in these states report that such work consumes a large part of their time and attention and can detract from their higher mission of defeating Democrats in the general election.[8]

The Southern Republican Primary Today

By almost any measure one chooses to apply—number of voters, number of candidates,[9] news media attention, or relevance to the outcome of the general election—the modern Republican primary has become a larger and more important event in the world of southern politics. Tables 6.1 and 6.2 demonstrate how the number of Republican primary voters has grown since the late 1970s, both in absolute numbers and relative to Democratic primary turnout.

Between the late 1970s and early 1990s, voting in Republican gubernatorial primaries increased, both relatively and proportionately, in all eight states for which comparisons were possible. In five states, the Republican turnout more than doubled, while Democratic turnout actually dropped in five. When returns for all eight states are aggregated, the overall Democratic turnout declined by 2.7 percent, while GOP primary activity rose 160.8 percent. The Republican share of the two-party primary vote rose to 25.7 percent, as compared with 11.4 percent for the earlier period. The size and distribution of these gains strongly imply that southerners have come to look upon the Republican primary as an electoral arena that is worthy of their attention and participation.[10]

Hypotheses to Be Tested

Why have increasing numbers of southerners chosen to vote in Republican primaries in recent years? Probably a micro analysis would yield the most authoritative answer—that is, a scientific random survey of those who are now voting in those primaries (and perhaps also those who still do not). However, the researcher who lacks the resources for such an undertaking may find both solace and insight in a macro study, one that uses a larger, more easily measurable, unit of analysis. The county is the obvious choice for such a project, as election returns and demographic data are most readily available in that form.

In 1952, Alexander Heard predicted that the Republican Party would ultimately emerge as a serious political force in the South and would do so with a distinctly middle-class base of support.[11] This vision has been amply validated by more recent studies of southern electoral behavior that document a strong relationship between socioeconomic level and support for the Republican Party and its candidates.[12] Accordingly, those counties that have

Table 6.1. Votes Cast in Southern Gubernatorial Primaries, by Party, 1976-1979, and 1990-1992

	1976-1979[a]				1990-1992[b]			
	Democrat		Republican		Democrat		Republican	
State	No.	%	No.	%	No.	%	No.	%
				OPEN PRIMARY STATES[c]				
Alabama	899,917	97.2	25,850	2.8	741,710	85.6	125,177	14.4
Arkansas	525,961	95.8	22,797	4.2	491,146	85.0	86,977	15.0
Georgia	695,911	96.3	26,605	3.7	1,052,315	89.9	118,118	10.1
Mississippi	737,163	95.8	32,452	4.2	726,465	92.0	63,561	8.0
Texas	1,812,790	92.0	158,403	8.0	1,487,260	63.5	855,231	36.5
Total	4,671,742	94.6	266,107	5.4	4,498,896	78.3	1,249,064	21.7
State M	—	95.4	—	4.6	—	83.2	—	16.8
				CLOSED PRIMARY STATES				
Florida	1,037,533	73.0	382,831	27.0	1,074,056	61.6	668,181	38.4
Kentucky	566,786	81.0	133,125	19.0	491,949	75.3	161,107	24.7
North Carolina	677,931	85.4	115,852	14.6	701,606	72.7	262,963	27.3
Total	2,282,250	78.3	631,808	21.7	2,267,611	67.8	1,092,251	32.2
State M	—	79.8	—	20.2	—	69.9	—	30.1
			TOTALS FOR OPEN AND CLOSED PRIMARY STATES					
Total	6,953,992	88.6	897,915	11.4	6,766,507	74.3	2,341,315	25.7
State M	—	89.6	—	10.4	—	78.2	—	21.8

Note: These data were compiled from Richard M. Scammon and Alice V. McGillivray, eds., America Votes, vols. 12, 13, 19, and 20 (Washington, D.C.: Congressional Quarterly, 1976-1979). South Carolina and Tennessee are not shown here because the number and distribution of uncontested gubernatorial primaries precludes any direct comparison between the periods under study. No meaningful data are available for Louisiana because of that state's unique electoral system, in which all candidates, regardless of party, appear on the same primary ballot. Virginia is not listed because most recent statewide nominations have been made by party conventions.

[a] These totals are from 1978 primaries except those shown for Arkansas and North Carolina (1976) and Kentucky and Mississippi (1979).

[b] These totals are from 1990 primaries except those shown for Kentucky and Mississippi (1991) and North Carolina (1992).

[c] Alabama, Arkansas, Georgia, Mississippi and Texas are classified as open primary states because no advance party affiliation is required for voting in a given party's primary. Florida, Kentucky and North Carolina are classified as closed primary states because voters must declare a party affiliation when registering to vote if they wish to participate in that party's primary.

Table 6.2. Net Change in Gubernatorial Primary Turnout,
1976–1979 and 1990–1991 (percent)

State group	Democrat	Republican	Total[a]
Open primary	–3.7	369.4	16.4
Closed primary	–0.8	72.9	15.3
Total	–2.7	160.8	16.0

[a]Minor parties such as the Libertarians are not considered here. These parties are rarely able to conduct primaries because state election laws make it difficult for them to maintain formal ballot status, and it appears that few of the statewide primaries they do hold are contested (*American Votes*, various volumes).
Source: Table 6.1.

undergone the sharpest "middle classification" between the late 1970s and the early 1990s should also be the ones with the greatest growth in Republican primary voting.

To test this thesis, I have constructed three census-based independent variables that exemplify what observers had in mind when they anticipated the emergence of a middle-class South. A standard product-moment correlation technique (Pearson's R) will be used to measure the degree of county-level association between these factors and Republican primary turnout. A correlation of .25 will be used as an approximate benchmark for determining whether a given variable has a meaningful association with Republican primary turnout. The formal hypotheses under examination are:

1. The greater the 1980–1990 increase in the median value of owner-occupied housing, the greater the growth in Republican primary voting over the same period.
2. The greater the increase in median household income, the greater the growth in Republican primary voting.
3. Growth in the absolute number of white-collar employees (that is, the U.S. Census category of "managerial and professional specialty occupations") will correlate strongly with growth in Republican primary voting.

Each of these hypotheses is designed to measure the relationship between a certain type of socioeconomic development and the dependent variable. However, drawing our target so narrowly carries the risk that some larger, more broadly based, demographic force will be overlooked. Specifically, a county's population growth may explain the rise in Republican primary voting as much as or more than its gravitation to middle-class living standards. To check for this possibility, a fourth hypothesis will be tested:

4. The greater the population growth, the greater the growth in Republican primary voting.

Scope of the Study

I have chosen to limit this study to the Deep South because two-party
competition in these states has developed more slowly, and has been more
prone to reversal, than in the Outer South. At least through the 1980s, this
distinction held true for every level of election (apart from the presidency)
and also for participation in Republican primaries. For example, the GOP's
share of the two-party primary vote in the Deep South averaged less than 5
percent during the late 1970s, the period that provides the baseline for this
study. By focusing the analysis on the Republican party's "worst case" states,
I hope the results will at least hint at part of an answer to the puzzle of the
party's slow, uneven rise to power in the South.

There is no formal demarcation of "Deep" versus "Outer" South, but a
variety of geographic, historical, political, and even demographic factors
lead most political scientists and historians to designate Alabama, Georgia,
Louisiana, Mississippi, and South Carolina as Deep South states. There is
also cause to add Arkansas to this list, not least for political reasons. For
example, the Razorback State has fewer Republican legislators (nineteen,
or 18 percent of the total) than any other state in the South.

Four of these states—Alabama, Arkansas, Georgia, and Mississippi—use
the "open" primary, whereby voters select the party ballot of their choice
when they appear at the polling station on primary day. In "closed" primary
states, voters must formally declare a party affiliation at least thirty days
beforehand if they wish to participate in the party's primary.[13]

However, this interparty mobility also requires that the primaries studied
involve at least some degree of simultaneous competition in both gubernatorial primaries. The combination of an unopposed nomination in one
party (usually involving an incumbent) and an active contest in the other
seems likely to depress turnout artificially for the former primary and to
inflate it for the latter. This was precisely the case in South Carolina for both
1986 and 1990, so primary turnout patterns for that state cannot be analyzed here. Finally, Louisiana must be set aside because it does not hold
party primaries as such. Instead, all candidates are placed together on a
single primary ballot, and the top two finishers (regardless of party) advance to a runoff if no one wins a majority.

Two other research design issues require comment. First, why compare
returns from 1976–1979 with those from 1990–1991? The period centering
on 1978 is a good time for establishing a baseline for Republican primary
growth because the development of southern two-party competition was

then in a lull. One phase of major Republican breakthroughs had ended in 1972, and the effects of Watergate, recession, and Jimmy Carter's ascent to the White House forestalled the start of a second, more lasting phase of Republican growth until the 1980s. A four-year window has been established here because of the need to use Arkansas data from 1976—the nearest GOP gubernatorial primary contest—and Mississippi's odd-year election cycle, which fell due in 1979. Most important, it would be very difficult to assemble a multistate set of contested Republican primaries in the South prior to that time. The elections of 1990–1991 are used for comparison because they are the most recent gubernatorial elections for which data are available.

Second, I have chosen to limit this study to gubernatorial primaries because they are far more likely to feature seriously contested, high-visibility contests than primaries for lesser statewide offices and because they permit more cycle-to-cycle comparisons than U.S. Senate primaries. Also, I am setting aside presidential primaries because I believe the array of offices contested in "regular" primaries—governor, lesser state offices, U.S. Congress, and state legislature and county offices—offers a more broadly based measure of the relative significance voters attach to the respective parties' primaries. By contrast, recent southern presidential primaries have usually been single-office, and in some cases single-party, events.

Recent Republican Primary Turnout Data

Before testing the hypotheses introduced above, we will consider the magnitude and distribution of the increase (table 6.3) in Republican primary turnout for the four states used in this study. In these four states, aggregate GOP primary growth was actually greater than for the eight-state South analyzed in tables 6.1 and 6.2 (265.6 percent versus 160.8 percent). This result is not surprising, as Republican support has always started from a smaller base in the Deep South than in the Outer South. However, a closer look is in order if we are to appreciate how this aggregate growth was distributed among the 383 counties we will use to test our hypotheses. Table 6.4 classifies Republican primary turnout by magnitude for both time periods.

When both parts of table 6.4 are compared, it is apparent that the state-level primary turnout gains noted above are reflected in a widely dispersed pattern of turnout growth at the county level as well. The one-hundred-vote mark seems to be a watershed: the number of counties reaching this figure more than doubled from the first period to the second. However, these gross numbers do not permit us to draw direct conclusions about Republican primary turnout trends in individual counties. Table 6.5 provides some

**Table 6.3. Republican Gubernatorial Primary Voting
in Four Deep South States, 1976–1979 and 1990–1991**

			Gain	
State	1976–79	1990–91	No.	%
Alabama	25,850	125,177	99,267	384.0
Arkansas	22,797	86,977	64,180	281.5
Georgia	26,605	118,118	91,513	344.0
Mississippi	32,452	63,561	31,109	95.9
Total	107,704	393,773	286,069	265.6

Source: Official statements of the vote issued by the respective secretaries of state for the years indicated.

guidance on that issue by tabulating percentage growth in county-level turnout patterns.

The range of county-level percentage increases shown in table 6.5 confirms the general impression of widely distributed growth in Republican primary voting suggested by table 6.4.[14] Apart from its descriptive utility, this distribution is important because it allows us to test our hypotheses without worry that a small number of large counties accounted for most or all of a given state's total primary growth, thereby rendering any correlation results suspect.

The Hypotheses Considered

We now test the four hypotheses introduced above. The correlations presented in table 6.6 reflect calculations involving all of the 360 counties for which usable data are available. Three of the variables tested demonstrate a fairly vigorous, and roughly equal, degree of association with Republican primary turnout growth. Not surprisingly, housing value, income, and population correlate with each other at very high levels (between .495 and .557). How strongly do these variables associate with GOP primary growth within individual states? Table 6.7 presents the results.

The four variables maintain approximately the same ranking that was shown in table 6.6: housing value and population remain the strongest, and white-collar employment the weakest. Perhaps of greater significance is the aberrant pattern produced by Arkansas. In sharp contrast to the other three states, Arkansas provides almost no support for any of the hypotheses tested; even the generally strong population measure is barely noticeable. One possible explanation—though surely not a complete one—lies in the state's lack of distinctly suburban (hence middle-class) counties.

**Table 6.4. Republican Gubernatorial Primary Votes, Counties
by Number of Votes Cast, 1976–1979 and 1990–1991**

County[a]	Ala.	Ark.	Ga.	Miss.	Total
			1976–1979		
10,000 or more	1	0	0	1	2
1,000–9,999	3	6	4	7	20
100–999	12	25	20	27	84
1–99	50	43	113	47	253
Zero	1	1	21	0	23
Total	67	75	158[b]	82	382
			1990–1991		
10,000 or more	3	1	4	2	10
1,000–9,999	13	13	16	11	53
100–999	30	39	59	24	153
1–99	21	22	76	44	163
Zero	0	0	4	0	4
Total	67	75	159	82	383

[a]By number of votes cast.
[b]The 1978 turnout total was missing for one Georgia county.
Source: Official statements of the vote issued by the respective secretaries of state for the years indicated.

It is clear that the variables tested do show some strength, but there is also considerable variance among the scores within at least two states and for each of the variables when compared across the states. When the results of table 6.5 are reviewed, the suspicion arises that a certain "tyranny of small numbers" is at work here. Indeed, fifteen counties registered Republican turnout percentage increases of over 5,000 percent, while another eighty—over a fifth of the initial pool—had gains of at least 1,000 percent. Changes of such magnitude are rarely encountered in the study of mass electoral behavior, and their presence here points to the possibility that the associations we are trying to measure may be masked by the impact of some statistically idiosyncratic cases.

In fact, such distortion is readily apparent when individual counties are examined. The most extreme increase was found in Crisp County, Georgia, whose GOP primary turnout rose an astounding 14,200 percent. However, only one resident marked a Republican ballot in 1978—truly a primary that could be held in a phone booth! While the 1990 turnout of 143 represented impressive growth, it was hardly the stuff of which analytically significant five-figure growth rates are made. In similar fashion, three of the four coun-

Table 6.5. Percentage Increase in Republican Primary Voting, by County, 1976–1979 and 1990–1991

Range of increase (%)	Ala.	Ark.	Ga.	Miss.	Total
Infinity[a]	1	1	20	0	22
5000 or more	5	0	10	0	15
1000–4,999	25	8	44	3	80
500–999	16	16	27	5	64
100–499	15	27	41	17	100
0–99	4	21	13	30	68
Decrease	1	2	3	27[b]	33
Total	67	75	158[c]	82	382

[a]Because no Republican primary votes were cast in these twenty-two counties in 1978–1979, any increase would be expressed as an infinite (and therefore statistically meaningless) percentage.
[b]See note 14 for discussion of this anomaly.
[c]The 1978 turnout total was missing for one Georgia county.
Source: Official statements of the vote issued by the respective secretaries of state for the years indicated.

Table 6.6. County-Level Correlations Between Changes in Republican Primary Voting and Changes in Selected Demographic Variables

Independent variable	R
Housing value	.328
Income	.254
Population	.308
White-collar employment	.128

Note: $N = 360$. The twenty-two "infinity" counties noted in table 6.5 are omitted, as is the one "missing" county from Georgia.
Source: Data calculated by the author.

ties with increases of over 10,000 percent started from a 1978 base of one vote each, while eleven of the fifteen with gains of at least 5,000 percent began with fewer than ten votes apiece.

In hopes of correcting for these statistical anomalies, a method of truncation was devised. All counties with a 1978–1979 Republican primary turnout of ten or fewer were dropped from the pool of counties, and the hypotheses were retested. Table 6.8 presents the results. The truncation technique significantly strengthens the relationships between the independent variables and Republican primary turnout growth. Increases are widely distributed in terms of specific scores (eleven values went up, four went down, and one was unchanged) and among the states. Population is

**Table 6.7. County-Level Correlations by State
for Selected Demographic Variables**

Independent variable	Ala.	Ark.	Ga.	Miss.
Housing value	.31	.13	.22	.12
Income	.16	−.07	.18	.18
Population	.28	.06	.27	.44
White-collar employment	.07	−.24	.17	.15

Source: Data calculated by the author.

the big winner among the variables, as each of its scores rose by at least .09. Eliminating those counties with the smallest base Republican vote also removed many of the smallest counties in each state, and this step serves to amplify further the association between population growth and GOP primary turnout growth.[15]

It may be argued that the concept of truncation gains validity from the fact that its application has moved the two outlier categories—Arkansas and white-collar employment—somewhat closer to the others. While this method also widened the range of correlation scores within each state (and rather significantly in two of them), this effect is entirely a function of the enhanced population scores noted above.

Conclusions

None of the three middle-class variables produced consistently strong correlation values. The scores for housing value growth fell within a narrow range (.08), indicating that this variable had a similar effect upon Republican primary turnout growth in all four states. However, this relationship was not especially robust, as it exceeded .25 in only one untruncated case. On the other hand, income growth and white-collar employment growth correlated with turnout strongly in one state (Georgia) but produced modest, minimal, or even slightly negative associations in the others.

By contrast, the population growth variable recorded consistently strong correlations across state lines (at or above .25 in three states before truncation and in all four afterward). It also produced the highest values within each state in five of the eight cases.

In view of these results, I am prepared to argue the following points:

1. The three middle class variables clearly explain some of the recent growth in Republican primary voting, but their correlation values are highly variable and relatively modest. A multivariable "middle classification"

**Table 6.8. County-Level Correlations by State, Using
Truncated County Populations for Selected Demographic Variables**

Independent variable	Ala.	Ark.	Ga.	Miss.
Housing value	.20	.12	.20	.15
Income	.18	−.05	.34	.16
Population	.53	.25	.42	.53
White-collar employment	.07	.00	.44	.17

Note: Total *N* of counties retained after truncation was 261 (or 68.1 percent of original pool of 383). State totals: Alabama 42 (62.7 percent); Georgia 76 (47.8 percent); Arkansas 69 (92.0 percent); Mississippi 74 (90.2 percent).
Source: Data calculated by the author.

index would probably help control for the distorting effects of state- and election-specific factors.

2. If the net increase in a county's population is the strongest single predictor (particularly after we control for the effects of "small base" counties), then growth in Republican primary turnout is being carried by forces widely distributed within each state. This "rising tide lifts all boats" pattern indicates that something more broadly based than the expansion of the South's middle-class electorate is at work here.

Additional support for the rising tide thesis comes from an examination of the relative influence each state's leading metropolitan area enjoys within that state's Republican primary. Since these metropole counties rank highly on each of the middle-class growth indicia we have tested, the underlying premise of our middle-class growth model means that the metropole share of Republican primary votes should register significant growth between the late 1970s and the early 1990s. This idea is tested in table 6.9.

Metropole vote shares have declined moderately in Alabama and Georgia, have increased a bit in Mississippi, and have risen sharply only in Arkansas. The aggregate metropole increase for the four-state group is only 6.4 percent, which is less than simple population growth would predict. Also, the metropole vote shares have undergone a considerable convergence across state lines. What had been an enormous range of Republican primary vote shares during the first cycle (from 17 to 71 percent) narrowed dramatically during the second (now 40 to 70 percent).[16] Does this mark the emergence of a stable, even "mature," profile of Deep South Republican primary turnout (that is, roughly half coming from the state's leading metro area and half from elsewhere)? More data from future primaries will be needed before we can draw such a conclusion, but the general pattern presented here adds credence to the rising tide interpretation.

Table 6.9. Metropole Share of Republican Primary Vote by State, 1978–1979 and 1990–1991

State	N^a	Percent	
		1978–79	1990–91
Alabama	3	56.1	49.7
Arkansas	3	17.3	40.0
Georgia	14	70.9	70.1
Mississippi	3	39.4	45.1
Total[b]	23	46.5	52.9

[a]Those counties traditionally recognized as comprising the largest metropolitan area in each state or counties that are now considered such because of recent suburban growth. They are: Birmingham, Alabama (Jefferson, Saint Clair, Shelby); Little Rock, Arkansas (Faulkner, Pulaski, Saline); Atlanta, Georgia (Barrow, Cherokee, Clay, Cobb, DeKalb, Douglas, Fayette, Forsyth, Fulton, Gwinnett, Henry, Newton, Rockdale, Walton); Jackson, Mississippi (Hinds, Madison, Rankin).
[b]The twenty-three-county share of the entire Republican primary vote cast across the four-state region.
Source: Official statements of the vote issued by the respective secretaries of state for the years indicated.

Directions for Future Research

What are the sources of this rising tide of Republican primary voting that is washing across the Deep South? Neither of the models tested in this study directly addresses the impact of political factors upon Republican primary turnout. At least four different—though possibly overlapping—political scenarios may lend themselves to systematic observation and analysis. They are:

1. *Supply Side.* Republican primary turnout is primarily affected by factors specific to a given year's primary election campaign. This would include the number and attractiveness of candidates both for statewide and for local offices; how much money their campaigns are able to spend; and the amount of ideological polarization and group-based appeals the campaigns feature. Each party's primary turnout will rise (or fall) from one election to the next, depending upon the potency of these factors.

2. *Influence-seeking.* Voters will go where the action is. They want to cast their primary vote where they believe it will have the greatest effect, perhaps even without regard to their general election voting preferences. The more the Republican primary is seen as the place where important electoral decisions are made, the higher the turnout for that primary will be. This statement may especially be true with respect to local races. One possible method for testing this theory is to track GOP primary turnout (both abso-

lutely and relative to Democratic turnout) in a county before and after the party wins its first local office.

One curious by-product of such behavior would be the phenomenon of mischievous voting, that is, partisans of one party voting in the other party's primary for reasons of strategic advantage, ideological preference, or animosity against a prominent officeholder. At least two of these factors appeared to be at work in Georgia's new sixth congressional district in 1992, when primary-switching Democrats probably helped account for Cong. Newt Gingrich's near defeat in the Republican primary. The GOP's recent domination of county and state legislative elections in that area surely made it easier for loyal Democrats to justify ignoring their own party's primary.

Two other models proceed from a common assumption that increases in Republican primary turnout are not pushed by demographic change or pulled by short-term electoral stimuli but reflect changes in the underlying loyalties of the voters themselves.

3. *Party Identification.* Those who start voting in Republican primaries do so because they have come to think of themselves as Republicans at least to the degree that they would give that answer to a survey question about party identification. However, conventional surveys would only tell us how many respondents identify themselves as Republicans, and what their demographic profile is. Further questioning would be required to probe why they have decided to vote in that party's primary and whether they expect to do so in the future.

4. *Consolidation.* Those who have tended to vote Republican in general elections eventually start voting in Republican primaries, regardless of self-identification. In this way, the party's base of support, perhaps highly unstable and situational to begin with, consolidates over time into something more stable and reliable.

One way to test this premise, or at least the magnitude of primary vote growth it accounts for, would be to measure growth in those counties where the 1978–1979 Republican gubernatorial candidate ran the farthest behind the party's 1980 presidential vote. This approach should give a good measure of the "situational Republican" vote that existed at the eve of the Reagan era.

However, this scenario also raises questions of causality not answerable here (or perhaps by any analysis): does a history of Republican voting eventually lead a voter to the self-conscious conclusion that he or she has a stake, obligation, or rational imperative to vote in that party's primary? Also, does voting in Republican primaries, once adopted, serve to reinforce the voter's proclivity to support the party's nominees in November?

7

Dixie Versus the Nonsouthern Megastates in American Presidential Politics

Thomas F. Eamon

Following the 1992 election the American South found itself in a position that it had occupied all too often in the first two-thirds of the twentieth century. The former Confederate states were on the losing side in a presidential race and that in an election where the victors had won an electoral college landslide. However, in 1992 most southern states had voted for the Republican candidate in an election won by the Democrats. There was further irony. For the first time since the Civil War, both the presidential and vice-presidential candidates of a major political party—in this case the Democrats—were from the South. In contrast the Democratic ticket amassed its greatest pluralities in the big electoral vote states outside the South, all of which were Republican leaning before 1932 and major two-party battlegrounds afterward. As in earlier days, these larger states—especially Pennsylvania, Michigan, and Ohio—were the most heavily courted by both the Democrat and Republican tickets.

This most recent of elections was a driving force behind our investigation of modern presidential politics. So too was the stimulating and provocative book *The Vital South* (1992), in which Earl and Merle Black argued that the South had emerged as a crucial region in American politics.[1] At least on first glance the 1992 election appeared to raise serious questions about the validity of their central thesis.[2]

We thought also about a winter 1989 article in *Polity* that was in partial conflict with the Blacks' position. In "Go West, Young Democrat," C. B. Holman asserted that "the time has come for national Democrats to look away from Dixieland and toward the Golden West."[3] On the basis of long-term electoral trends and public opinion surveys, Holman concluded, "There is closer harmony between eastern and western Democrats on a variety of issues and . . . the Democrats should reconstruct their party coalition along these geographic lines."[4]

Furthermore, Holman was implicitly calling into question a political axiom of the 1980s, namely that the GOP held an electoral lock on presidential elections.[5] A monolithic and Republican South and West were said to be the centerpiece of this coalition. At least superficially the Clinton-Gore victory of 1992 smashed the lock. In our view the lock thesis was always an oversimplification. However, we do believe that two diverse groupings of states are crucial to the dynamics of the electoral college and will continue to be. To complicate matters a bit further, they do not always act in tandem with one another. The first is regional and consists of the eleven former Confederate states. Once the bedrock of the Democratic Party, they have since 1952 been up for grabs. Diverse though they are, these states usually display a tendency to move in the same general direction. The southern grouping includes two superstates, Florida and Texas. Yet most fall close to the national median in population rank. Together, they now have 147 electoral votes—over half of the electoral votes needed to win the presidency.

Following convention we classify the states of Alabama, Georgia, Louisiana, Mississippi, and South Carolina as Deep South.[6] We label Arkansas, North Carolina, Tennessee, and Virginia as the Peripheral South. Unlike other studies we place Florida and Texas in a separate group, which we simply label "Florida-Texas."[7] More colorfully it might be called the "wavering South," the "wondering South," or the "fleeing South." The closest call was Virginia. We feel confident in placing the Old Dominion, on the basis of overall population characteristics and political culture, with the Peripheral South despite the changes wrought by expanding Washington suburbs. Other observers might place it in the group with Florida and Texas or by itself. They could cite Virginia's relatively high income (which we consider a result of the Washington overspill) or the tendency of Virginia in recent times to take its own path whatever the rest of the South might be doing.

The second grouping, which is not strictly speaking a regional one, we call the megastates. More accurately, they are the nonsouthern megastates, as Florida and Texas are excluded. The megastates are New York, Pennsylvania, Illinois, Michigan, Ohio, and California. Together, they currently have 171 electoral votes, nearly two-thirds of the number needed for victory. All are characterized by ethnic diversity and huge urban populations. For decades they have figured prominently in national electoral strategy. While they do not always vote for the same presidential candidates, there is typically a narrow range in their popular vote percentages.

This chapter examines the roles of the megastates and the southern states from 1952, a watershed year in southern presidential voting, to 1992. Together, the two groupings are the largest in the electoral college. We shall evaluate their relative influence. While the practicalities of a presidential victory demand a close focus on their behavior in the electoral college, we must also examine the groups' relative contribution to the popular vote results. Psychologically, the popular vote contest is the more crucial of the two for a president who wishes to govern effectively. We shall also evaluate the impact of changing demographics and recent election trends.

Our thesis suggests that the nonsouthern megastates remain the centerpiece of any successful strategy to win the presidency. However, the South—notwithstanding the 1992 election—is well positioned to remain a major player. More specifically the region's own superstates, Florida and Texas, are among the nation's most rapidly growing. Georgia, North Carolina, and Virginia boomed in the 1980s. While by no means supplanting the nonsouthern megastates, the South could over a period of time become an equally important force. Such a thesis begs the question as to whether the South will behave as a unit. Perhaps the real truth lies somewhere between the Black and Holman positions.

Regionalism and the New Party System

The New Deal party system did not die without a fight. Political scientists were reluctant to acknowledge that a system based on the politics of the early Roosevelt era was vanishing even as fissures appeared in the 1940s. As late as the 1960s and 1970s, the normal political party system was still seen as one with a Democratic majority. Superficially, Jimmy Carter in 1976 had revived the coalition with an electoral lead based on the South and the megastates of New York, Pennsylvania, and Ohio. In fact the old New Deal coalition was dealt a devastating blow in 1968 if not before.[8] From 1968 through 1988 the Democrats lost five of the six elections. Black and Black and Holman agreed that the Democratic loss largely reflected the defection of previously Democratic voters in the South. Beyond this, their prescriptions for the Democrats differed.

Holman asserted, "The future of party politics rests with the south and the west."[9] On the basis of trends through 1988 he saw the Northeast as Democratic and the Rocky Mountain states as safely Republican. Looking at what he saw as the pivotal regions, Holman thought the deeply ingrained social conservatism of the South made Democratic prospects there bleak. He concluded that a liberal social and foreign policy could propel the Democrats to victory in the West.

Viewing many of the same electoral trends, Black and Black suggested a Democratic strategy to make the party competitive in the South. For this to happen, Democratic presidential candidates would need to focus on white swing voters who took moderate positions on political issues. Democrats have successfully appealed to such voters in state and congressional races.[10] The strategy demands progressive rhetoric and action on educational and infrastructure issues while at the same time selling such expenditures as long-term investments. Democrats would also need to call for a strong defense posture. While expressing support for equal rights for all, a strong commitment to specific affirmative action programs, especially those that involve racial quotas for blacks, would be avoided. Black and Black saw race as the most difficult issue of all.[11]

While accepting the prevailing view that southern defections have contributed to Democratic electoral losses, we believe that many of the major studies have given inadequate attention to the nonsouthern megastates. Since 1952, the GOP has more than held its own in such states as Pennsylvania, Illinois, and Ohio. (Even during the New Deal, the Republicans maintained a reservoir of support in these historically two-party states.) Eisenhower and Reagan swept the nonsouthern megastates. There, as in the south, the Democrats usually did better in state and local elections. Today the megastates of the country's northeastern quadrant from New York to Illinois continue to exert a strong pull on presidential politics. Arguably, they still hold the key to presidential outcomes. When joined with California, a state whose political behavior is quite like that of Illinois and Ohio, the states are worthy rivals to the South.

All students of politics can appreciate the emphasis that presidential candidates place on winning the six megastates, but some might question a grouping that places together states whose geographic locations and images are as diverse as those of Pennsylvania, Illinois, and California. Yet we feel the grouping is not only defensible but indeed logical, especially if we contrast them with the South.

Aside from having tremendous populations in long-established metropolitan centers, the megastates differ from Dixie in numerous ways. First, all of the megastates have central cities with high population density at the heart of their largest conurbations. This includes California. Except for New York, San Francisco has the highest residential density of any large American central city. Even Los Angeles, the archetypal spread city, has a central-city population density as high as or higher than that of older core cities of Cleveland, Detroit, and Pittsburgh. If the San Fernando Valley suburbs did not make up a substantial portion of the "city" population, its residential density would approach that of such established eastern cities as Baltimore and Philadelphia. From a sociodemographic standpoint, Los Angeles is more akin to Chicago or New York than to Houston. By contrast, the great southern cities except Miami have low population densities. All of the megastates have huge suburban populations that are not politically part of the main city. The backbone of the southern urban population is in middle-sized cities and smaller towns.

The megastates have a history of heavy manufacturing in their large metropolitan centers and often strong union penetration. The South's manufacturing was from the beginning more spread out, and to this day unions are less potent. In the megastates nearly all blacks live in the central cities or in nearby suburbs. In the South blacks are more evenly distributed between cities and rural areas. (The same is true of Hispanics in Texas.) Except for parts of the Central Valley of California, the vast rural and small-town stretches of the megastates are predominately of European background.

Non-African ethnics, whether of European, Asian, or Latino ancestry, are a major force in all of the megastates. In the South this statement is partly true in only three states: Florida, Louisiana, and Texas. Until recently, their real political impact was minimal in all three states. (Even Louisiana did not have a Catholic governor until the 1970s.) In the megastates, including California, urban settlements and booms were shaped largely by railroads. Southern urban centers owe their national status more to highway networks or air transport. (New Orleans is an exception.) Megastates—again including California—were major players in the electoral college by 1932. In the South only Texas held this status. The megastates with the exception of Republican Pennsylvania prior to 1936 were two-party battlegrounds during the period from 1880 to 1950. With rare and easily explained exceptions, the southern states from Virginia to Texas voted the straight Democratic ticket. (Even today Democrats often maintain at least a shaky monopoly on county and legislative elections.) Despite pockets of pro-Confederate, or "copperhead," sentiments, the megastates were emotional centers of the antislavery crusade. Their political cultures were individualistic, with a puritan-moralistic streak in some areas.[12] The southern states—pockets of moralistic and individualistic culture notwithstanding—were predominately traditional.

Megastates Versus the South: Power Shift?

Through 1960 the megastates commanded 181 electoral votes as compared with 128 electoral votes in the old Confederacy. As table 7.1 shows, the megastates held their advantage through the 1970s. This edge largely reflected growth in California, but even Michigan and Ohio gained electoral power as a result of the 1960 census. During the same period the South's relative position stayed about the same despite strong growth in Florida and Texas. If we exclude these two states, the Deep South and Peripheral South states saw their electoral positions erode in the 1950–1970 period. A fundamental shift began occurring in the 1970s. As a result, the 1980 census required a 9 percent reduction of electoral votes in the five megastates lying in the country's northeastern quadrant. Even California could muster only two additional electoral votes. For the first time in the twentieth century, metropolitan areas had grown more slowly than the

Table 7.1. Electoral Vote Shift, 1952-1992, in Megastates and the South

	1952-60	1964-68	1972-80	1984-88	1992
Megastates	181	185	185	175	171
Deep South	49	47	46	46	46
Peripheral South	45	42	41	42	44
Florida-Texas	34	39	43	50	57

Source: Data drawn from Richard M. Scammon, ed., *America Votes: A Handbook of Contemporary American Election Statistics,* 20 vols. (vols. 1-2: New York: Macmillan, 1956, 1958; vols. 3-5: Pittsburgh: University of Pittsburgh Press, 1959, 1962, 1964; vols 6-20 [with Alice V. McGillivray]: Washington, D.C.: Congressional Quarterly Press, 1966-93).

country as a whole. The pattern was most convincingly seen in the megastates' decline in the electoral college. The exception to the general pattern was the South, where most metropolitan areas grew at a rapid clip. Again the trend was most pronounced in Florida and Texas. Even the five Deep South states held steady with forty-six electoral votes. While their rural populations lagged, their cities and suburbs experienced steady and in some cases dramatic population growth.

Despite a 1980s economic boom in their coastal urban centers, New York and Pennsylvania saw little population increase and lost electoral power in the 1990 census. The drop was even more pronounced in the recession-weary Midwest. California's massive population gains kept the megastates from repeating their losses of the 1970s. Led by Florida the South's relative position improved further. But even Texas, battered by a petroleum recession in much of the eighties, managed to gain three electoral votes. The Deep South states maintained forty-six electoral votes, while the Peripheral South went from forty-two to forty-four votes. Though a gain, this figure was still below its 1950 total of forty-five.

Table 7.1 shows the megastates dropping from 181 electoral votes in the 1952-1960 period to 171 in 1992. Excluding California, the drop was of near massive proportions, from 149 to 117. Most of this decline occurred following the 1980 and 1990 censuses. While the South moved in the same period from 128 to 147 electoral votes, there was a net loss of four outside Florida and Texas. These losses reflected out-migration prior to 1970. Since then the Deep South and Peripheral South have held their own and in some cases have grown more rapidly than the country as a whole.

Though electoral votes determine the winner, public perceptions of politics are shaped largely by the popular vote lead. Opposition politicians may remind the president and public that a clear mandate is lacking if the electoral winner achieved a plurality victory but not a majority. In 1993 Robert

Dole frequently spoke of Bill Clinton as a "minority president," despite Clinton's electoral college landslide. John Kennedy and Jimmy Carter also had to govern in the shadow of narrow popular vote leads. Likewise national polling reflects roughly what the popular vote is at a particular time. Consequently, it behooves us to look closely at how heavily our regional groupings have contributed to the popular vote from 1952 to 1992 (table 7.2).

Despite an 18 percent population growth over a forty-year period, the northeastern megastates' raw vote stayed about the same. Indeed, New York saw a slight decline. The Great Lakes megastates experienced a 38 percent population growth rate and a 20 percent voting increase during the same period. California, with a population gain near 200 percent, had a 116 percent expansion in voting between 1952 and 1992. (The greater lag of voters compared with population in California and New York can be explained in part by the tremendously increased proportions of recent immigrants from overseas or Latin America.) The South's electoral participation increased dramatically in all areas. Florida's was up 395 percent over the forty years, a figure that kept pace with its population growth. The 167 percent growth in the Texas electorate was well above its 120 percent population increase. (Texas enforced a poll tax until the mid-1960s.) The Peripheral South states had gains ranging from 104 percent in North Carolina to 295 percent in Virginia. In all four states the increases far surpassed population growth. Virginia experienced a surge after the abolition of the poll tax in 1964–1965 and again in the 1980s, when the Washington area saw rapid growth. Regionally, the most explosive growth in voters came in the Deep South. Part of the gain can be attributed to the aftermath of the Voting Rights Act of 1965. Not only did this make it possible for more blacks to vote, but it also mobilized whites. Alabama, with a modest 32 percent population increase, led the way with a 292 percent voter gain between the presidential elections of 1952 and 1992.

In an era when American presidential voting has struggled to keep up with population increases, the South stands out as an exception. The region has contributed more heavily to the popular presidential vote in this period than at any other time in modern history.

A Note on the Classification of Elections

We would classify American presidential victory spreads of 10 percent of the popular vote or more as landslides. A cliff-hanger or tight election is one in which the winner's margin falls below 4 percent. Victory margins between 4 percent and 10 percent are considered "normal." By this standard no presidential election from 1952 through 1984 was normal. Republican

Table 7.2. Change in Popular Vote and Population in Megastates and Southern States, 1952–1992 (percent)

State or megastate	Popular vote	Population
New York	–2.8	21.3
Pennsylvania	7.8	13.1
Northeastern Megastates	*1.5*	*17.9*
Illinois	3.8	31.2
Michigan	40.8	45.8
Ohio	23.7	36.4
Great Lakes Megastates	*20.0*	*37.8*
California	*116.4*	*181.1*
Alabama	291.6	31.9
Georgia	236.5	88.0
Louisiana	167.8	57.2
Mississippi	226.3	18.0
South Carolina	231.1	64.7
Deep South	*238.2*	*51.9*
Arkansas	119.3	23.0
North Carolina	104.0	63.1
Tennessee	115.3	48.1
Virginia	295.3	86.4
Peripheral South	*159.0*	*55.1*
Florida	394.7	366.9
Texas	167.5	120.2
Florida/Texas	*274.1*	*185.4*

Source: Author's election files.

landslides occurred in 1952, 1956, 1972, 1980, and 1984. Lyndon Johnson's 1964 victory over Barry Goldwater was the lone Democratic landslide and indeed one approaching avalanche proportions. By contrast, the contests of 1960, 1968, and 1976 were among the closest in American history but produced the presidencies of Democrat John Kennedy, Republican Richard Nixon, and Democrat Jimmy Carter. With victory margins of about 6 percent, George Bush in 1988 and Bill Clinton in 1992 were near the middle of the normal range. However, their electoral college victories exceeded a 2 to 1 margin. The only tight electoral vote victories were Kennedy's 303–219 margin over Nixon in 1960 and Carter's 297–240 lead over Gerald Ford in 1976. While the Kennedy-Nixon cliff-hanger has assumed legendary status, Carter in fact came close to electoral defeat. Shifts of a few thousand voters in Ohio and Mississippi would have carried Ford to victory even though he trailed by 1.5 million popular votes.

The Decline of the Solid Democratic South: A Convergence?

From 1880 through 1924 the South cast a majority of its electoral votes for the winning presidential candidate in only four elections: the victories of Grover Cleveland in 1884 and 1892 and of Woodrow Wilson in 1912 and 1916. In this Republican era the South voted with the winner only in elections where aberrations produced Democratic presidencies. In other elections, the South was almost unanimous in its support for the Democratic loser. (The qualification "almost" is necessary because Tennessee went for Republican Warren Harding in 1920.) Even as the South revolted against the perceived evils of papacy and liquor in the 1928 battle, the Catholic Democrat Al Smith and Republican Protestant Herbert Hoover finished with a 64–64 split in the region, with Smith dominant among die-hard Deep South Democrats. With the advent of the Roosevelt era, the southern states at last became members of a winning Democratic coalition. In 1948, seven southern states were a crucial part of the Truman coalition. The four states—Alabama, Louisiana, Mississippi, and South Carolina—that backed Dixiecrat Strom Thurmond did so under the Democratic ballot emblem in their home states.

The year 1952, in which Republican Dwight Eisenhower defeated Democrat Adlai Stevenson 55 percent to 45 percent, marked a new era in southern presidential voting (see table 7.3). From that time forward the Republican candidate would be competing in large portions of the South. Driven by marked GOP gains in nearly all urban centers of the former confederacy, Eisenhower won the states of Virginia, Florida, Tennessee, and Texas. He ran especially well for a Republican, albeit a Republican military hero, in other southern states. Yet the election returns reveal a South quite distinct from the rest of the country. The South's electoral votes split 71 to 57 for Stevenson. Stevenson won three-fifths of the Deep South's popular vote and about half in the Peripheral South. However, Eisenhower narrowly carried Florida and Texas.

The megastates joined the rest of the country in providing solid support for the Republican ticket. Together they provided two-thirds of Eisenhower's electoral vote. The GOP standard-bearer held a 12 percent lead in the megastates. The urbane Stevenson, a hero of the intellectual Left, was saved from total annihilation by the rural South. It was enough to qualify him for a rematch four years later.

In 1956 for the first time Eisenhower, a Republican, won a majority of the South's electoral (and popular) votes, with an electoral vote lead of 67 to 61. He received 38 percent of the popular vote in the Deep South and 50 percent in the Peripheral South and swept Florida and Texas. In addition to holding the four states he won in 1952, Eisenhower carried Louisi-

Table 7.3. The Eisenhower Victories: Electoral Vote in the Megastates and Dixie, 1952 and 1956

Region	1952			1956		
	Dem.	Rep.	Pop. vote for Eisenhower (%)	Dem.	Rep.	Pop. vote for Eisenhower (%)
Megastates	0	181	55.5	0	181	57.8
Deep South	49	0	39.6	39	10	37.8
Peripheral South	22	23	48.9	22	23	50.1
Florida-Texas	0	34	53.7	0	34	55.9
All South	71	57	45.9	61	67	44.0
United States	89	442	55.1	73	457	57.4

Source: Data drawn from Richard M. Scammon, ed., *America Votes: A Handbook of Contemporary American Election Statistics*, 20 vols. (vols. 1–2: New York: Macmillan, 1956, 1958; vols. 3–5: Pittsburgh: University of Pittsburgh Press, 1959, 1962, 1964; vols 6–20 [with Alice V. McGillivray]: Washington, D.C.: Congressional Quarterly Press, 1966–93).

ana and barely lost North Carolina. Ironically, in view of future developments, Eisenhower's victories resulted in part from strong black support in the urban South. Yet Eisenhower's southern victory paled in comparison with his national electoral landslide, 457 votes to Stevenson's 73.

The megastates (especially New York) provided massive majorities for the Republican ticket, as Eisenhower's popular vote margin there was fourteen points. With a 57 to 42 percent popular vote in the final national totals, Eisenhower's reelection depended on no one region or stratum.

The megastates more than ever before were targeted by the Democratic strategists in 1960. On balance, Kennedy's Catholic identification was a slight plus in most of the large states. Despite losses to Vice President Richard Nixon in California and Ohio, Kennedy led, with 124 to 57 electoral votes in the six most populous nonsouthern states (see table 7.4). His popular vote lead was below 1 percent in the same state. With Lyndon Johnson's vice-presidential candidacy the ticket also stressed the South where the ghost of Al Smith's candidacy lurked. Special emphasis was placed on returning Texas to the Democratic fold and retaining the Carolinas. The strategy worked in the sense that the South was neutralized with a 67 to 47 Democratic electoral lead. States'-rights-oriented electors won Mississippi. (Six Alabama unpledged Democratic electors also backed this slate.) Kennedy had a big popular vote lead in the Deep South based largely on Democratic loyalist strength in Georgia and Catholic support in Louisiana. Elsewhere in Dixie, the election was tight. The Civil Rights movement would shortly come to a head in the South.

In the South the elections of 1964, 1968, and 1972 brought partisan reversals of near record magnitudes. Polling only 38 percent of the national popular vote and trailing 486 to 52 in the electoral college, the GOP's 1964 standard-bearer Barry Goldwater was competitive in all of the South outside Lyndon Johnson's Texas. Nevertheless, he failed to carry Florida or any Peripheral South states. In the Deep South, Goldwater won all forty-seven electoral votes. His vote proportions ranged from about 55 percent in Georgia and Louisiana to 87 percent in Mississippi. The Mississippi landslide represented the highest popular vote proportion ever received by a presidential candidate in any state between 1952 and 1992! All of these developments came at the climax of the civil rights revolution. Senator Goldwater of Arizona had voted against the Civil Rights Act of 1964. In less than a year the Voting Rights Act of 1965 would lead toward less monolithic voting behavior in the Deep South, as blacks joined the electorate in large numbers. Yet the newly franchised blacks would lack the numbers needed to transform the Deep South states into liberal Democratic strongholds.

The six megastates provided Lyndon Johnson with over two-thirds of the votes needed for an electoral college victory. Roosevelt in 1936 had carried all of these states for the Democratic ticket, but never was he able to achieve

Table 7.4. The Kennedy Cliffhanger: Electoral Vote in the Megastates and the South in 1960

Region	1960 Dem.	Rep.	States' Rights	Pop. vote for Kennedy (%)
Megastates	124	57	0	50.2
Deep South	35	0	14	53.5
Peripheral South	22	23	0	48.9
Florida-Texas	24	10	0	49.7
All South	81	33	14	47.7
United States	303	219	15	49.7

Source: Data drawn from Richard M. Scammon, ed., *America Votes: A Handbook of Contemporary American Election Statistics,* 20 vols. (vols. 1–2: New York: Macmillan, 1956, 1958; vols. 3–5: Pittsburgh: University of Pittsburgh Press, 1959, 1962, 1964; vols 6–20 [with Alice V. McGillivray]: Washington, D.C.: Congressional Quarterly Press, 1966–93).

commanding popular vote majorities on the level of Johnson's. Johnson's popular vote lead in the megastates was 63 percent to 37 percent.

Four years later, the Republican victor Richard Nixon and American Independent George Wallace were strong in the South. A last-minute surge gave Humphrey a plurality win in Texas. Nixon carried Florida on the basis of strength in central and southern sections. In the Peripheral South, only Wallace's Arkansas edge kept Nixon from a full sweep. In the Deep South Strom Thurmond, now a Republican, saved South Carolina for Nixon. As expected, the other Deep South states were pro-Wallace. The closeness of the contest was reflected in the returns from the megastates. They split 93 to 92 in Humphrey's favor. Indeed, we would argue that neither of the state groupings under discussion was decisive in 1968. However, modest voter shifts in Illinois, Ohio, and California would have produced a Humphrey victory. Wallace victories in South Carolina and several Peripheral South states, where he ran second, might have led to a deadlock in the electoral college. In an election where Nixon had 43 percent of the popular vote, he led Humphrey 301 to 191 in the electoral college.

Carrying every jurisdiction outside of the District of Columbia and Massachusetts in 1972, Richard Nixon won an electoral college victory similar to Democrat Roosevelt's in 1936, and his 61 percent popular vote total was in the same range. Despite the post-1965 surge of black and pro-Democratic voters in the Deep South, Nixon's best popular vote showing was his 72 percent in that region. In this election with a Democratic Party "tainted" by social liberalism in general and civil rights for blacks in particular, Mississippi provided a telling footnote. In 1972 and 1964 it was the union's most Republican state. Heavily for George Wallace in 1968, Mississippi was the

Table 7.5. From Democratic Landslide to Republican Victory: Electoral Vote in Megastates and the South in 1964 and 1968

Region	1964			1968			
	Dem.	Rep.	Pop. vote for winner (%)	Dem.	Rep.	Wallace	Pop. vote for winner (%)
Megastates	185	0	62.8	93	92	0	45.5
Deep South	0	47	34.2	0	8	39	23.8
Peripheral South	42	0	55.5	0	35	7	39.0
Florida-Texas	39	0	58.2	25	14	0	40.1
All South	81	47	51.3	25	57	46	34.6
United States	486	52	61.1	191	301	46	43.4

Note: 1964 Winner = Democrat. 1968 Winner = Republican.
Source: Data drawn from Richard M. Scammon, ed., *America Votes: A Handbook of Contemporary American Election Statistics*, 20 vols. (vols. 1–2: New York: Macmillan, 1956, 1958; vols. 3–5: Pittsburgh: University of Pittsburgh Press, 1959, 1962, 1964; vols 6–20 [with Alice V. McGillivray]: Washington, D.C.: Congressional Quarterly Press, 1966–93).

least Republican state! The Peripheral South, Texas, and Florida gave Nixon a 2 to 1 edge. (The 1972 election is excluded from tables 7.5 and 7.6 as Nixon carried all states.)

With Georgian Jimmy Carter heading the Democratic ticket, the Deep South and Peripheral South were more Democratic than the country as a whole in 1976 and 1980. Carter won all five Deep South states in 1976. He carried Florida, Texas, and all of the Peripheral South states except Virginia. Only 27 votes over the number needed for electoral college victory, Carter's 118 to 12 lead over Gerald Ford in the South was the most salient feature of the election. Carter and Ford both had about 49 percent of the megastates' popular vote. The megastates split their electoral votes evenly, 93 Democratic and 92 Republican.

In a reversal of fortune, the southern states voted electorally 118 to 12 for Reagan in 1980, with Carter's Georgia the only holdout. Even so, in all of the other southern states except Florida, Louisiana, and Texas, Carter was much more competitive in the South than in the country as a whole. All six nonsouthern megastates jumped on the Reagan bandwagon. Only New York and Pennsylvania were close.

Reagan would become a hero of the cultural Right. If the Carter era had suggested morning again for the Democrats in Dixie, the Reagan era made the perception seem a mirage. As Reagan led Walter Mondale in 1984, 59 percent to 41 percent in the popular vote, the South and the Rocky Mountain West were the most Republican states. The South had joined all states except Minnesota (and the District of Columbia) in supporting Reagan. Reagan had over 60 percent of the vote in all southern subregions. Survey research information hinted that around this time white Southerners who identified as Republicans numbered as many as or more than Democrats. There were no major differences in the various southern subregions. (No table is shown for the 1984 election, as Reagan carried all states examined.)

Even in the face of Republican George Bush's seven-point popular victory and 425 to 111 electoral vote landslide in 1988, there were hints of a new political landscape in the megastates. Only New York among these states cast its electoral vote for Democrat Michael Dukakis. Yet Pennsylvania and Illinois were very close. In the six nonsouthern megastates, Bush had a modest 3 percent lead. The Bush-Quayle campaign's stress on defense, patriotism, and fighting crime produced a solid South—solidly Republican. The cold technocratic approach of Dukakis was no match for the GOP's socioemotional approach.

The Clinton campaign of 1992 saw the economy as the issue providing the most direct road to the White House. The election outcome offered evidence of their wisdom. As students of books blaming the Democratic decline on cultural liberalism and high taxes, especially Edsall and Edsall, the Clinton campaign strategists moved to the political center on many is-

Table 7.6. The Carter and Reagan Victories: Megastates and the South in 1976 and 1980

Region	1976			1980		
	Dem.	Rep.	Pop. vote for winner (%)	Dem.	Rep.	Pop. vote for winner (%)
Megastates	93	92	48.8	0	185	50.2
Deep South	46	0	56.9	12	34	47.5
Peripheral South	29	12	54.5	0	41	50.1
Florida-Texas	43	0	51.4	0	43	55.3
All South	118	12	55.1	12	118	49.6
United States	297	240	50.1	19	489	50.7

Note: 1976 Winner = Democrat. 1980 Winner = Republican.
Source: Data drawn from Richard M. Scammon, ed., *America Votes: A Handbook of Contemporary American Election Statistics*, 20 vols. (vols. 1–2: New York: Macmillan, 1956, 1958; vols. 3–5: Pittsburgh: University of Pittsburgh Press, 1959, 1962, 1964; vols 6–20 [with Alice V. McGillivray]: Washington, D.C.: Congressional Quarterly Press, 1966–93).

sues (abortion was an exception).[13] The shift worked on a national level. Yet the election returns suggested a nation fraught by a deep cultural divide. A Bush campaign akin to that of 1988 in issues, if not skill, returned dividends in the white South. Elsewhere its successes were confined to usual Republican strongholds and some conservative ethnic communities.

With Ross Perot polling 19 percent of the popular vote in the 1992 election, Bill Clinton became the fifth minority president of the twentieth century. Yet in a two-way race his lead over Republican George Bush would likely have remained in the 5 to 6 percent range. As it was, Clinton led Bush 43.3 percent to 37.7 percent. Having landslide wins in New York, Illinois, and California, comfortable wins in Pennsylvania and Michigan, and a narrow victory in Ohio, Clinton held an overall lead exceeding 11 percent in the megastates. These six states alone put him within ninety-nine votes of an electoral majority. All six states had suffered in the recent recession. (See table 7.7.)

The electoral college allocation system did not work to Clinton's advantage in his home region, where he trailed Bush 108 to 39. The southern popular vote was close. In the Peripheral South Clinton's wins in Arkansas and Tennessee were not enough to overcome losses in North Carolina and Virginia. He trailed Bush 27 to 17 despite a 1.6 percent popular vote lead. In the Deep South the popular vote and electoral votes were well matched. Bush had a 2.5 percent popular vote margin; he led 24 to 22 in the electoral college. With modest wins in Texas for thirty-two electoral votes and in Florida for twenty-five electoral votes, Bush was propelled to a sweeping victory in Dixie.

Questions raised about Clinton's patriotism, most notably his draft record, and morality were widely discussed in the election. In the South, if nowhere else, such talk might have determined the outcome. Yet the closeness of the popular vote in most of the South is telling. The region remained competitive for much of the campaign. In part this characteristic reflected cultural identity with two sons of the South, Clinton of Arkansas and Gore of Tennessee. In addition, Clinton's moderate image and coolness toward civil rights leader Jesse Jackson enhanced his standing among white voters. It could be argued that the southern superstates of Florida and Texas were close enough to be within the grasp of the Democratic ticket. What if they had been targeted by Clinton in the same way as Michigan and Ohio?

Still the overall southern result begs a chilling question for loyalist Democrats in Dixie: if the Clinton-Gore ticket could not win a majority in the region, what national Democratic ticket could do so? Outside the candidates' home states, only their razor-thin margin in Georgia was a real accomplishment. The other victory was in Louisiana, one of the nation's most economically distressed states.

A graph of voting in the megastates and southern subregions between

Table 7.7. The Rise and Fall of George Bush: Electoral Vote from the Megastates and the South, 1988–1992

Region	1988			1992		
	Dem.	Rep.	Pop. vote for winner (%)	Dem.	Rep.	Pop. vote for winner (%)
Megastates	36	139	50.9	171	0	46.0
Deep South	0	46	58.5	22	24	42.5
Peripheral South	0	42	58.3	17	27	44.3
Florida-Texas	0	50	58.1	0	57	37.9
All South	0	138	58.5	39	108	42.8
United States	111	426	53.4	370	168	43.0

Note: 1988 Winner = Republican. 1992 Winner = Democrat.

Source: Data drawn from Richard M. Scammon, ed., *America Votes: A Handbook of Contemporary American Election Statistics,* 20 vols. (vols. 1–2: New York: Macmillan, 1956, 1958; vols. 3–5: Pittsburgh: University of Pittsburgh Press, 1959, 1962, 1964; vols 6–20 [with Alice V. McGillivray]: Washington, D.C.: Congressional Quarterly Press, 1966–93).

1952 and 1992 shows a nation more united than our analysis might suggest (figure 7.1). After deep divisions in the mid and late 1960s, there was a considerable degree of popular convergence through 1988. Except for the Carter aberration, the southern states established a firmly Republican pattern. So did the megastates for awhile. The next big regional cleavage came in 1992, when the megastates were much less Republican than the South. Even then the gaps between the Deep South and the megastates were much less than in the 1960s and a bit less than in the more passive 1950s. However, presidential politics works on a winner-take-all system for each state. If the South has firmly established itself as a Republican-leaning region, the future of the Democratic Party could well lie elsewhere. We shall next focus on such a possibility.

Comments on Trends

Prior to the 1992 elections, several themes stand out when we look at voting in the South and megastates. Nationally there have been shifts from the Right to the Left and back. Personality and style also matter. After twenty years of welfare-oriented Democratic policies and the conflicts of World War II and Korea, the country was ready to turn to the mildly conservative general and certified nation hero Dwight Eisenhower in 1952. The megastates led the way, and the states of the Outer South were receptive. Isolated somewhat from national trends by the burden of history, the Deep South states were unable to support a candidate who probably shared many of their values on social and economic issues. (Some very conservative areas of the Deep South did join the Eisenhower bandwagon. One example was South Carolina, where Eisenhower came close to winning under an independent label.) As the nation continued its love affair with Eisenhower in 1956, the South was divided. Because of a coalition of more nationally oriented white conservatives and gains among blacks, Eisenhower was able to hold his own in the South.[14]

In 1960, most southern blacks and whites saw little difference between Kennedy and Nixon on racial questions. Superficially, Kennedy had revived the Roosevelt coalition, but this time most economic conservatives in the South's growing urban areas stuck with Republican Nixon. Kennedy depended on liberal whites and blacks and tradition-bound whites to win. In the megastates, economic issues and a cultural identification with Kennedy likely carried the day.

From 1964 to 1972, southern elections centered on issues of race and cultural conservatism. This was the era of the civil rights revolution, black power, the Vietnam War, drugs, and hippies. The Deep South states were

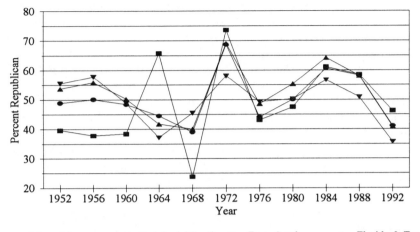

Figure 7.1. Megastates Versus the South in Presidential Elections: 1952–1992.
Source: Data drawn from Richard M. Scammon, ed., *America Votes: A Handbook of
Contemporary American Election Statistics,* 20 vols. (vols. 1–2: New York: Macmillan,
1956, 1958; vols. 3–5: Pittsburgh: University of Pittsburgh Press, 1959, 1962, 1964;
vols. 6–20 [with Alice V. McGillivray]: Washingon, D.C.: Congressional Quarterly
Press, 1966–93).

the most resoundingly conservative in the country in all three elections. By
now the Peripheral South states behaved more along the lines of the country as a whole, supporting Johnson and Nixon.

The megastates were close to national trends: they favored Johnson in
1964, were evenly divided in 1968, and resoundingly backed Nixon in 1972.
At this point, however, there were signs that New York was becoming decidedly more Democratic than the nation as a whole.

In 1976, national malaise and southern regional pride combined to make
Carter the president. Superficially, there was minimal difference in the behavior of the South and the megastates. However, the trends of the 1970s—
economic and international humiliation—would come to haunt the body
politic by the end of the 1970s. By 1984, the South had emerged as a heart-
land of political support for the Reagan revolution. Instead of lagging in
national trends, the white South was leading the way. While the new pros-
perity among middle- and upper-class southerners contributed to this role,
we believe that Reagan had made the underlying southern cultural conservatism respectable. The South was no longer isolated from the national
mainstream. The southern states and megastates were with the nation as a
whole in supporting Reagan.

In what Burnham called "Reagan's valedictory," Bush achieved solid southern support in 1988.[15] But this time cracks appeared in the megastates. While only New York failed to support Bush, his showing was lackluster in the other megastates.

Several points stand out in our 1992 examination of the South. The electoral college distorted the results heavily toward Bush, the reverse of what happened in the nation as a whole. Second, a candidate who loses both Florida and Texas is at a severe disadvantage in the region. Third, Bush received his highest popular vote proportions in the region; yet Clinton did as well as in some other parts of the country, gaining over 40 percent in all southern states except Florida and Texas. This gain was possible in part because of Perot's weakness in the South outside of Florida and Texas. Consequently, the South has reasserted its post-1968 position as the most Republican of regions in presidential politics. This is a sharp reversal from the period up to 1960 and also contrasts with Jimmy Carter's crucial southern base in 1976. Fourth, it is possible for a Democrat to win a big electoral victory without the South. To support this point we should emphasize that if the Clinton-Gore ticket had lost the entire South—including Arkansas, Tennessee, Georgia, and Louisiana—it would have still had an electoral college lead of 331 to 207. Yet Clinton-Gore's popular vote edge would have been a respectable though hardly overwhelming 5 percent. This fact shatters at least temporarily the thesis holding that the GOP has an electoral lock. Furthermore, it suggests that 1992 was not the most fortuitous year for the publication of Black and Black's *The Vital South*. Still the cautious observer should be hesitant to dismiss their thesis out of hand. (See below.)

Looking at the United States as a whole, the 1992 election proves conclusively that the nonsouthern megastates remain a powerful force in the 1990s. As in 1952 and 1960, a substantial victory in the megastates provides the most direct route to the White House.

The megastates are at the center of the political stage for several reasons. First, they have a consistent history of two-party competition and well-organized political parties on the state and local levels. Second, even in this day of instant electronic communications, their size combines with their physical and psychological closeness to major news and money centers to give them more attention in presidential politics. Third, their citizens still vote at a higher rate than in the southern states, though our figures suggest the gap is narrowing. Fourth, the megastates have tremendous cultural diversity, reflecting their many ethnic groups and varied political traditions. In contrast the South as a whole remains heavily Protestant, and its ethnic stock is predominantly northwest European or African. (Certain portions of Florida and Texas of course are exceptions to the rule.) Most other areas of the country, whether northern or western, lack the rich population mix of the megastates. As in the nation generally, the dynamics of the megastates make it difficult for one group to dominate. Fifth, the megastates despite erosion outside California are the largest electoral vote bloc in the United States and are likely to remain so. A caveat is that several megastates, notably California and New York, were suffering crises of confidence and considerable population flight in the early 1990s. Yet they continued to be magnets for new immigrants. Should the new immigrants and other noncitizens not yet able to vote become mobilized in the next decade or two, the popular vote totals for New York and California would swell. Furthermore, the megastates in general and California and New York in particular remain among the most powerful economic engines in the world. The rumors of their doom are premature.

This analysis leaves us with qualms about the analyses of both Black and Black and Holman.[16] To Black and Black one might respond, "Yes, the South is more central to American politics than at any point since 1865, but it has rarely determined the winner of an American presidential election." With the arguable exception of Jimmy Carter and the still more questionable exception of John Kennedy, no president since 1920 has really owed his election to the South. True, Truman, Kennedy, Nixon in 1968, and Carter were in a sense put over by the South. Yet in all cases except the latter, other areas were more "vital."[17] Indeed, the 1992 election might have put an overly confident South back in its place even while electing two southerners.

Be that as it may, dismissal of the well-crafted and provocative Black and Black study would be foolhardy.[18] They were on to something not the least of which was the meteoric rise of Florida and Texas. These are states whose population and political clout increase even when they are suffering serious recessions. And there are no signs of change in the near future. Both are already among the four top states in population. As recently as the 1960 election, Florida had only ten electoral votes as compared with today's twenty-five. At that rate it could be tomorrow's worthy rival to California. Up to this point the political cultures of Florida and Texas have the imprint of their southern heritage. Will they in the future be more akin to California?

Perhaps Holman's advice should have been "Go to California, young Democrat."[19] Until California fell into the Democrats' arms almost by default in 1992, modern presidential Democrats were simply unwilling to make the needed effort in the nation's largest states. Politically, one might infer from this chapter that we consider California more akin to Illinois than to Arizona or Montana. So it is today. But at this very time, Californians are pouring into other western states from New Mexico to Washington. This exodus has the potential of shifting the politics of the Rocky Mountain region as it already has the Pacific Northwest. The relative population, and consequently the electoral vote of the West, is likely to rise over the next twenty years. California itself will remain an empire within a nation. Never has one state been so strong in the electoral college.[20] Whether its explosive population mix will be receptive to Holman's liberal prescription remains a big question.

As for the politics of electing presidents through 2000, the six nonsouthern megastates anchored by California and New York remain the "big leagues."

8

Increasing Liberalism Among Southern Members of Congress, 1970–1990, with an Analysis of the 1994 Congressional Elections

Layne Hoppe

From 1970 until 1990 and beyond, during a period in which a mainly conservative Republican Party has flourished in presidential elections and a competitive two-party system has emerged in the American South, Congress as a body has become more liberal. The largest contribution to this increasing liberalism has been made by southern Democrats, who have moved closer to the mainstream of their party. Using interest group ratings, this chapter portrays these regional patterns and contrasts the mean scores of the members of each party. A possible, partial explanation of increased liberalism of southern members during this period may be related to the fact that the Democratic Party in Congress held all the committee and subcommittee chairperson positions during most of this period. Some data relating to this speculation are presented.

Some data are also presented that bear on the changes in Congress that have followed in the wake of the 1994 congressional elections. It appears possible that the seeds of change that bore fruit in these elections were sown in the years preceding, as a reaction to the increasing liberalism of Congress, including that of its southern Democratic members.

Survey of the Literature

Ideology

Early studies of Congress did not focus on ideology, probably because ideological divisions in the United States were not important.[1] Party and regional differences were among the first to be studied,[2] and these are still important.[3] More recent studies have examined ideological patterns,[4] and *Congressional Quarterly's* Conservative Coalition (CC) scores have been used often.[5] The primary focus has been on the ideological orientation of each member. Individual beliefs tend to be stable—they are "sticky" variables[6]—and members are likely to change parties rather than their beliefs.[7] This chapter focuses on the collective ideological orientation of Congress, and of its southern members in particular.

Group Ratings

The rating scores assigned by interest groups are being used more frequently, especially those of the liberal Americans for Democratic Action (ADA). Liberal scores are also a measure of lack of conservatism. Either way, interest group scores have the virtue of focusing clearly on important votes identified by very close observers.[8] The validity of ADA scores has been tested and found to be high.[9] Another study found ADA scores to be more valid than CC scores.[10] A caveat is that the concept of liberalism unfortunately remains somewhat vague.[11]

Regional Differences

The South was long the most politically distinctive region,[12] and current studies have shown its ideological character emerging from the shadows of its race-based, one-party past.[13] Initially one-party cohesion declined,[14] but as a two-party system emerged, the importance of party increased again.[15] Conservatives moved into the Republican Party, leaving the Democratic Party, once the home of conservative southern whites, to liberals.[16] As a result of these changes, southern political patterns are increasingly resembling national political patterns.[17]

Influences

In seeking to explain Congress's ideological orientation, we must consider a number of possible influences. Constituency characteristics (including regional differences) and party influence are two of the most important.[18] Constituency characteristics have been examined for evidence of influences on the ideological orientation of southern members of Congress. In House districts, race and urbanization have been identified as influences, with urban, black districts being more liberal.[19] More recently, Grofman, Griffin, and Glazer found that, for southern House districts, the higher the percentage of blacks in a district, the more likely the district was to elect a liberal Democrat, and the lower the percentage, the less likely any Democrat was to be elected.[20] Fleisher also found that the racial composition of the district had some explanatory value but deemed racial composition to be less crucial than the willingness of white voters of a district to support liberal Democrats.[21]

The institutional dynamics of Congress create a variety of influences. Some of these appear to bring about changes independent of constituency influences. One recent study, "Something's Happening Here: What It Is Ain't Exactly Clear," identifies the revival of party organization in Congress as the source of some of the influence, causing more southern Democrats to pursue "good public policy."[22] Studies of cohort behavior have identified differing moods and priorities as also contributing to some ideological difference.[23] The ability of committee chairs to generate political action committee (PAC) campaign contributions has been found to be especially important in the House.[24] This finding may lend support to the idea, outlined later in this chapter, that the organization of Congress helps contribute to its ideological orientation.

The findings on the influences of PACs appear to be crystallizing. PACs have settled on helping likely winners.[25] It is usually the case now that incumbents with high group ratings are favored over challengers.[26] Business PACs are especially likely to be "accommodationists" rather than Democratic or Republican "partisans" or ideological "adversaries."[27] Ideological PACs behave in a similar way.[28] These patterns of PAC behavior have allowed the Democrats, who have generally controlled Congress, to be the chief PAC beneficiaries.[29]

Data

The main part of this study examines three sets of data. These include group rating scores for members of Congress in 1970, 1980, and 1990—a period of time for which these scores were accessible to the author. The ratings collected included those by the following groups: the ADA and the liberal AFL-CIO's Committee on Political Education (COPE), the conservative Americans for Constitutional Action/American Conservative Union (ACA/ACU), the National Association of Businessmen (NAB) combined with the U.S. Chamber of Commerce (COC), and the environmentalist League of Conservation Voters (LCV). A smaller database was also assembled for Senate ADA scores in 1986, when Republicans had had control for six years.

Each member was also coded by region (South or non-South), party, body (House or Senate), and leadership status (whether or not a member was a committee or subcommittee chairperson). The South was defined as the eleven states of the Confederacy.[30] For 1990, PAC contributions as a percentage of total campaign contributions were also coded.

In order to take into account the dramatic results of the 1994 congressional elections, two additional sets of data were created, one consisting of

ADA scores for the 103rd (1993–1994) Congress and another for ADA scores based on issues voted on during the first one hundred days of the 104th Congress.

Findings

Ideology and Region

Table 8.1 contains the mean group rating scores for the Congress as a whole, for southern members, and for members from outside the South, for 1970, 1980, and 1990.[31] While only one time point in each decade is used, and some of the differences are not large, table 8.1 shows that the group rating scores for the entire Congress became somewhat more liberal overall: liberal ADA and COPE scores went up, and conservative ACA/ACU scores declined. LCV scores, a measure of support for environmental policies, increased. Only the business groups' rating scores became slightly more conservative. Despite obvious difficulties that might stem from comparing scores based on different votes, a factor analysis (see table 8.2) revealed high intercorrelations among the scores generally; therefore, for purposes of clarity, further analysis will be limited to ADA scores.

Figure 8.1 shows clearly and simply that Congress became more liberal between 1970 and 1990. The mean scores of members of Congress from the South increased even more. Here, as for the South in many other respects as well, there is evidence of national convergence. It should also be noted, however, that the increase in liberalism for southern members of Congress was modest; conservative scores, though declining during this period, were still considerably higher in the South than in the rest of the nation (table 8.1).

A Leftward Shift

The data analyzed here show what was, between 1970 and 1990, a shift away from conservatism by the members generally, rather than the increased mean values' simply being a result of a few more extreme individual scores. An analysis of southern members' ADA scores by quartiles (of the members) reveals evidence of a notable shift—of the ideological center of gravity, one might say—to the left over the time period being studied. Figure 8.2 portrays that shift, by displaying the average ADA scores of the twenty-fifth, fiftieth, and seventy-fifth percentiles of members of Congress ranked by their ADA scores. The percentile values and years they represent are reversed, so that the shift does indeed move to the left, although the figure could have been presented in the normal order just as well.

**Table 8.1. Mean Group Scores for the United States
and by Region, 1970–1990**

Organization	United States			South			Non-South		
	1970	1980	1990	1970	1980	1990	1970	1980	1990
ADA	41	44	51	16	25	36	49	50	56
COPE	54	49	58	31	34	47	63	53	62
ACA/ACU	47	48	41	65	57	52	41	45	37
NAB/COC	47	51	49	60	68	57	43	46	46
LCV	49	48	56	28	30	47	56	54	60

Notes: ADA = Americans for Democratic Action (liberal); COPE = Committee on Political Education (labor, liberal); ACA = Americans for Constitutional Action (1970); ACU = American Conservative Union (1980, 1990); NAB = National Association of Businessmen (1970, 1980); COC = U.S. Chambers of Commerce, 1990 (conservative); LCV = League of Conservative Voters (environmental, liberal).
Source: Data compiled by the author from Michael Barone, Grant Ujifusa, and Douglas Matthews, *The Almanac of American Politics, 1972* (Boston: Gambit, 1972); Michael Barone and Grant Ujifusa, *The Almanac of American Politics, 1982* (Washington, D.C.: Barone, 1981); Michael Barone and Grant Ujifusa, *The Almanac of American Politics, 1992* (Washington, D.C.: National Journal, 1991).

**Table 8.2. Factor Loadings for Group Scores for the United States
and by Region, 1970–1990**

Organization	1970			1980			1990		
	U.S.	South	N-S	U.S.	South	N-S	U.S.	South	N-S
ADA	.93	.88	.93	.96	.92	.96	.97	.96	.97
COPE	.97	.91	.97	.94	.94	.93	.95	.93	.96
ACA/ACU	-.95	-.91	-.95	-.93	-.88	-.95	-.97	-.97	-.97
NAB/COC	-.93	-.91	-.95	-.95	-.91	-.95	-.95	-.93	-.95
LCV	.82	.76	.79	.79	.54	.78	.79	.71	.80

Notes: ADA = Americans for Democratic Action (liberal); COPE = Committee on Political Education (labor, liberal); ACA = Americans for Constitutional Action (1970); ACU = American Conservative Union (1980, 1990); NAB = National Association of Businessmen (1970, 1980); COC = U.S. Chambers of Commerce, 1990 (conservative); LCV = League of Conservative Voters (environmental, liberal).
Source: Calculations, using the Statistical Package for the Social Sciences (SPSS), based on data compiled by the author from Michael Barone, Grant Ujifusa, and Douglas Matthews, *The Almanac of American Politics, 1972* (Boston: Gambit, 1972); Michael Barone and Grant Ujifusa, *The Almanac of American Politics, 1982* (Washington, D.C.: Barone, 1981); Michael Barone and Grant Ujifusa, *The Almanac of American Politics, 1992* (Washington, D.C.: National Journal, 1991).

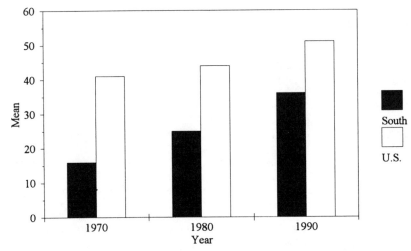

Figure 8.1. Mean ADA Scores for the United States and the South, 1970–1990.
Source: Data compiled by the author from Michael Barone, Grant Ujifusa, and
Douglas Matthews, *The Almanac of American Politics, 1972* (Boston: Gambit, 1972);
Michael Barone and Grant Ujifusa, *The Almanac of American Politics, 1982* (Washing-
ton, D.C.: Barone, 1981); Michael Barone and Grant Ujifusa, *The Almanac of American
Politics, 1992* (Washington, D.C.: National Journal, 1991).

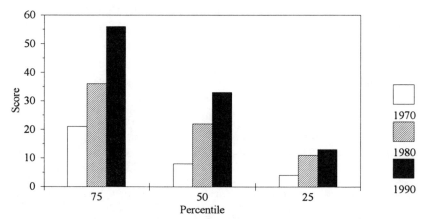

Figure 8.2. Liberal Shift: Mean ADA Scores by Percentile for the South, 1970–1990.
Source: Data compiled by author from Michael Barone, Grant Ujifusa, and Douglas
Matthews, *The Almanac of American Politics, 1972* (Boston: Gambit, 1972); Michael
Barone and Grant Ujifusa, *The Almanac of American Politics, 1982* (Washington, D.C.:
Barone, 1981); Michael Barone and Grant Ujifusa, *The Almanac of American Politics,
1992* (Washington, D.C.: National Journal, 1991).

Ideology and Party

Perhaps the most important aspect of the increased liberalism that has been identified is its relationship to party. Were the mean ADA scores of both southern Democrats and southern Republicans increasing? Not really. As can be seen in figure 8.3, the increase in liberalism was almost all attributable to the increase in the mean scores of southern Democrats. During the period of time covered by this study, the ideological gap between the southern parties has widened. Of course, it would be possible for the Republican Party to become more homogeneously conservative and the Democratic Party more homogeneously liberal without any overall increase in liberalism, but that was not the case, according to the data presented here.

Ideology and the Two Houses of Congress

So far, the data presented have been House and Senate scores taken together. One reason is that the differences in mean scores between House and Senate are small (see table 8.3). However, when the ADA scores of southern members are broken down by body, controlling for party, the patterns that we have been examining are again present. Figure 8.4 demonstrates that the increasing liberalism of the southern members of Congress from 1970 to 1990 was not confined to one house. Also, note that the ideological differences between Democrats and Republicans widened in each house. This phenomenon obviously merits closer study.

Ideology and Committee Leadership

What differences do the ideological orientations of members make? From the review of the campaign finance literature, we learn that incumbents and likely winners are favored, especially committee chairpersons in positions to influence directly public policies in their areas. The databases used in this study have very little direct information about campaign finance. (A variable measuring the PAC contributions as a percentage of total receipts showed no correlation with the other variables.[32]) However, it might be possible to gather some inferential evidence by examining the ideological scores of members according to their committee leadership status, taking into account their party and controlling for both body and region.

Let us examine the House first (table 8.4), for the years 1972, 1982, and 1992. These years are for the new Congress that follows the years for which scores have been collected. This procedure allows us to use the 1970, 1980, and 1990 scores, reported in the 1972, 1982, and 1992 *Almanac of American Politics,* respectively, rather than having to create three additional data-

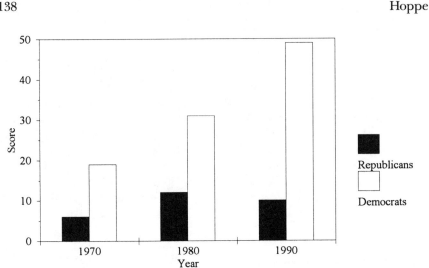

Figure 8.3.   Mean ADA Scores for the South by Party, 1970–1990. *Source:* Data com-
piled by author from Michael Barone, Grant Ujifusa, and Douglas Matthews, *The
Almanac of American Politics, 1972* (Boston: Gambit, 1972); Michael Barone and Grant
Ujifusa, *The Almanac of American Politics, 1982* (Washington, D.C.: Barone, 1981);
Michael Barone and Grant Ujifusa, *The Almanac of American Politics, 1992*
(Washington, D.C.: National Journal, 1991).

Table 8.3. Mean ADA Scores for the United States, by Chamber, 1970–1990

Chamber	United States			South			Non-South		
	1970	1980	1990	1970	1980	1990	1970	1980	1990
House ADA	40	44	51	16	24	35	49	51	57
Senate ADA	43	44	50	16	33	40	50	46	53

Note: ADA = Americans for Democratic Action.
Source: Data compiled by the author from Michael Barone, Grant Ujifusa, and Douglas
Matthews, *The Almanac of American Politics, 1972* (Boston: Gambit, 1972); Michael Barone
and Grant Ujifusa, *The Almanac of American Politics, 1982* (Washington, D.C.: Barone, 1981);
Michael Barone and Grant Ujifusa, *The Almanac of American Politics, 1992* (Washington, D.C.:
National Journal, 1991).

bases. Table 8.4 shows that in the House, liberalism scores for those southern members holding committee chair positions increased threefold, from
sixteen to forty-eight, with only a slightly smaller increase for nonchairs.
Republican scores, although low, almost doubled; Republicans held no chair
positions during this period.

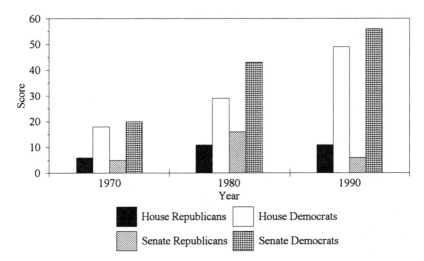

Figure 8.4.   Mean ADA Scores for the South by Party and Body, 1970–1990. *Source:* Data compiled by author from Michael Barone, Grant Ujifusa, and Douglas Matthews, *The Almanac of American Politics, 1972* (Boston: Gambit, 1972); Michael Barone and Grant Ujifusa, *The Almanac of American Politics, 1982* (Washington, D.C.: Barone, 1981); Michael Barone and Grant Ujifusa, *The Almanac of American Politics, 1992* (Washington, D.C.: National Journal, 1991).

Table 8.4. Increasing Liberalism: Mean ADA Scores, U.S. House of Representatives, 1970–1990, for the South, by Party and Leadership Status, 1972–1992

Group	1972	1982	1992
Dem. Chairs	16	29	48
Dem. Nonchairs	22	29	50
Rep. Chairs	—	—	—
Rep. Nonchairs	6	11	11

Note: ADA = Americans for Democratic Action.
Source: Data compiled by the author from Michael Barone, Grant Ujifusa, and Douglas Matthews, *The Almanac of American Politics, 1972* (Boston: Gambit, 1972); Michael Barone and Grant Ujifusa, *The Almanac of American Politics, 1982* (Washington, D.C.: Barone, 1981); Michael Barone and Grant Ujifusa, *The Almanac of American Politics, 1992* (Washington, D.C.: National Journal, 1991).

Now let us turn to the Senate, which has the more interesting patterns, since party leadership did change, the Republicans being in control from 1981 to 1986. In table 8.5, note the low Democratic chair and Republican mean scores for 1972, when the Conservative Coalition held sway, and the dramatic increase in 1992, by which time the Coalition had become unrav-

Table 8.5. Zigzag Liberalism: Mean ADA Scores, U.S. Senate, 1970–1990, for the South, by Party and Leadership Status, 1972–1992

Group	1972	1982	1986	1992
Dem. Chairs	18	—	—	57
Dem. Nonchairs	41	43	52	47
Rep. Chairs	—	23	5	—
Rep. Nonchairs	5	17	10	5

Note: ADA = Americans for Democratic Action.
Source: Data compiled by the author from Michael Barone, Grant Ujifusa, and Douglas Matthews, *The Almanac of American Politics, 1972* (Boston: Gambit, 1972); Michael Barone and Grant Ujifusa, *The Almanac of American Politics, 1982* (Washington, D.C.: Barone, 1981); Michael Barone and Grant Ujifusa, *The Almanac of American Politics, 1992* (Washington, D.C.: National Journal, 1991).

eled. Note also that there was actually an increase in the mean scores of Republican chairs in 1982. However, by 1986 (recall that a separate data set was created for this analytical purpose), the last year of Republican control, the mean ADA scores for chairs had dropped almost as far down as it could go—only to rise dramatically by 1992 by over fifty points. The contrast, or swing, in the leadership mean score—a liberalism-conservatism zigzag—when a change of party control occurs and takes hold, is large (see figure 8.5).[33]

Now, taking into account the literature on PAC campaign contributions, and bearing in mind the data presented in table 8.5, it might be possible to speculate as follows: increased liberalism or conservatism in Congress, the South included, may in part be generated by a ratchet effect stemming from the advantage of party control of leadership positions. That is, the combined effect of generous PAC campaign funding to committee chairs with continuous party control may work to drive ideological rating scores up or down, depending on which party is in control. It happens that the Democrats, the more liberal party, have mainly been in control in recent years, and the scores of their chairs have clearly risen. In the instance when that wasn't the case, the ADA scores of Republican chairs just as clearly declined.

Summary

The data examined in this study point toward several conclusions: (1) Congress, including its southern members, became more liberal between 1970 and 1990; (2) the increase in liberalism (beginning from low levels) among members of Congress from the South has been notable and tended to converge with the overall national pattern during this period; (3) the ideological center of gravity in Congress among southern members shifted

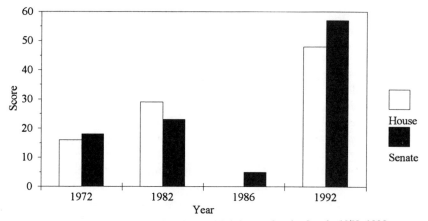

Figure 8.5. House and Senate Chair Mean ADA Scores for the South, 1972–1992.
Note: No House scores were coded for 1986. *Source:* Data compiled by the author from
Michael Barone, Grant Ujifusa, and Douglas Matthews, *The Almanac of American Politics,
1972* (Boston: Gambit, 1972); Michael Barone and Grant Ujifusa, *The Almanac of Ameri-
can Politics, 1982* (Washington, D.C.: Barone, 1981); Michael Barone and Grant Ujifusa,
The Almanac of American Politics, 1986 (Washington, D.C.: 1985); Michael Barone and
Grant Ujifusa, *The Almanac of American Politics, 1992* (Washington, D.C.: National
Journal, 1991).

somewhat to the left during this period in both houses of Congress; (4) the
increase in liberalism was traceable mainly to southern Democrats—and, as
a result, there was an increasing ideological gap between Democrats and
Republicans; and (5) the change in party control in the Senate showed major swings (albeit perhaps partly as a result of small *n*s) in ADA scores for
committee chair positions held by southern members.

The descriptive statistics presented here are minimal; ideally, group rating scores for every Congress, not just those at ten-year intervals, ought to
be examined. Additional data are needed to study the causal speculations
above. In particular, a comparison between PAC contributions and committee leadership positions should be formulated that might make it possible
to help pin down the suggested connection between party control and ideological swing.

Discussion and Analysis of the 1994 Congressional Elections

Perhaps the present debate over campaign finance reform, with the party
in power (mainly the Democrats during this period) discreetly favoring the
continuation of PAC funding, is reflected indirectly in the data presented
here. In an era in which conservatism has more electoral appeal than liberalism, an increasingly liberal Democrat-controlled Congress (until 1995),

with increasing support from its southern delegation, had exploited its opportunities by winning urban and black southern seats, instilling party discipline, protecting the present campaign finance system, and, until 1995, retaining control of Congress.

The results of the 1994 congressional elections appear to support the conclusion of this study that liberalism in Congress, especially that of its southern Democratic members, was (then) increasing but vulnerable. The Democrats needed to keep their majorities, and they failed. Given the increasingly close correspondence between ideology and party, party control of Congress has become one key to ideological effectiveness and policy direction. And the South continued to play a major part in these developments. In the Congress overall, seventy Democrats and twenty-three Republicans were replaced by eighty Republicans and thirteen Democrats; in the South twenty-one Democrats and four Republicans were replaced by twenty-two Republicans and three Democrats.[34]

Some additional data exist—ADA scores for the 103rd Congress and ADA scores for the first 100 days of the 104th Congress—permitting an extension of the preceding analysis.[35] This extension has been made in figure 8.6, which builds on figure 8.1. In figure 8.6, it is plain that after two decades of increasing liberalism Congress is again becoming more conservative. What is perhaps more surprising is the extent to which the liberalism of southern members has remained relatively high, buffering what would otherwise be an even steeper decline in the country as a whole, a reversal of recent historical fortunes.

The present ideological orientation of the southern members of Congress is vividly highlighted in figure 8.7 (an extension of figure 8.3), which shows a Democratic southern membership becoming increasingly liberal, even into the 104th Congress. Unfortunately for the Democratic Party, the size of its southern membership has diminished as its liberalism has increased, and many reasons in addition to the forces discussed in this chapter have been put forward to explain this development, including the creation of so-called majority-minority districts.[36] A second aspect of the ideological orientation of Congress—its increasing polarization, especially among Southern members—is also apparent in figure 8.7. The polarized pattern lends further support to the thesis that the two major parties in the South have more or less realigned along ideological lines. And the gap is very large.[37] This can be seen in figure 8.8, which may also serve as a visual summary of the patterns that have been examined in this chapter, along with a comparison—for perspective—of changes among nonsouthern members.

Taking into account the evolving patterns portrayed here, it may be that an American variant of party government, long desired by many and long feared by many others, is at hand. If, as has been argued by Rohde[38] and others, the liberal Democrats used their party organization and majority

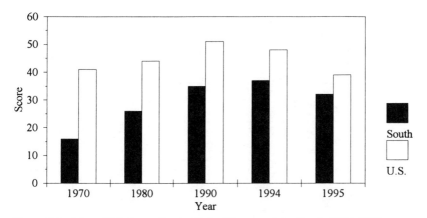

Figure 8.6.   Mean ADA Scores for the United States and the South, 1970–1995.
Source: Data compiled by the author from Michael Barone, Grant Ujifusa, and
Douglas Matthews, *The Almanac of American Politics, 1972* (Boston: Gambit, 1972);
Michael Barone and Grant Ujifusa, *The Almanac of American Politics, 1982* (Washing-
ton, D.C.: Barone, 1981); Michael Barone and Grant Ujifusa, *The Almanac of American
Politics, 1992* (Washington, D.C.: National Journal, 1991); ADA press release, "ADA
Voting Record Reveals Congress Divided, Stymied by Partisanship: 104th Congress to
be Most Extreme in Recent Memory," December 11, 1994; House and Senate election
returns reported in the *Washington Post*, "Election 1994," November 10, 1994, pp. A31
and A37; unpublished ADA scores for the first one hundred days of the 104th Congress, released to the author by the ADA, July 15, 1995.

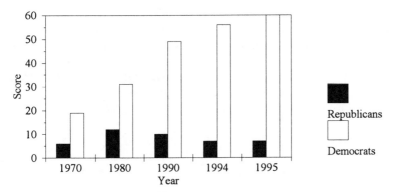

Figure 8.7.   Mean ADA Scores for the South by Party, 1970–1995. *Source:* Data compiled by
the author from Michael Barone, Grant Ujifusa, and Douglas Matthews, *The Almanac of American Politics, 1972* (Boston: Gambit, 1972); Michael Barone and Grant Ujifusa, *The Almanac of
American Politics, 1982* (Washington, D.C.: Barone, 1981); Michael Barone and Grant Ujifusa,
The Almanac of American Politics, 1992 (Washington, D.C.: National Journal, 1991); ADA
press release, "ADA Voting Record Reveals Congress Divided, Stymied by Partisanship:
104th Congress to be Most Extreme in Recent Memory," December 11, 1994; House and Senate election returns reported in the *Washington Post*, "Election 1994," November 10, 1994,
pp. A31 and A37; unpublished ADA scores for the first one hundred days of the 104th Congress, released to the author by the ADA, July 15, 1995.

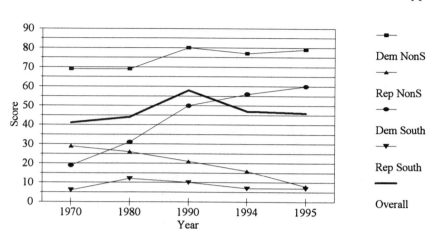

Figure 8.8. Mean ADA Scores Overall and by Party and Region, 1970–1995. *Source:* Data
compiled by the author from Michael Barone, Grant Ujifusa, and Douglas Matthews,
The Almanac of American Politics, 1972 (Boston: Gambit, 1972); Michael Barone and Grant
Ujifusa, *The Almanac of American Politics, 1982* (Washington, D.C.: Barone, 1981); Michael
Barone and Grant Ujifusa, *The Almanac of American Politics, 1992* (Washington, D.C.:
National Journal, 1991); ADA press release, "ADA Voting Record Reveals Congress
Divided, Stymied by Partisanship: 104th Congress to be Most Extreme in Recent Mem-
ory," December 11, 1994; House and Senate election returns reported in the *Washington
Post,* "Election 1994," November 10, 1994, pp. A31 and A37; unpublished ADA scores for
the first one hundred days of the 104th Congress released to the author by the ADA, July
15, 1995.

status to mount their policy offensives, it appears that conservative Republicans took careful note, honed their own partisan skills, and laid the
groundwork for a successful electoral campaign that has provided them
with the policymaking opportunities they sought. In that case, increasing
liberalism among southern members of Congress may have been a spur to
the conservative counteroffensive.

9

Representation and Party in the Virginia General Assembly Since the Civil Rights and Reapportionment Revolutions

Clifton McCleskey

A good argument can be made that the single most important development in American politics in the second half of the twentieth century has been the collapse of the Democratic one-party systems in southern states and the emergence of the Republican Party there as an equal (and sometimes more than equal) competitor in elections for national and, often, statewide office. In presidential elections, the South has become the strongest and most dependable source of Republican votes, with a role fairly summed up by the title of Merle and Earl Black's second masterful volume on the politics of the region: *The Vital South: How Presidents Are Elected*.

When John Tower won a special Texas election in 1961 to replace Lyndon Johnson in the U.S. Senate, he became the first Republican senator from the former Confederacy in the twentieth century. In that same year, a grand total of seven southern Republicans served in the U.S. House: two each from Virginia and Tennessee, and one each from Florida, North Carolina, and Texas. When Congress convened in January 1995, 13 of the South's 22 senators and 64 of its 125 representatives in the House had been elected as Republicans.

In contests for governorships, Republican candidates have not been as successful as in national elections, but the gains have been substantial. Over the past quarter century, every southern state except Georgia has elected at least one Republican governor, and in a majority the governor's office has been held by Republicans for at least two terms. Other statewide offices have been much harder to win, however, as have been elective offices in the state judiciaries and in local and district governments.

State legislatures in the South have also proved to be a tough nut for Republicans to crack. In 1964 Republican representation in southern state legislatures was barely perceptible, consisting of about 6 percent of all lower house seats and about 5 percent of all upper house seats. Thirty years later, after the 1994 elections, the respective percentages for Republicans were 38 percent and 37 percent.[1]

But buried in these aggregate figures for the entire South are highly significant variations among the eleven states. Republican progress in the Arkansas legislature has been quite modest and not markedly better in Alabama and Louisiana. In other state legislatures, Republicans have gained considerable ground, winning majorities in 1994 in the Florida Senate and in the North Carolina and South Carolina Houses.

Virginia is prominent among those states experiencing a growth in Republican representation. The last state senate elections in 1991 gave the GOP eighteen of the forty seats (45 percent); after the House of Delegates elections in 1993, the Republicans held forty-seven seats and the Democrats fifty-two, with one long-time Independent.

My objective in this chapter is to describe the coming of party competition to the Virginia General Assembly and to shed such light as I can on the dynamics of the changes that have taken place in assembly elections over the past thirty years—changes slow in coming but nevertheless quite remarkable, at least for those of us old enough to remember the southern one-party system in its heyday.

The Republican Party in Virginia

The Republican Party's rise in Virginia politics is all the more extraordinary when one considers the political context in which it was achieved.[2] Party warfare in the Old Dominion was periodically sharp and intense in the century that followed the emergence of party politics in the 1790s. However, in the last decade or so of the nineteenth century, Democratic control of electoral policy and machinery, coupled with machine-style organization and tactics and the use of racial issues, gradually eroded Republican capacity to compete effectively, even in fusion with Populists and dissident Democrats. From a high of 49.3 percent of the two-party vote in the 1888 presidential election, Republican strength ebbed to 43.9 percent in 1890 and—after highly restrictive suffrage changes launched by the constitution of 1902—to 38.7 percent in 1908.

The continued decline of the GOP in twentieth-century Virginia shifted political conflict from general elections to Democratic Party primaries. And particularly after Harry Byrd, Sr., assumed leadership of the Democratic machine in 1922, the winners in those intraparty battles were mostly conservative in their policy orientations. By the time World War II came, Republican gubernatorial candidates could poll only 18 percent of the vote, and Republican representation in the General Assembly dropped to token levels, almost always from across the Blue Ridge Mountains. The Byrd Machine's conservatism, however, brought it more and more into conflict with the national Democratic Party and with moderate and liberal Democrats convinced that the low level of public services—roads, education, welfare, and so on—was endangering Virginia's economic development. The result in 1949 was the most serious challenge to the organization in thirty years, with Francis Pickens Miller's strong but ultimately unsuccessful bid for the Democratic nomination for governor. Four years later, Republican Theodore Roosevelt Dalton polled 44.3 percent of the vote for governor against organization candidate Thomas Stanley.

But prospects for change were pushed back for a decade by the Democratic organization's response to the desegregation battles triggered by *Brown v. Board of Education* in 1954. Its unyielding opposition to racial desegregation brought renewed white support of a sort that effectively postponed reform of Virginia policies and politics until the mid-1960s. The changes that finally came to Virginia in the 1960s are intimately bound up with the civil rights revolution. The movement for racial equality and for the better treatment of blacks in public policy and administration stirred the African-American population of Virginia to political activity on a level not seen since the late nineteenth century; it also brought support for such changes from many whites and hostility and opposition from a great many others. The door to better realization of civil rights objectives was opened further by the statutory, administrative, and judicial actions that ended decades of suffrage restrictions in Virginia.

The most immediate result was an upheaval in the Democratic Party with far-reaching consequences. The minority of moderate and liberal Democrats who had struggled futilely against the Byrd Organization in Democratic primaries was suddenly bolstered by an influx of African-American Democrats. The result in 1966 was the defeat of Byrd Democrats in key contests for the U.S. House and Senate. As time went on, the conservative Democrats found it harder and harder to win in party primaries, as their ranks were thinned by defections to a Virginia Republican Party more and more receptive to them and as liberals and moderates gained support from newcomers to the Commonwealth in Northern Virginia and elsewhere.

The ensuing collapse of Virginia's one-party Democratic system in the 1960s and 1970s with respect to national and statewide elections needs only to be summarized here. In national elections, the most revealing generalization is that no Democratic presidential candidate has carried Virginia since Lyndon Johnson in 1964, and even Johnson was preceded by Republican victories in 1952, 1956, and 1960. Since Republicans elected their first U.S. senator of the twentieth century in 1972, they have continually held at least one Senate seat and, from 1982 to 1988, have held both. GOP strength in the U.S. House elections began building in the late 1960s, reaching its apogee in 1980, when nine of the ten seats then allotted to Virginia were won by Republicans. After that, the party division became more even (Democrats held a 6–5 majority after the 1994 House elections), settling into a fairly stable pattern in which each party keeps four seats fairly safe, with the remainder—now three after the 1991 redistricting—competitive enough to be subject to periodic shifts.

Nor have Republicans lacked for success in contests for the three offices filled by statewide elections. Three different Republican candidates won consecutive gubernatorial victories in 1969, 1973, and 1977 (Virginia governors are constitutionally barred from serving a second consecutive term). Republicans also won the office of lieutenant governor in 1973 and of attorney general in 1977.

While the growth of Republican sentiment among Virginia voters in the 1960s and 1970s was quite real, the Republican statewide victories then owed a great deal to skillful exploitation of Democratic Party factionalism. Thus, Republican Linwood Holton's election as governor in 1969 was greatly aided by the bitter divisions in a Democratic gubernatorial primary in which a moderate with ties to the Kennedy administration narrowly defeated a liberal and a staunch conservative. When Democrats backed a liberal, as they did for governor in 1973 (even though Henry Howell was officially listed as an Independent), Republicans offered disgruntled Democrats a conservative alternative in the person of Mills Godwin, the former Democratic governor who had accepted the GOP nomination. In 1977, when a Democrat once closely tied to the Byrd Organization (Ed Lane) won the Democratic nomination for attorney general, Republicans presented a moderate "Valley" Republican (Marshall Coleman) whose support from liberal and moderate Democrats enabled him to poll a comfortable 53.5 percent of the vote.

However, in the 1980s, this route to Republican electoral success began to be closed off. Democratic factionalism in Virginia declined considerably, as some of the older issues—especially those related to civil rights—began to fade and as activists in both factions saw more clearly the consequences of their feuding. At the same time, the increasing conservatism of the Republican Party left it less capable of flexibility in responding to conflicts in the Democratic Party. First in the 1981 elections, and then again in those of 1985 and 1989, the less divided Democrats won all three statewide offices, although their black gubernatorial candidate in 1989 (L. Douglas Wilder) won by an exceedingly close margin (50.1 percent). Still, what is worth remembering is that the Republicans were able to remain quite competitive in the losing elections of the 1980s. That strong electoral base enabled them to win the office of governor and attorney general in 1993 without having to depend on the Democratic penchant for self-destruction (or at least the form of it that involved ideological factionalism).

With this review of Republican progress in elections for national and statewide offices providing a bit of context, I turn now to changes in the partisan composition of the Virginia General Assembly.

The Virginia House of Delegates

The one hundred members of the House of Delegates are elected for two-year terms in November of odd-numbered years. Regular sessions are now held annually, beginning in January and lasting for sixty days in the first year and for thirty days in the second, with an additional thirty days possible in each case by a two-thirds vote. Candidates of the major parties may be nominated either by caucus/conventions or in direct primaries for which a plurality suffices (that is, no runoff primary is used). Campaigns vary greatly in cost, with an occasional candidate spending next to nothing and others tens of thousands of dollars.[3] There are no limits on individual contributions and no prohibition on funds from corporations, banks, or labor unions.

Like most state legislatures, the Virginia General Assembly has been considerably affected by the reapportionment revolution triggered by *Baker v. Carr* in 1962. In the 1960s, Virginia was still governed under the constitution of 1902, which, in spite of—or, more likely, because of—a century of political agitation over representation in the General Assembly, established no basis at all for the redistricting required after every decennial census. However, a long tradition stretching back to the early years of the colonial House of Burgesses (first convened in 1619) tied representation in the lower chamber of the assembly to counties and, later, cities. Though by the early 1960s each local jurisdiction could no longer be assured of having its own delegate, the principle was honored by keeping city and county boundaries intact when they had to be combined to create a district. To accommodate more populous jurisdictions, multi-member districts were created, but rural resistance and the practical problems created by the unwillingness to breach city and county boundaries resulted in considerable inequality of representation for Virginia's urban areas. Though not as outrageous as in some states,[4] these inequalities were poorly addressed by the redistricting act of 1962, and almost immediately four members of the General Assembly, later joined by citizen activists from Norfolk, sued in federal district court on the basis of *Baker v. Carr,* decided shortly before. The three-judge federal court found the 1962 act to be unconstitutional for both the House of Delegates and the Virginia Senate but allowed the 1963 elections to proceed under it pending review by the U.S. Supreme Court.[5]

The decision by the Supreme Court in *Mann v. Davis* (1964) upholding the lower court forced the General Assembly to prepare new districting plans for the 1965 elections. The new act, passed in a special session late in

1964, and accepted by the federal court with only very minor changes, continued the mix of single-member and multimember districts but sharply reduced (without eliminating) the population disparity among districts.

For all practical purposes, African-Americans and Republicans were on the sidelines in the 1960s redistricting battles fought in the General Assembly and in the federal courthouse. Redistricting after the 1970 census was still very much in the hands of white Democrats, but the moderating influence of the civil rights revolution made them more sensitive to the political dangers in racial discrimination, while the presence of a Republican in the governor's office and a 24 percent Republican bloc in the House of Delegates made them alert to the partisan consequences of their redistricting efforts. Their favorite tool in 1971 continued to be the multimember House of Delegates district, useful not only to avoid breaching city and county lines but also to submerge minorities—Republicans especially.

Once again, those dissatisfied with the outcome in the General Assembly took their grievances to a federal court, which accepted the assembly's heavy reliance on multimember districts but rearranged their boundaries as necessary to obtain population equality, even when it meant breaking city and county lines. That judicial "improvement" on the 1971 act governed the 1973 elections, but a U.S. Supreme Court decision the following year reversed the lower court with respect to the House of Delegates and allowed the 1971 act to be used in the 1975 elections and subsequently.

By the time the General Assembly returned to redistricting in 1981, the influence of African-Americans in the Democratic Party had greatly increased, although they still had only four members in the House of Delegates.[6] Republicans, with twenty-five seats, had only one more than they had had in 1971, but their continuing control of the governor's office and success in federal elections gave them an unmistakable respect. Perhaps for those reasons, the house plan continuing a heavy reliance on multimember districts won broad support from its members, which continued even after the Justice Department forced changes in ten Southside districts designed to improve black representation. However, groups external to the General Assembly, including the American Civil Liberties Union (ACLU), the National Association for the Advancement of Colored People (NAACP), and several counties and one town, betook themselves to the federal courthouse, winning in late August 1981 a decree allowing the 1981 elections to go forward as scheduled in November but limiting the term of office to one year and ordering the assembly to ready a new plan. That plan, or a judicially decreed substitute, would then form the basis for another set of elections in November 1982 for one-year terms, so that the regular two-year cycle could be resumed with 1983 elections.

The court's rejection of the 1981 plan was primarily based on the disparities in population (in the extreme case, a deviation of 26.6 percent between the least and most populous districts). When the General Assembly returned to the redistricting task in late November 1981, it attempted to remedy the population inequalities by reducing still more the number of single-member districts and increasing the use of multimember districts. By this time, however, the Republicans were becoming converts to the idea of single-member districts, and Governor Dalton vetoed this November version. When the effort to override his veto failed (Republicans were almost unanimous against overriding, Democrats divided), a new plan was devised in the house that provided for single-member districts for all except eight urban areas that had been allocated twenty-three seats. Six weeks of negotiation between the house and the governor resulted in a compromise plan relying almost entirely on single-member districts that was adopted just before their terms of office expired in January. This plan, however, was rejected by the Justice Department for shortcomings related to black representation. Finally, in March 1982, with a new governor (Democrat Charles Robb) and a bloc of Republicans in the house that had been expanded to thirty-three, a new plan was devised utilizing only single-member districts that satisfied the Justice Department and various litigants by creating nine majority black districts.

When redistricting was again taken up in 1991, the legal and constitutional framework had been altered by the 1982 amendments to the 1965 Voting Rights Act regarding minority representation and by the Supreme Court decision in *Davis v. Bandemer* (1986) regarding partisan gerrymandering. Though Republicans held none of the three statewide elective offices, they had increased their delegation in the house to thirty-nine. The first redistricting act for the house mostly reflected the status quo, adjusted here and there to reflect population change, to improve black representation a bit, and to accommodate incumbents. It drew the wrath of Republicans, the governor, the NAACP and ACLU, and—most important—the Justice Department, necessitating another special session in late July. The plan that emerged satisfied everyone except Republicans, whose suit seeking a judicial remedy was finally dismissed in September 1991, less than two months before the General Assembly elections.

Party Competition

Let us turn now to closer consideration of the growth of party competition in the House of Delegates, the course of which is charted in table 9.1. It was in 1962 still very much a white, male-dominated institution, with a large majority of the delegates integrated into the Byrd Machine, with no black members and only one female. Republicans had always maintained a

Table 9.1. Partisan Composition of the Virginia House of Delegates, 1961–1993

Election year	Democrats	Republicans	Independents
1961	95	5	—
1963	89	11	—
1965	88	12[a]	—
1967	85	14	1
1969	75	24	1
1971	73	24	3
1973	65	20	15
1975	78	17	5
1977	76	21	3
1979	74	25	1
1981	66	33	1
1982	65	34	1
1983	65	34	1
1985	65	33	2
1987	64	35	1
1989	59	39	2
1991	58	41	1
1993	52	47	1

[a]Wilkinson reports (*Harry Byrd,* 279, n. 48) that one of the twelve Republicans elected in 1965 had been on the ballot as an Independent because he had missed the filling deadline.
Source: J. Harvie Wilkinson III, *Harry Byrd and the Changing Face of Virginia Politics, 1945–1966* (Charlottesville: University Press of Virginia, 1968), 221, 279, for the years 1961 through 1965; Commonwealth of Virginia, *The General Assembly of the Commonwealth of Virginia, 1962–1981* (Richmond, 1983); *Manuals of the House of Delegates* (Richmond, various years); reports of the state Board of Elections.

presence in the House of Delegates, but in the 1962 session it was merely a token five members, three from traditionally Republican areas of Southwest Virginia and the Shenandoah Valley, plus one each from Fairfax County in Northern Virginia and from Albemarle County in central Virginia. The stringent requirements flowing from *Baker v. Carr* and subsequent decisions had not yet been felt, but even so, the 1963 House of Delegates election yielded Republicans six additional seats, four from southwestern Virginia and the Shenandoah Valley, plus two from a multimember district encompassing Richmond City and Henrico County.

The next two election years produced a net Republican gain of only three seats, but the 1969 contests brought a major increase from fourteen to twenty-four seats. The ten-seat jump was achieved by holding two open Republican seats and electing eleven freshman Republicans while suffering the defeat of only one incumbent. Significantly, nine of the eleven newcomers were elected from metropolitan areas east of the Blue Ridge (four from districts wholly or partially in Fairfax County, four from Arlington County, and one from Richmond/Henrico County).

Results over the next decade were undoubtedly discouraging to Republicans. At a time when the party was winning most statewide races and was building toward a near sweep of U.S. House seats, Republican representation in the House of Delegates first leveled off and then receded. After maintaining the level of twenty-four seats in 1971 elections, Republicans experienced a slide to 20 seats in 1973 and to seventeen seats in 1975. A four-seat gain in 1977 and another four seats in 1979 finally recovered and barely exceeded the ground first won by the GOP in 1969.

That the gains of the late 1970s were no fluke was amply demonstrated by the outcomes of the 1981 House of Delegates elections, for even as they lost all three statewide races, the Republicans emerged with thirty-three seats—a net gain of eight—and the potential for an enhanced role in the legislative process. The geographical distribution of these new seats is significant, for they came in the expanding Northern Virginia complex and the Richmond area, with beachheads in Southside and in Virginia Beach that could be expanded later. While retaining most of its traditional bases in southwestern Virginia and the Shenandoah Valley, the Virginia Republican Party was more and more becoming the party of Northern Virginia and the suburban part of the urban corridor stretching from Fairfax County southeast to the North Carolina border.

The durability of these Republican gains was demonstrated a year later when the legal and political battles over redistricting necessitated new elections for all one hundred house seats. These 1982 house elections for one-year terms resulted in thirty-four GOP winners—a net gain of one. The GOP found itself on a plateau not significantly changed through the next three elections, with the Republicans holding steady in 1983, dropping one seat in 1985, and adding two in 1987, for a new total of thirty-five. There followed Republican gains of four seats in 1989, two in 1991, and six in 1993, producing a new high of forty-seven of the one hundred seats in the house and the possibility of Republican control. No matter what their ages, Democratic delegates had never before had to consider that prospect seriously.

I will not attempt in this chapter to deal with the impact of the Republican threat to Democratic control on the operation of the house, for it is much too early to tell. Some indication of the potential for change is offered, however, by the press reports that the eight African-American Democrats in the house used their enhanced bargaining position in 1994 to extract better committee assignments from the Democratic leadership.

It is worth considering as well how the level of competition has changed. The easiest and simplest measure is the number of seats contested by both major parties. Table 9.2 reports the results for the period 1971 to 1981, a

Table 9.2. Number of Party Candidates, and Winners, for the House of Delegates by Type of District, 1971–1981

| | Type of District | | | | | | | | |
| | Single Member | | Two Member | | Three Member | | Four or more Member | | Total | |
Election year	No.	Win-ners	No.	Win-ners	No.	Win-ners	No.	Win-ners	No.	Win-ners
1971										
Seats	21	—	34	—	18	—	27	—	100	—
Democratic	21	18	30	22	18	15	27	18	96	73
Republican	7	2	29	11	9	2	26	9	71	24
1973										
Seats	24	—	36	—	18	—	22	—	100	—
Democratic	19	13	27	22	17	14	22	16	85	65
Republican	10	3	27	10	7	1	16	6	60	20
1975										
Seats	24	—	36	—	18	—	22	—	100	—
Democratic	21	18	32	25	18	18	22	17	93	78
Republican	5	3	25	9	8	0	10	5	48	17
1977										
Seats	24	—	36	—	18	—	22	—	100	—
Democratic	22	18	30	23	18	18	22	17	92	76
Republican	9	5	22	11	11	0	12	5	54	21
1979										
Seats	24	—	36	—	18	—	22	—	100	—
Democratic	20	18	30	24	18	18	22	14	90	74
Republican	13	6	18	11	11	0	10	8	52	25
1981										
Seats	18	—	34	—	30	—	18	—	100	—
Democratic	17	12	30	26	25	13	18	15	90	66
Republican	10	6	12	7	27	17	9	3	58	33

Note: The number of winners does not always equal the total number of seats because Independents won three seats in 1971, fifteen in 1973, five in 1975, and one in 1979 and 1981.
Source: Compiled from reports of the state Board of Elections.

time when representation in the House of Delegates was based on a mixture of single-member and multimember districts ranging in size from two to seven members. During the period covered by table 9.2, the Democratic Party normally contested 90 percent or more of the one hundred seats. (The apparent decline in 1973 is misleading, since several independent candidates that year were actually Democrats.) The Democratic Party was especially attentive to the larger multimember districts, where it often won disproportionately, at least until the 1981 redistricting, when Democratic miscalculation in creating several additional three-person districts allowed the Republicans to win almost 60 percent of the seats in those districts.

Republicans made their most ambitious effort of the era in 1971, when they offered seventy-one challengers for House of Delegate seats concentrated in the two-person districts and those with four or more members; in later years they were contesting fewer seats (usually fifty to sixty) more evenly spread among the different-sized districts.

It is instructive, therefore, to consider the patterns of challenge after single-member districts became universal in 1982. Table 9.3 shows a distinct trend toward convergence in the number of candidates offered by the two parties, with a modest decline in the number of Democratic contenders after the onset of single-member districts and a corresponding increase in the number of Republican candidates, resulting in a gradual but irregular increase from 1982 to 1993 in the number of districts with party competition (column 3). What the data in table 9.3 do not make clear is the extent to which activists in both parties consistently write off one-third to two-fifths of the one hundred House of Delegates districts. For example, about forty districts (three-fourths of them Democratic) had no major party opposition in at least four and often all five of the elections from 1982 to 1989.

The logic behind such abstentions is obvious enough in some cases. The Republican Party is least likely to challenge in the majority black seats, now totaling ten, plus certain ones in Southside Virginia. Democratic challengers are conspicuously absent in areas of the Shenandoah Valley and in suburban-dominated areas of Northern Virginia and Chesterfield County and around Lynchburg and Virginia Beach. However, such districts do not begin to account for all of those in which competition is rare. The fact that candidates of one party sometimes run and win in districts left unchallenged in the preceding two or three elections suggests a certain amount of coordination and strategizing among party leaders and activists.

We need to know something not only about the number of districts where major party candidates confront each other but also about the level of competition in them. Two measures may be helpful. One involves the size of winning votes. I have classified as competitive those House of Delegates elections in which the winner had less than a 10 percent margin of victory. By that measure, only a relative few districts can be seen as competitive. Specifically, the average number of competitive districts in each of the seven elections, since single-member districts were adopted is only about thirteen (out of one hundred), though the number is substantially higher (twenty-one) in the first such election in 1982 and lower in the next two (seven and eight, respectively).

A more exacting measure of competition asks how many seats change partisan hands from one election to another, either by the defeat of incum-

156

McCleskey

Table 9.3. Party Competition for 100 Single-Member Districts, Virginia House of Delegates, 1982–1993

Year	Democratic No.	Democratic Winners[a]	Republican No.	Republican Winners[a]	Number of districts with major party competition
1982	87	65	66	34	53
1983	81	65	56	34	37
1985	83	65	61	33	44
1987	78	64	59	35	37
1989	80	59	62	39	42
1991	82	58	65	41	47
1993	79	52	78	47	57

Number of candidates offered (spanning Democratic and Republican columns)

[a]Winners do not total 100 because one Independent was elected in every year except 1985 and 1989, for which there were two each. Although they were elected as Independents who defeated Democratic incumbents, one delegate in 1985 and another in 1989 affiliated with the Democratic Party in the House and won reelection in subsequent years as a Democrat.
Source: Compiled from reports of the state Board of Elections.

bents or by the capture of open seats. In the Virginia House of Delegates, as in most American representative bodies, the defeat of incumbents by the opposition is quite difficult. In the period from 1979 through 1993 (chosen for the convenience provided by identification of state Board of Elections' incumbents), an estimated 325–350 incumbent house members sought reelection. Only forty-four of them, or roughly one in eight, were defeated in the general election by a candidate of the opposition party (two others—both Democrats—were defeated by Independents who in the next election ran and won as Democrats). Republican challengers defeated twenty-five Democratic incumbents; Democratic challengers defeated nineteen Republican incumbents. A net gain of six "conquered" seats for the Republicans over the course of fourteen elections is a slow way of increasing representation.

But incumbents do not go on forever, and Virginia Republicans have been especially adept at capitalizing on the opportunities presented by open Democratic seats while minimizing losses of their own. If we look at the period 1982–1993 (to avoid the complications involved in identifying open seats in the years when multimember districts were prevalent), we find in those seven elections a total of sixty-two open seats, with thirty-seven of them held by Democrats and twenty-five by Republicans going into the election. The postelection distributions yielded twenty-seven Democratic and thirty-five Republican seats—a net GOP gain of ten seats over a period in which Republican representation in the house increased by a net of thirteen seats.[7] These "conquered seats" and "open seats" are not mutually exclusive categories (hence the combined Republican gains exceed the net), but the proportions leave no doubt of the greater opportunity provided by open seats.

What factors are at work in bringing about the defeat of incumbents or in creating open seats? In many cases, the defeats can be accounted for by broad shifts in the balance of party strength in the district; no doubt, some open seats are created when incumbents decide not to swim against the tide or when redistricting has adverse effects. Both defeats and open seats may result from the failure of incumbents to live up to the expectation of supporters. Some defeats are clearly rooted in intraparty conflict, leading in extreme cases to independent candidates who split the vote; such conflicts may also create open seats in the general election by denying an incumbent renomination. Ambition often creates open seats as incumbents decide to pursue higher office, just as ambition presumably is at work when a challenger successfully takes on an incumbent. Flagging interest may contribute to an incumbent's defeat, and the same factor, or illness or death, may produce open seats.

The Independent Route to the House

One indication of the unsettled state of Virginia politics in the early 1970s is the record number of candidates who sought and won seats in the House of Delegates as Independents. While independent candidates had occasionally surfaced earlier in the time period covered here, none was successful until 1967, when incumbent Lacey Putney abandoned the Democratic Party to seek and win reelection as an Independent. Despite the presence of American Independent Party candidates in statewide races in 1969, there was no substantial increase in the number of Independents seeking House of Delegates seats that year, and only Putney was (re)elected.

In 1971, however, the number of Independent candidates increased to twenty-one (only one of them in single-member districts), and two more were elected to join Putney—one from a multimember district in Richmond City and Henrico County, the other from Southside Virginia.

The number of Independent candidates for the house ballooned in 1973 to thirty-seven, of whom a record fifteen were elected. The fact that the Republican delegation dropped at the same time from twenty-four to twenty, and the Democratic delegation from seventy-three to sixty-five, raises questions about the relationship of the 1973 Independents to the major parties. Were they closet Republicans seeking an acceptable way station en route to open affiliation with that party? Were they really conservative Democrats cut adrift by the collapse of the Byrd Organization? Or were they moderate Democrats seeking to distance themselves from the shambles of the Democratic Party created by the 1972 presidential campaign and the 1973 guber-

natorial race? Did they merely reflect peculiarly local and individual considerations?

The answer seems to be "all of the above." The single largest bloc of 1973
Independents consisted of five incumbent members who had originally
been elected as Democrats, who promptly affiliated with the Democratic
caucus when the house convened in January 1974, and who ran as Democrats when they sought reelection in 1975. Two of these Democrats were
apparently distancing themselves from the confusion of the gubernatorial
election; three of them may have had similar concerns but were also more
identified with the Byrd Organization. A sixth incumbent Democrat who
turned Independent kept that status for a term but aligned himself with the
Democrats thereafter. Two other incumbent Democrats who became Independents in 1973 retained that status until they left the house, at which
point one of them (French Slaughter) was elected to the U.S. House as a
Republican. Two other Democratic incumbents elected as Independents in
1973 kept this status in the 1974 session but were not candidates in the 1975
general elections.

Of the three freshmen elected as Independents in 1973, two were defeated in 1975 when they sought reelection as Independents; the third won
reelection as a Democrat in 1975. And the two incumbent Independents
retained this status throughout their house service, though one became a
Republican when she moved to the senate.

It seems fair to conclude that the great "Independent" epidemic of 1973
turned out to be mostly advantageous to the Democratic Party, though a
further and more detailed analysis focusing on the impact of the twenty-two
Independent *losers* on the outcomes in their districts might require some
recasting of that generalization.

Whatever its causes and impact, the Independent alternative soon faded.
Only five incumbent Independents were reelected in 1975, one of whom
aligned with the Democratic Party when the House convened. By 1979, the
only Independent left was the one who had started it all in 1967. He has
continued to serve in his unique role with no opposition from the Republicans and only a little from the Democrats.[8]

"Coattails" and Midterm Falloff

To what extent might the Republican gains in the House of Delegates
over the past thirty years be related to "coattails" provided by Republican
candidates for governor? A glance at the returns makes such a connection
seem plausible, for the largest gains in Republican membership came in the
gubernatorial election years of 1969 (ten), 1981 (eight), and 1993 (six).
And for all seven gubernatorial elections since 1969, the GOP netted an
increase of twenty-seven House seats, compared with a net of only six in the

seven off-year elections. Still, there are worrisome anomalies: Republicans lost four seats in one winning gubernatorial year (1973) while winning four in each of two different off-year elections. And gubernatorial coattails seemed not to work at all for Democrats, whose gubernatorial victories in 1981, 1985, and 1989 were accompanied by the net loss of twelve seats in the house.

Hoping to get a clearer understanding of coattail effects, I examined the thirty-seven districts in which two-party competition occurred in 1991 and 1993. In most districts, the 1993 voter turnout was substantially higher than in the off year. Nevertheless, the outcomes seemed not very different: Democratic candidates as well as Republicans in 1993 typically increased their margins of victory over 1991. In the eleven districts in which the winning candidate's 1991 majority was reduced in the later election, almost as many Republicans (five) suffered as did Democrats (six). In short, I find little basis for a coattail interpretation, though I would be reluctant to argue that it is totally absent.

Is it possible to gain further understanding by looking for a phenomenon associated with congressional elections, namely, the midterm falloff? As sketched by those who first authoritatively dissected the midterm falloff, the party that controls the executive branch usually loses seats in the midterm elections because the less committed and less motivated voters who are mobilized for presidential elections—disproportionately in favor of the winner—are less likely to participate in the midterm house elections, thus undermining candidates of the president's party.

A glance over the data indicates that no pattern of midterm falloff in House of Delegates elections seems to exist. If we take the three Republican administrations that began with Holton's election in 1969, we find that one midterm election (1971) provided no change in Republican seats in the House of Delegates, another brought a three-seat loss (1975), and the third a four-seat gain (1979). The results for the Democratic administrations of the 1980s are not so muddled but provide little support for the importance of midterm falloff, for in one such election (1983) the Democrats had no change in seats, while in each of the other two they lost a single seat. My conclusion is that midterm elections have probably not made much difference; when notable changes have occurred, as in 1975 and 1979, other factors were probably more important.

The Virginia Senate

Tracing the shift in party representation in the Virginia Senate is easier and simpler than for the house, partly because it has only forty members, partly because its elections for four-year unstaggered terms are determinedly off cycle (in odd-numbered years when the governor and other statewide officials are not on the ballot), and partly because it has always relied mostly on single-member districts.

Prior to the adoption of the 1971 Virginia constitution and the language in article II, section 6, requiring house and senate districts to be compact, contiguous, and equal, no basis was specified for the required decennial redistricting. Senate representation was as much an issue as that of the House of Delegates in the epic political battles fought in the antebellum period.

In the twentieth century, however, redistricting has typically been easier in the senate than in the house. The smaller number of seats meant that most of the time, a senate district would be composed of two or more counties and cities; only rarely would a city or county have enough population to warrant two or more members, and when that did happen, the aversion to breaking local government boundaries led to the creation of multimember districts.

Even so, the inequities of representation in the senate were substantial, and the changes brought by the reapportionment revolution were immediately felt. A federal court allowed the 1963 senate elections to proceed on the basis of the 1962 act of the assembly but cut the terms of those elected to two years and ordered a new round of senate elections in 1965, also for two-year terms. Both the 1962 act and the court-approved plan made use of multimember districts, with the latter providing for twenty-eight single-member districts and five multimember ones with a total of twelve seats.

In redistricting for 1971, the senate opted to use only single-member districts, breaking city and county boundaries in the process. The plan was largely sustained by the courts except for an order requiring, ironically enough in the light of later judicial rulings, a three-person multimember district for Norfolk to avoid problems in creating single-member districts caused by the difficulty of fixing residences for several thousand sailors of the Atlantic Fleet.

Senate redistricting in 1981 was much less controversial than in the house, though Justice Department insistence on a black majority district in Norfolk forced a revision before the forty single-member districts were finally approved. The senate's redistricting effort in 1991 proved to be rather contentious, for Governor Wilder vetoed the first plan—an action reflecting not only his stated concern to obtain more black representation but also his ongoing feuds with certain senate leaders. The plan finally agreed upon appeared to have been helpful with regard to minority representation, for two additional black senators were elected in 1991, bringing the total to five.

Through the first twenty postwar years, Republican representation in the Virginia Senate was stable at either two or three members; as table 9.4 re-

Table 9.4. Partisan Composition of the Virginia Senate, 1961–1991

Election year[a]	Democrats	Republicans
1961	38	2
1963	37	3
1965	36	4[b]
1967	34	6
1971	33	7
1975	35	5
1979	31	9
1983	32	8
1987	30	10
1991	22	18

[a]Election years only, except 1961, which is included for purposes of comparison. The 1965 senate election was court ordered.
[b]Wilkinson reports that the fourth seat in 1965 came in a December 1965 special election.
Source: J. Harvie Wilkinson III, *Harry Byrd and the Changing Face of Virginia Politics, 1945–1966* (Charlottesville: University Press of Virginia, 1968), 221, 279, for the years 1961 through 1965; Commonwealth of Virginia, *The General Assembly of the Commonwealth of Virginia, 1962–1981* (Richmond, 1983); *Manuals of the Senate* (Richmond, various years); reports of the state Board of Elections.

veals, the next thirty years altered that picture greatly. Redistricting changes, along with other forces, helped to pull the GOP to seven seats by 1971, but it was another eight years before that level was exceeded (nine seats in 1979) and another eight years before the tenth seat was won in 1987. The next step turned out to be a giant one, for the 1991 elections sent eighteen Republicans (45 percent of the total) to the senate.

The same sort of geographical shift noted with respect to the House of Delegates also took place in Republican senate representation. In the late 1960s, the six Republican senators were all from southwestern Virginia and the Shenandoah Valley except for one who came from the Lynchburg area—east of the Blue Ridge but just barely. The decline in and slow recovery of Republican seats in the early 1970s also brought some geographical displacement; of the nine Republicans elected in 1979, only three were from west of the Blue Ridge. The remainder had seats scattered from Alexandria to Virginia Beach, covering much of the urban corridor, though the Republican districts drew upon suburban and rural support rather than upon that of the central cities. The shift eastward continued in the 1980s, so that by 1987 only two of the ten Republican districts were in the party's traditional strongholds of southwestern Virginia and the Shenandoah Valley. The sharp increase of eight seats in 1991 necessarily brought more geographical diversity, including an additional two members from west of the Blue Ridge and one from the central Piedmont. Still, most of the new seats were near the major population concentrations of Northern Virginia, Richmond, and the Tidewater.

Table 9.5 shows for the senate that the Democratic Party can no longer be counted on to offer a candidate for every seat, though the number missed is small. Republican candidates can be regularly found in one-half to three-fourths of the districts. The number of party-contested districts accordingly varies from one-half to three-fifths of the total.

More useful, however, are the data in table 9.5 on the number of seats for which the party contests are in fact competitive (that is, the margin between party winners and party losers is 10 percent or less of the vote). The average number of competitive seats over the six elections covered by table 9.5 is not quite seven, with the earlier years having fewer and the later years more than that. Over time the parties have divided these competitive seats almost evenly, with Democrats winning twenty-one and Republicans twenty of them. However, there is considerable variation from one year to another, as is reflected in the fact that in 1983 the Democrats won five of six party-competitive districts, while in 1991 the Republicans won eight of thirteen.

These figures raise the question of the relative importance in the senate of defeating incumbents and winning open seats. In the period from 1971 through 1991, a total of fourteen incumbents suffered defeat by a party opponent. Republicans defeated ten incumbent Democrats while losing only four of their own incumbents, for a net gain of six "conquered" seats. With respect to open seats, Democrats held six and Republicans three going into the elections involved; the postelection distribution was zero Democratic and nine Republican, for a net Republican gain of six.[9] (These two categories are not mutually exclusive, and hence the combined defeated seats and open-seat gains for Republicans exceed the actual total of eleven seats gained from 1971 through 1991.) Thus Republican gains in the senate have been achieved about equally by defeating incumbent Democrats and by capturing open seats.

In the House of Delegates, it will be recalled, Republicans gained more ground by successfully contesting open seats (a net gain of ten seats from 1981–1993) than by defeating incumbents (a net gain of six seats from 1979–1993). It is interesting to speculate as to why Republican gains in the senate depend on open-seat victories less than in the house. One possibility is that the much smaller population of house districts makes it easier for the Democrats in control of redistricting to protect their incumbents, though I have seen the opposite argued. It may be too that because retirements are apt to be fewer in the more prestigious senate, Republicans feel forced to challenge incumbent Democrats in the senate rather than waiting for the open-seat opportunity. And it has been suggested that the greater visibility of senators increases their vulnerability to defeat.

Table 9.5. Party Competition in the Virginia Senate, 1971–1991

Election year	Candidates		Party contests	Party competitive districts		
	Dem.	Rep.		Total	Dem. won	Rep. won
1971	39	27	26	4	2	2
1975	40	20	20	2	—	2
1979	39	26	25	9	5	4
1983	38	23	21	6	5	1
1987	36	23	19	7	4	3
1991	38	30	28	13	5	8

Note: Status is as of the completion of the general election in the year indicated.
Source: Compiled from reports of the state Board of Elections.

Concluding Observations

The growth of the Republican Party to competitive status in both houses of the Virginia General Assembly has been mostly a gradual affair marked by occasional "breakthrough" elections (1969 and 1993 in the house; 1991 in the senate). In neither chamber has there been close competition across even a majority of districts; the real battles in each election rarely involve more than twelve to fifteen house districts and six to eight senate districts (thus making the senate the more competitive body, given the differences in size). In the senate, Republicans have advanced about equally by defeating incumbents and by capturing open seats; in the house, GOP gains have come more often through the capture of open seats.

I found little evidence that either gubernatorial coattails or midterm fall-off were at work in House of Delegates elections, and of course they are irrelevant for the senate, given its election schedule. Independent candidacies have been much more frequent in the house and have resulted in some successes there, but the house total of fifteen Independents elected in 1973 gives a misleading picture, for they quickly faded with little disturbance of the preexisting partisan alignments.

I have not tried to measure the influence of the civil rights revolution and the reapportionment revolution on the partisan balance in the General Assembly, treating them rather as part of the context within which narrower and more manageable questions can be explored. There can be no doubt, however, that both played a major role in breaking up the Democrats' near monopoly of seats in the General Assembly. In Virginia, as elsewhere, the two revolutions turned out to be highly interactive, particularly in the 1980s and 1990s. Republicans, of course, from the outset saw the potential for their party in both revolutions (some perhaps saw the dangers as well). The reception accorded Nixon's "Southern strategy" was uneven, but Republicans moved early to exploit the liberal/conservative tensions in the Democratic Party. They were equally quick to see that the creation of majority black legislative districts would make other districts whiter and more Republican, leading them in some cases to join black and liberal legal attacks on Democratic redistricting plans.

I suppose two things impress me most about the rise of the Republican Party to competitive status in the General Assembly. One is the difficulty inherent in trying to undo a one-party system, even one that is faction-ridden. So much has to be overcome: popular attitudes and prejudices, institutional arrangements favoring the majority party, the intrusion of unfavorable outside events (for example, Watergate), a dearth of experienced leadership, undeveloped political skills, and so on. The second thing that impresses me—and a thirty-year perspective helps—is the inexorable quality of the Republican advance. The fact is that the Republican Party in Virginia has found the route to assembly power very slow and difficult going. The comparison that comes to my mind—I hope my Confederate forebears and "old Virginia" friends will excuse the comparison—is Grant's campaign against the Army of Northern Virginia in the spring and summer of 1864: lots of fighting and lots of slogging, not very pretty to watch, often bogged down and at cross-purposes, sometimes confused strategically but always moving, a slow and relentless tide.

But all tides have their limits, even political ones. Deep conviction, along with skillful politicking and much grit and determination, have helped to move the Republican Party to a point where control of either or both houses of the General Assembly in the near future is a distinct possibility. Though impressed by the qualities that have brought Republicans this far, I remain skeptical of their capacity to fashion a permanent governing majority in Virginia. To win the votes necessary to displace those in power is no easy task, but it is even harder once in power to meet the ideological demands of the faithful and at the same time to satisfy the broader, less ideological public. The GOP has adapted quite well to the role of the loyal opposition—for a good many Virginians, that party is still primarily a convenient stick with which to beat a Democratic dog that is often ill behaved and unresponsive but one with which the household has nevertheless learned to live. My guess, then, is that GOP control of the General Assembly may turn out to be more elusive than now projected and that no solid and continuing Republican control of the statehouse and assembly will be possible. What we must expect is a great deal of divided and near-divided government.

10
Electoral Competition and Southern State Legislatures

The Dynamics of Change

R. Bruce Anderson

In recent research into changes in southern state legislatures, two strands stand out: changes in the electoral contestation, competitiveness, and success of Republican candidates and organizational changes in the legislatures themselves. In nearly all southern electoral environments, Republicans have made important progress toward moving legislatures closer to true two-party status through their increasing presence, competitiveness, and success in elections. During the 1994 elections, Republicans seized control of several chambers that have been, in recent memory, wholly the preserve of their Democratic counterparts. This essay examines the dynamics of the electoral environment in state house elections over the past twenty years in an attempt to uncover some of the underlying conditions that have characterized these changes.

I will ask to what degree Republican inroads in the electoral arena have changed the face of the southern electoral environment—that "external" arena in which increasing tension is hypothesized to produce internal stress in the chambers themselves. I will then briefly examine the type of elections associated with each party's success or failure across three general arenas: uncontested elections, contested elections, and competitive ("marginal") elections.

Electoral Competition

The development of a competitive two-party system is one of the most significant changes to occur in southern politics in the last fifty years. It may be asked whether the electorate in the South is in a state of dealignment, realignment, or some combination.[1] From an officeholding perspective, "[at] all levels, officeholders have become substantially more Republican" in the South.[2] The rate of electoral success, however, has not been constant across all offices. Rather, there is a "striking difference" between GOP performance at the state office level and that at the federal level. The accepted wisdom is that "an affinity for the GOP began at the top and has percolated downward."[3]

However, in recent years the Republican Party has made significant inroads in being elected to southern state senates and houses. By the 1992–1993 period, for example, Republicans held at least 20 percent of the seats in seven houses and seven senates. In three senates and five houses the minority party had accumulated at least 33 percent of the chamber seats, a tipping point thought to be extremely important in terms of partisan organization within the legislatures.[4] In the 1994 election, three chambers (the Florida Senate, the North Carolina House, and the South Carolina House) shifted to Republican control, and Republicans are within a few seats of a majority in the Virginia House and Senate and in the Florida House. The substantial minority party gains are not confined to the states in which Republicans have had a viable minority presence for many years. For example, there were no Republicans in either the Alabama House or Senate in the mid-1970s. Currently, they constitute over one-third (39 percent)of all legislators in both chambers. At the state legislative level, the once Solid South is a thing of the past.

The increased party competition has not gone unnoticed by academic researchers. Rather, a once dormant area of study has been the object of a great outpouring of research in recent years,[5] a phenomenon due in no small way to the creation and availability of excellent databases. In this chapter, the focus is on political party competition for state legislative seats in the South from 1968 to 1991.

Party Competition

A key issue in the study of state elections and state legislatures in the South is the extent to which there is two-party competition. While this is a seemingly simple concept, a perusal of the research literature reveals the absence of any agreement as to its operational definition.

The dimension of electoral party competition indicates the level of competition, or the percentage of votes received by each party. In general, studies that focus on the level of competition as the dependent variable for southern elections try to account for the share of the two-party vote received by one party at the legislative district level. Models incorporate national and state political and economic factors, along with characteristics of the district and the candidates.[6] Another method of viewing competition that incorporates the district-level approach is concerned with indexes of party competition.[7] Holbrook and van Dunk's study was issued in reaction to the widespread use of indexes of competition that are not directly based on electoral data[8] and is therefore only tangentially concerned with many of the issues presented here.

While many researchers have criticized such aggregations,[9] few have attempted to generate a district-level approach that takes into consideration the multifaceted problems associated with such a party competition index. Criticisms are generally decomposed as: the limited time frame (that is, the use of cross-sectional data to describe or explain dynamic events or short over-time analysis that picks up time-bound "noise"), limited samples of the units (that is, the use of a few cases—states—to describe regional or sectional features), and limited samples of the districts. This last method has been most frequently confounded by the presence of multimember free-for-all districts (MMFFA), which defy simple analysis of competition because of the multiplicity of candidates and confusion over vote choice.

In this study, I have sought to address these problems straightforwardly by (1) increasing the time frame to a larger number of elections (1968–1991); (2) using the complete set of units where data are available (ten states of the former Confederacy)[10]; and (3) resolving the measurement problems in MMFFA districts so that all districts within the array may be utilized (see appendix).

Operational Definitions: Electoral Material

In these measures I have followed the earlier work of Hamm and Anderson,[11] which is loosely conceptualized from theoretical work initiated by Jewell.[12] I examine three dimensions of legislative elections:

1. The first is the level of contestation. While some authors[13] have defined a contested race as one in which the candidate of that party received at least 10 percent of the general-election vote, the more typical approach is to determine whether one or both parties entered a candidate. In this chapter, I measure each party's contestation as the percentage of legislative district general elections in which the political party fielded a candidate. Separate calculations were made for the Democrats and Republicans. Then a measure of two-party contestation is calculated as the percentage of constituency-level general elections in which both major parties were represented.

2. The second dimension taps the percentage of district-level races in which the party's nominee made a very credible showing. I operationalized each party's (Democratic or Republican) competitiveness as the percentage of the total races including those contested by only one party, in which the party's candidate received 40 percent or more of the two-

party general-election vote. Two-party competitiveness occurred when both parties received at least 40 percent of the total general-election vote.

3. The third dimension is the level of electoral success. It is defined as simply the percentage of the general-election races in which the party's candidate had the greatest number of votes. In those rare cases in which an independent candidate won, I opted to make that race part of the base calculation.

The issue of electoral *success* will be examined in terms of distribution of the victories by type of race. That is, what proportion of seats won are in uncontested, minimally competitive, or competitive races, and what trends, if any, are displayed across time in the various southern states and across the two parties?

The time variable for the over-time comparisons is operationalized as being a counter variable, starting at (time = 1) in the first year for which we have data (that is, 1968) and continuing by increments of one to where (time = 24) in the last year (that is, 1991). The South consisted of the eleven original Confederate states minus Louisiana.

I have also included in several of the tables four nonsouthern states for the sake of comparison. These states were chosen on the basis of two simple criteria: (1) that they fall into the upper tier of states across the full array in terms of overall competition and (2) that they be geographically disparate. The states chosen were Illinois, New York, Ohio, and Washington. I make no claim that this is a complete or even representative sample—rather the reverse. It is meant as a simple (and admittedly incomplete) gauge of how the southern states under investigation compare to their nonsouthern neighbors and is carefully chosen to skew the sample into the upper end of that nonsouthern distribution.

This analysis of the political parties in state legislative elections has been immensely aided by the availability of the state legislative election data for the time period 1968–1987 from the Inter-University Consortium for Political and Social Research (ICPSR). Keith Hamm and I have augmented these data by obtaining additional data for elections held during the 1988–1991 period.

Analysis

To what extent did candidates from the two parties contest elections in the ten southern states under investigation? To answer this question, I will examine each variable independently and then together. I will then attempt to suggest ways in which the competition in these chambers may affect the organizational aspects.

Contestation

Overall, during the time period studied, Republicans contested on average 40.9 and 40.4 percent of the seats in the southern senates and houses, respectively (see table 10.1). Substantial variation exists, however, with the range between a low mean of 15 percent (Arkansas) and a high of 61.7 percent (North Carolina) in the senates across the time frame and a corresponding range being between means of 19.4 percent (Mississippi) and 64.5 percent (North Carolina) in the state houses. A comparison with the selected nonsouthern states reveals near parity in Democratic contestation, but when we turn to Republican and two-party contestation, the seat strength in each state is a good indicator of the strength of contestation. Mean contestation figures fall dramatically (as expected) in states where seat strength is low. There is some variation among the units, with the North Carolina Senate and House slightly higher in contestation in relation to the other states than might have been predicted. In two-party contestation, both chambers in Tennessee reveal lower figures than is strictly expected, and North Carolina's chambers are both higher than others in their range.

Competition

The measure of competition follows a slightly different path (table 10.2). As some researchers have suggested, the southern states start at a much higher level of Democratic competition than their nonsouthern counterparts—this tendency is most evident for states that are closest to the one-party dominant ideal. The figures on mean Republican competition seem to suggest that this supposition holds. Mean Republican competition in North Carolina is slightly above others in that range though not dramatically. Two-party competition is low overall and lowest among those states falling toward the one-party dominant end of the spectrum.

Over-Time Measures

An intriguing question is whether the percentage of contested seats increased with the passage of time.[14] The trend of Democratic contestation has been downward across the array of the selected northern states. Among these states that have had significant minorities in the chamber for the longest time, two states have positive—but not significant—coefficients in the senates, two are positive (Illinois significantly so) in the house, and the rest are generally negative. Contestation in the Illinois House is rising across the board, with Democratic, Republican, and two-party contestation all positive

Table 10.1. Levels of Contestation in Selected State Legislatures, 1968–1991, by Chamber

State	Democratic contestation M	Republican contestation M	Two-party contestation M	Republican seats, 1991 (%)
		SENATE		
IL	**0.947**	**0.885**	**0.831**	—
NY	**0.939**	**0.952**	**0.892**	—
OH	**0.980**	**0.976**	**0.956**	—
WA	**0.946**	**0.912**	**0.858**	—
TN	**0.678**	**0.561**	**0.243**	**39.3**
VA	*0.954*	*0.583*	*0.538*	*45.0*
FL	**0.808**	**0.590**	**0.398**	**45.0**
TX	0.830	0.443	0.273	29.0
NC	0.990	0.617	0.607	28.0
SC	0.982	0.422	0.404	28.2
GA	0.886	0.285	0.171	19.6
MS	0.971	0.206	0.177	17.3
AR	0.967	0.150	0.117	11.4
AL	0.971	0.236	0.208	20.0
South	0.903	0.409	0.313	28.8
		HOUSE		
IL	**0.734**	**0.720**	**0.454**	—
NY	**0.948**	**0.963**	**0.912**	—
OH	**0.970**	**0.916**	**0.886**	—
WA	**0.949**	**0.920**	**0.867**	—
TN	**0.719**	**0.581**	**0.300**	**42.4**
VA	*0.853*	*0.560*	*0.427*	*41.4*
FL	**0.812**	**0.538**	**0.351**	**38.3**
TX	*0.837*	*0.444*	*0.275*	*38.0*
NC	*0.984*	*0.645*	*0.629*	*32.5*
SC	*0.943*	*0.422*	*0.365*	*35.2*
GA	0.884	0.279	0.163	19.4
MS	0.971	0.194	0.167	19.0
AR	0.963	0.121	0.084	9.0
AL	0.973	0.259	0.232	21.9
South	0.893	0.404	0.299	29.7

Note: Bold indicates that the chamber had reached the 33.3 percent margin of Republicans by 1968; italic indicates that it had done so by 1990.

Source: Data include raw elections figures (win-loss) through 1987 from the Interuniversity Consortium for Political and Social Research State Legislative Elections Study, Malcolm Jewell, principal investigator.

**Table 10.2. Levels of Competition in Selected State Legislatures,
1968–1991, by Chamber**

State	Democratic competition M	Republican competition M	Two-party competition M	Republican seats, 1991 (%)
		SENATE		
IL	**0.702**	**0.610**	**0.312**	—
NY	**0.617**	**0.609**	**0.228**	—
OH	**0.726**	**0.667**	**0.392**	—
WA	**0.954**	**0.769**	**0.421**	—
TN	**0.606**	**0.508**	**0.118**	39.3
VA	*0.896*	*0.400*	*0.292*	*45.0*
FL	**0.743**	**0.479**	**0.222**	**45.0**
TX	0.790	0.327	0.116	29.0
NC	0.938	0.430	0.368	28.0
SC	0.950	0.271	0.220	28.2
GA	0.844	0.214	0.058	19.6
MS	0.945	0.100	0.045	17.3
AR	0.967	0.098	0.066	11.4
AL	0.931	0.110	0.041	20.0
South	0.861	0.293	0.154	28.8
		HOUSE		
IL	**0.614**	**0.541**	**0.155**	—
NY	**0.728**	**0.513**	**0.241**	—
OH	**0.728**	**0.550**	**0.279**	—
WA	**0.754**	**0.654**	**0.409**	—
TN	**0.651**	**0.503**	**0.152**	42.4
VA	*0.809*	*0.439*	*0.261*	*41.4*
FL	**0.740**	**0.446**	**0.187**	**38.3**
TX	*0.786*	*0.347*	*0.132*	*38.0*
NC	*0.933*	*0.435*	*0.368*	*32.5*
SC	*0.891*	*0.270*	*0.161*	*35.2*
GA	0.852	0.229	0.081	19.4
MS	0.955	0.116	0.072	19.0
AR	0.953	0.073	0.031	9.0
AL	0.939	0.149	0.088	21.9
South	0.850	0.300	0.153	29.7

Note: Bold indicates that the chamber had reached the 33.3 percent margin of Republicans by 1968; italic indicates that it had done so by 1990.
Source: Data include raw elections figures (win-loss) through 1987 from the Interuniversity Consortium for Political and Social Research State Legislative Elections Study, Malcolm Jewell, principal investigator.

and strongly significant. The results for southern states that have had significant minorities in the chamber are also mixed. A clearer pattern emerges among states still leaning to one-party dominance. In these states Democratic contestation is generally falling, while Republican contestation is rising. Two-party contestation is also up, in several cases (in both of Alabama's chambers, in the Georgia House, and in the North Carolina Senate) significantly.

The general picture of contestation seems to be reflected in the finding that of the twenty southern chambers considered, Republican contestation has risen in sixteen, significantly so in eight; Democratic contestation has fallen in seventeen chambers, significantly so in twelve. These trends are reversed in Tennessee, which has had a significant Republican minority for the longest time.

How frequently did the two parties square off against one another in these elections for southern state legislatures? The mean level of contestation in the South was 31.3 percent in the senates and 29.9 percent in the state houses. As shown in table 10.3, contestation did not increase consistently with the time variable, but an interesting pattern emerges nonetheless. In the individual correlations for two-party contestation the senates and houses vary widely, from strongly significant increases in the Alabama House (and Senate) and the North Carolina Senate to a significantly negative reading in the Florida Senate. It is critical to note that these are just the sort of readings one would expect if it could be established that there is a linkage between the length of time during which a state has had a significant minority party and the degree of competition. Across the findings, fourteen of the chambers reveal positive increases. Of these, four are statistically significant. Six chambers disclose negative results, one of which is significant—all but one of these (the Arkansas Senate) are chambers in states that have reached the 33 percent margin for the minority party. In states with the longest history of two-party competition, the features are markedly different from those of states without this history.

This trend becomes even more dramatic when we examine the dynamic measures for competition (see table 10.4). Here the general trend in Democratic competition is downward among northern states in all chambers but Washington (plus the Illinois House). Democratic competition is most significantly in decline in the southern chambers that have leaned to one-party dominance—especially so in the houses. Tennessee, the state that has had a significant minority party for the longest time, reveals a positive coefficient for Democratic competition in both chambers, and the measure is significant in the Tennessee House. This trend is reversed in all other southern states and in both chambers: the pattern that strongly emerges here is one of decreasing Democratic competition with attendant increases among the Republicans.

Table 10.3. Correlation Between Levels of Contestation and Time, 1968–1991

State	Democratic contestation	Republican contestation	Two-party contestation	Republican seats, 1991 (%)
		SENATE		
IL	**-.758*****	**-.799*****	**-.911******	—
NY	**-.807*****	**-.823*****	**-.865******	—
OH	**.103**	**-.199**	**-.082**	—
WA	**.105**	**.125**	**.215***	—
TN	**.292**	**-.302**	**.102**	39.3
VA	*-.900***	*.189*	*-.457*	*45.0*
FL	**-.678****	**-.023**	**-.594***	**45.0**
TX	-.697**	.808***	.444	29.0
NC	.544	.755**	.772***	28.0
SC	-.765*	.698	.507	28.2
GA	-.345	.389	.193	19.6
MS	-.842*	.644	.471	17.3
AR	-.841***	-.144	-.547	11.4
AL	-.597	.780*	.796*	20.0
		HOUSE		
IL	**.819*****	**.811*****	**.883*****	—
NY	**-.892******	**-.821*****	**-.867******	—
OH	**-.311**	**-.288**	**-.144**	—
WA	**.400**	**.048**	**.252**	—
TN	**.331**	**-.508***	**-.309**	42.4
VA	*-.639***	*.370*	*-.045*	*41.4*
FL	**-.480**	**.617****	**.256**	**38.3**
TX	*-.722****	*.834****	*.095*	*38.0*
NC	*-.644***	*.123*	*.008*	*32.5*
SC	*-.870*****	*.051*	*-.288*	*35.2*
GA	-.090	.569*	.603**	19.4
MS	-.830**	.694	.327	19.0
AR	-.799***	.514*	.300	9.0
AL	-.734*	.918***	.881***	21.9

Note: Bold indicates that the chamber had reached the 33.3 percent margin of Republicans by 1968; italic indicates that it had done so by 1990.
*p < .10.   **p < .05.   ***p < .01.   ****p < .001.
Source: Data include raw elections figures (win-loss) through 1987 from the Interuniversity Consortium for Political and Social Research State Legislative Elections Study, Malcolm Jewell, principal investigator.

Table 10.4. Correlation Between Level of Competition and Time, 1968–1991

State	Democratic competition	Republican competition	Two-party competition	Republican seats, 1991 (%)
		SENATE		
IL	**−.786***	**−.777***	**−.924****	—
NY	**−.341**	**−.155**	**−.343**	—
OH	**−.264**	**−.043**	**−.258**	—
WA	**.149**	**.322**	**.623***	—
TN	**.196**	**−.082**	**.250**	39.3
VA	*−.822**	*.671*	*−.756*	*45.0*
FL	**−.625***	**.346**	**−.469**	**45.0**
TX	−.635**	.777***	.489	29.0
NC	−.607*	.576*	.431	28.0
SC	−.810*	.482	−.650	28.2
GA	−.451	.351	−.088	19.6
MS	−.788*	.771*	.621	17.3
AR	−.841***	.084	−.637**	11.4
AL	−.851**	.878**	.912**	20.0
		HOUSE		
IL	**.717***	**−.713***	**.239**	—
NY	**−.262**	**−.902****	**−.847***	—
OH	**−.249**	**−.718***	**−.784***	—
WA	**.168**	**−.390**	**−.160**	—
TN	**.509***	**−.632***	**.346**	42.4
VA	*−.851****	*.669**	*−.158*	*41.4*
FL	**−.536***	**.566***	**−.026**	38.3
TX	*−.784***	*.924****	*.310*	*38.0*
NC	*−.558**	*.301*	*.110*	*32.5*
SC	*−.930****	*.604**	*−.276*	*35.2*
GA	−.222	.484	.514*	19.4
MS	−.830*	.628	.212	19.0
AR	−.854****	.746***	.359	9.0
AL	−.904***	.932***	.903***	21.9

Note: Bold indicates that the chamber had reached the 33.3 percent margin of Republicans by 1968; italic indicates that it had done so by 1990.

* $p < .10$.   ** $p < .05$.   *** $p < .01$.   **** $p < .001$.

Source: Data include raw elections figures (win-loss) through 1987 from the Interuniversity Consortium for Political and Social Research State Legislative Elections Study, Malcolm Jewell, principal investigator.

The pattern is quite clear. Among the southern states represented here, the variance in competitiveness over time beyond the general trend is quite small. Pairs of significant measures in Republican gains and Democratic losses may be found in the Alabama, Mississippi, North Carolina, and Texas senates, with similarly situated figures for the houses in Virginia, Florida, Texas, South Carolina, Arkansas, and Alabama.

Two-party competition is somewhat more problematic. Among the states where one might expect it to rise, it does so significantly in only three chambers (in both chambers in Alabama and in the Georgia House); further, it is significantly decreasing in the Arkansas Senate. Of the southern states under consideration, two-party competition is falling in eight of the twenty chambers: five of these (both chambers of Virginia and Florida and the South Carolina House) are chambers that have had minority representation for some time.

A tremendous difference exists between fielding a candidate for a general election and having that person be competitive. Republicans learned this lesson in the late 1960s and early 1970s in several southern elections. Mathematically, the level of competition cannot exceed the level of contestation, but in some cases these variables are closer to convergence than in others. In the Tennessee Senate, the mean level of Republican contestation (.561) is almost exactly reflected in the level of Republican competition (.508). In the North Carolina House, by contrast, the two figures are quite divergent: Republicans contested, overall, an average of 64.5 percent of races but were competitive in only 43.5 percent of these. Overall, correlations between mean competition and mean contestation are higher in the houses than in the senates.

There is a striking similarity between the figures for each *chamber* by state. In the case of Tennessee, for example, the senate contestation figure is .561, with competition at .508; the house figures are .581/.503. Divergence is present across both chambers in North Carolina, with the senate at .617/.430 and the house at .645/.435. Differing patterns *between* chambers in the same state, moreover, are *not* evident—suggesting that perhaps a similar strategy may be present in elections in each state. If so, then some unifying mechanism may be at work, but of course, from these data, no definitive conclusions may be drawn. In sum, there is divergence between *states* in terms of mean levels of contestation and competition, but at least on the face of it, there is systematic convergence between *chambers* in the same state across these figures.

While I have shown that contestation does not necessarily translate into competition, it is intuitively evident that competition is a prerequisite for success. The central question at this point in the analysis is how contestation and competition are converted into "money in the bank"—seats in the chambers. I have broken this section of the investigation into two overall portions: first, victories by type—simple correlations over time, by party, for those that are uncontested, those contested, and those with a competitive challenger (see table 10.5). Second, I have examined these types, over time, in terms of relative portion of total victories by party over time in order to try to discern patterns in the marginal (competitive) races and also to see how these types of races stack up in terms of the total apportionment of victories (see table 10.6). For total victories, I computed the proportion of victories to defeats for each party. For relative victories, the type of victory (that is, competitive victories, simply contested, but not competitive victories and unchallenged victories) is computed as percentages of the number of total victories by that party in a given state and year. In other words, the first figure reflects a party's number of victories expressed as a percentage of the total seats in that chamber. Relative competitive victories are then expressed as the party's percentage of total victories (that is, 100 percent) that were competitive.[15] Thus, since I have demonstrated that movement in elections in southern state legislatures has occurred along two other dimensions—in terms of contestation and competition over time—as well as simple seat transition, we need to examine the effect these changes may have on the type of victories parties are having.[16]

Tables 10.5 and 10.6 report the findings for these two broad sections—correlations between types of victory and time and correlations between the several types of victories (relative victory) and time. Under these sections, I have ordered the tables into subsections that report the correlations for *uncontested* races, that is, races in which the candidates of that party had no opposition, victories in noncompetitive elections (in which the candidates of that party faced nominal contestation but in which their opposite numbers were not competitive under the 60 percent cut point), and victories in competitive elections (the marginal races). These figures are reported for both chambers of the legislature in the ten southern states examined for 1968–1991.[17]

In table 10.5, we note that overall uncontested victories for Democrats have fallen off significantly; decline is present in all of the states under study with the exception of Tennessee and is significant in ten of the twenty chambers. The results for the houses are stronger than those for the senates. Among Republicans, these figures are reversed—it is clear that while the number of "safe" districts for Democrats has declined overall, the number of districts in which Republicans face no opposition has grown (with the exception of both Tennessee chambers and the North Carolina Senate). The pattern here is similar to that of the Democrats in that Republican gains in this regard are generally greater in the houses than in the senates; strong correlative significance is recorded for South Carolina, Arkansas, and the Texas House.

With the exception of Tennessee, Democratic victories that are contested

Table 10.5. Pearson Correlation Coefficients over Time for Victories by Type: Southern State Legislatures, 1968–1991

State	Uncontested Democratic victories	Democratic victories in non-competitive elections	Democratic victories in competitive elections	Uncontested Republican victories	Republican victories in non-competitive elections	Republican victories in competitive elections
			SENATE			
TN	**.271**	**.177**	**.225**	−.422	−.312	.183
VA	−.547	−.794*	−.615	.505	.419	.531
FL	−.263	−.566*	.360	.514	.249	−.129
TX	−.823***	−.704**	.637**	.417	.006**	.372
NC	−.755**	−.576*	.491	−.544	.730**	−.340
SC	−.698	−.482	−.644	.765*	.820**	−.072
GA	−.529*	−.437	.327	.286	.085	.145
MS	−.621	−.764*	.141	.836**	.302	.677
AR	−.240	−.393	.028	.804***	.821***	.272
AL	−.862**	−.923***	.794**	.771**	.750*	.760**
South	−.265**	−.239**	.152	.105	.167	.095
			HOUSE			
TN	**.508***	**.632****	**.044**	−.332	−.509*	−.650**
VA	−.368	−.664**	−.069	.638**	.850****	−.004
FL	−.617**	−.566*	.425	.480	.536*	.449
TX	−.845****	−.924****	−.192	.722***	.784***	.772***
NC	−.123	−.301	−.321	.644**	.558*	.491
SC	−.051	−.604**	−.438	.870****	.930****	.083
GA	−.569*	−.484	.689***	.090	.222	−.268
MS	−.406	−.628	.088	.791	.830*	.300
AR	−.514*	−.746***	−.071	.799***	.854****	.439
AL	−.918***	−.932***	.781**	.734*	.904***	.890***
South	−.187*	−.242**	.015	.262***	.308***	.058

Note: Bold indicates that the chamber had reached the 33.3 percent margin of Republicans by 1968; italic indicates that it had done so by 1990. "South" is overall.
* $p < .10$.   ** $p < .05$.   *** $p < .01$.   **** $p < .001$.
Source: Data include raw elections figures (win-loss) through 1987 from the Interuniversity Consortium for Political and Social Research State Legislative Elections Study, Malcolm Jewell, principal investigator.

but not competitive have also declined significantly; the overall coefficients for the South in both chambers are significant though not strongly so, and house races report a stronger showing in this regard than do those in the senates. On the Republican side, these numbers are soundly reversed: strong significance is reported for the house races in Virginia, South Carolina, and Arkansas, and contested but not competitive races are significant

Table 10.6. Pearson Correlation Coefficients over Time for Relative Victories by Type in Southern State Legislatures, 1968-1991

State	Relative Democratic victories: uncontested	Relative Democratic victories: contested, non-competitive	Relative Democratic victories: competitive elections	Relative Republican victories: uncontested	Relative Republican victories: contested, non-competitive	Relative Republican victories: competitive elections
			SENATE			
TN	**.043**	**−.345**	**.206**	−.397	−.345	−.312
VA	*−.098*	*.175*	*−.205*	*.354*	*.175*	*−.419*
FL	**−.168**	**−.228**	**.411**	.375*	−.228	−.249
TX	*−.739****	*.422*	*.663***	*.398*	*.422*	*.006*
NC	−.642**	.239	.590*	−.434	.239	.730**
SC	−.375	.661	−.421	.776*	.661	.820**
GA	−.517*	.531*	.339	.164	.531*	.085
MS	−.346	.269	.171	.797*	.269	.302
AR	−.107	.113	.068	.821***	XX+	−.073
AL	−.797**	.772**	.816**	.252	.772**	.404
South	−.238**	.184	.206**	.224**	.123	−.081
			HOUSE			
TN	**.156**	**−.185**	**−.099**	.361	−.192	−.492
VA	*−.011*	*−.116*	*.132*	*.185*	*.498**	*−.490**
FL	**−.642****	**−.483**	**.495**	.373	.056	−.499*
TX	*−.041*	*−.084*	*.182*	*.475*	*−.085*	*−.458*
NC	*.062*	*−.071*	*−.017*	*.533*	*.117*	*−.528*
SC	*.391*	*−.390*	*−.284*	*.352*	*.324***	*−.598***
GA	−.683**	−.500*	.693**	.106	.140	−.286
MS	−.023	−.151	.106	.500	.597	−.576
AR	−.219	.272	−.049	.082	−.004	−.123
AL	−.838**	−.830**	.808**	−.292	.695	−.465
South	−.068	.032	.092	.172*	.178*	−.266***

Note: Victories are relative to other types of victories; see the text for an explanation of variable constuction. Bold indicates that the chamber had reached the 33.3 percent margin of Republicans by 1968; italic indicates that it had done so by 1990. "South" is overall. XX^+ = too few observations to provide a reliable matrix.
* $p < .10$.   ** $p < .05$.   *** $p < .01$.   **** $p < .001$.
Source: Data include raw elections figures (win-loss) through 1987 from the Interuniversity Consortium for Political and Social Research State Legislative Elections Study, Malcolm Jewell, principal investigator.

in thirteen of the twenty chambers examined. All of the coefficients are positive, with the exception of Tennessee, and the figures for the house races are slightly more prominent than those for the senates.

The relative figures for these variables (see table 10.6) are also informative. For the Democrats, uncontested victories (as expected from the earlier results) are negative and significant overall, with several states reporting individually significant results. The results for relative Democratic victories that are contested but not competitive are generally in the positive direction, in line with our knowledge of the linkage between contestation and victory: the two are not necessarily related. When we link this last figure with the earlier figures for Republican contestation, the story that emerges is that, while Republicans are entering more races against Democrats (driving the uncontested victories by Democrats strongly downward), they are still not winning, and are not even competitive, in the majority of these races. Furthermore, Republicans are more competitive in the races in which they enter a candidate than heretofore, a trend that tends to reduce the overall number of contested but noncompetitive victories by Democrats. This increased Republican competitiveness also allows these victories to still compose, relatively, more of the *total* Democratic victories (which are also decreasing over time).

Uncontested victories are rising across the array for Republicans in seventeen of the twenty chambers (the exceptions are found in the Tennessee and North Carolina senates and the Alabama House). Elections that are contested but not competitive are also increasing across this time frame; this last conclusion corresponds with the Democratic findings. It may be due to elections in which Democrats were formerly competitive but are now simply contesting, as the reported results for the marginal elections suggest.

It is clear from both the simple and relative correlation figures that, though Republicans are running more competitive races in the one-party states, they are not winning them at a great rate—yet. While the overall rates for Republican contestation are up (see table 10.3), the direction of the share of competitive races contributing to victory is downward (table 10.6). As Cassie[18] has observed, where Republicans have focused their resources on a few districts ("targeting" these), they have generally been more successful than in states where the party has spread itself thinly across a multitude of districts and elections. For Republican victories, competitive election victories make up a smaller proportion over time than do other types of victories. This finding is most prominent in house races, where the share of this type of victories in the overall array is universally negative for Republicans and statistically significant in the general context of the South— there is a suggestion here that Republicans are not only targeting a smaller number of districts in states where they are successful (as suggested above) but that they are selectively targeting races where Democrats are weak—or perhaps where the quality of the Republican candidate is high. Although I have not tested Republican success at the individual district level, this pattern of competitive election victories also seems to indicate that Republicans are not giving up seats where they have held sway over time.

The notion that Republicans are challenging Democrats more than in the past is empirically borne out by the Democratic findings. The trend among all states in Democratic victories that are uncontested is down, generally, and sharply down in senate elections. This statement is also true in elections in which Republicans have entered a candidate who is not competitive. Still, though these numbers are down, often significantly, the share of Democratic victories in noncompetitive races is positive, though weakly so, over time (see table 10.6). Again, the important thing to notice is perhaps not the rate of Republican victory but rather the rate of Republican challenges. Democratic victories in the marginal races are generally positive, as expected from the results above for Republicans. Clearly, also, this rise of contestation and competition by Republicans has had a great impact on the way that the formerly dominant party is winning elections.

The general conclusion, then, should be that though Republicans are contesting more and becoming more competitive, contestation did not—in this period—generally pay off in seats.[19] Again, I would emphasize that winning is not always everything. Republicans are clearly becoming more like their Democratic counterparts in the areas of contestation and competition, if not always in seat gains, though it is clear that the capacity to contest and become competitive is a critical element for *future* success.

Appendix: The Election Data

A major difficulty in comparing results across different states is the variation in type of electoral system utilized. No problems were posed if single-member districts or multimember districts with individual races for specific positions were used by the state. The problem is created by the free-for-all multimember districts. While some researchers[20] have noted the similarities between voting behavior in single-member districts (or multimember post districts) and in MMFFA districts, it is important to note that the two are not precisely comparable, nor is it theoretically satisfactory in the measurement of district-level competition to observe that they are and to eliminate these districts from the sample.

To be fair, it is not entirely clear what Holbrook and van Dunk did when comparing these district types. If the MMFFA districts were included in their study, then of course this complaint is invalid; this does not seem to be the case, however. What does obtain is a .87 concurrence between the two types of districts—in some kinds of analysis, this might be considered a marginal difference; I believe that full inclusion is necessary for anything approaching precision in this case. Any district-level measure that leaves out some districts (particularly of a type that is unique to the array) and opts instead to use a *sample* of districts defeats its purpose of being inclusive. As a solution to this problem in earlier work, I opted to follow Niemi, Jackman, and Winsky's approach and create pseudo-single-member districts.[21] The Niemi, Jackman, and Winsky logic is simple—pair the Democrat with the highest vote and the Republican with the lowest vote and continue the rank/order in a descending-ascending pairing. Not only does this protocol match the election outcomes properly (and probably reflects voter preference), but it also provides the best measure of competitiveness.

One problem I encountered was that in some elections the number of candidates offered by a political party does not reflect the number of seats in the election. I solved this problem by creating a syntax that asks the statistical package to count the number of possible winners (in the original data set) and then to measure the number of candidates the party has put forward in the election. The resulting computation then places a line of false data in the observations with vote set to zero and will then match it with any opposing candidate. The other obvious problem here is that there may be instances in which a party may have more than the number of winners running under its label. In these cases, I removed the candidate with the least number of votes, forming the rectangular symmetry in the data required by the package for the pairings.

Conclusion

Southern Party and Electoral Politics in the 1990s: Change or Continuity?

Robert P. Steed,
Laurence W. Moreland, and
Tod A. Baker

In large part, this volume addresses regional political change. And as pointed out in the introduction, party and electoral politics in the South has changed greatly over the past half century. Each of the chapters explores that change in some way and underscores the conclusion that, at least politically, the Solid South of the first half of the twentieth century no longer exists. In addition, there is very little possibility that it will be reconstructed in a mirror image, with the Republicans becoming as dominant in the modern era as the Democrats were in the pre–World War II era.

First, the South's social and legal systems have changed dramatically. The most prominent manifestation of this change is in the area of race: African-Americans are no longer legally segregated in the social realm nor excluded in the political realm. While race remains a significant part of the southern (and national) political landscape, as Scher et al. and Gaddie and Bullock show, the context is quite different now from the period prior to the 1960s. The struggles over the issues of majority-minority districting and affirmative action, while important, are not comparable, in terms of either emotion-laden conflict or practical consequences, to the struggles over simple access to the ballot box, public accommodations, and schools. Since the one-partyism of the Solid South was firmly rooted in the Jim Crow system, it is highly unlikely that a similarly dominant one-partyism could be established in the contemporary South in the absence of such a similarly overriding concern with racial segregation buttressed by an interlocking network of laws and social customs and practices. The declining impact of race as a factor in southern participation bias, as discussed by Cotter, Fisher, and Williams, is consistent with such a view. Even the questionable constitutional status of majority-minority districts suggests nothing resembling a return to the old regime.

Second, the influx of in-migrants since World War II has altered the party and electoral systems. Republicans moving south have been important elements of that party's regional development over the past few decades, and Democrats moving south have contributed to changing that party's composition in some significant ways. Most notably, in-migrants in the Democratic Party constitute a more liberal group than native white southern Democrats.[1] Thus, these white in-migrants, combined with black Democrats, provide the Democratic Party a core of support that can be expected to resist any tide toward complete Republican dominance of the region's political system. Additional buttressing against Republican dominance will likely come from the persistence of party identification for traditional Democrats, at least in the short run, and, as discussed by Barth and McCleskey, from the persistence of election rules, popular attitudes and prejudices, and the power of incumbency (though declining through retirements and deaths), which retard Republican growth.

Third, it is certainly possible that the remarkable homogeneity displayed by the southern Republicans in recent years will erode as the party's coalition grows and comes to include more diverse people and groups.[2] This tendency has already surfaced in some areas in the form of competition for organizational dominance between long-standing Republicans, who are usually mainly concerned with economic conservatism, and newer Republicans from the Christian Right, whose main concerns are with such social and/or moral issues as abortion, school prayer, and control of pornography.[3]

While we must acknowledge that the replacement of the Democratic Solid South with a Republican Solid South is unlikely, there is evidence that some elements of the past continue to be sufficiently strong to work significantly to the advantage of the Republicans. For example, as Black and Black have argued, conservative symbolism (for example, family values, a strong defense posture, entrepreneurial individualism, light taxation, and restrained governmental regulation), long an important feature of southern politics, continues to play powerfully in the electoral arena among the region's majority white voters.[4] Republican success in coopting much southern symbolism has been amply demonstrated by voting patterns in recent presidential elections, which show the southern white vote going strongly Republican, frequently in the 80 percent range in those elections without a southerner on the Democratic ticket.[5] Even with two southerners on the ticket in 1992, the South was George Bush's strongest region. Although David Breaux, Stephen Shaffer, and Patrick Cotter have shown that at least in Mississippi and Alabama, voters are not as conservative as many of the Republican leaders in those states,[6] a conclusion consistent with earlier research showing that southerners are not much more conservative than nonsoutherners on a range of key issues, Edward Carmines and Harold Stanley have shown that conservative whites in the South have flocked strongly to the Republican Party over the past two decades.[7]

As noted above, perhaps the best evidence of this connection between southern conservatism (at least in the symbolic sense that is so important electorally) is the recent success of Republican presidential tickets in the South. Even though such a connection does not guarantee Republican victories—as Eamon demonstrates, the megastates constitute a formidable block of electoral votes also—it does pretty much guarantee that Republican candidates will continue to run hard and to run well in the South in recognition of the presence of a receptive audience controlling a significant number of electoral votes. There is increasing evidence of Republican success in down-ticket elections as well. For example, as data presented earlier in this volume show, and as the essay by R. Bruce Anderson demonstrates, Republicans are contesting more state legislative elections with increasing success.

An additional development that points toward continued Republican development in the South is the decline of the Democratic Party. The decline in Democratic support in terms of party identification and at the ballot box has been documented for some time,[8] and a number of chapters in this volume, especially those by Sturrock, McCleskey, and Anderson, address this pattern in some ways. But the decline in Democratic fortunes goes beyond these indicators of party support, extending, as well, to such matters as party organization. For example, recent research on southern party activists at the local level in all eleven southern states points consistently to the widespread perception among Democratic precinct officials that their party's organization has not improved appreciably over the past decade; more important, perhaps, large percentages of these officials in each state see their party organization as having declined over this period. In sharp contrast, local Republican Party officials are much more likely to see their organizations improving during the past decade. Data from several states illustrate the difference. In South Carolina, 87 percent of the Republican precinct officials feel that their overall party organization has improved during the previous ten years, as compared with only 27 percent of the Democratic precinct officials who see improvement in their party's organization over the same period. Conversely, a majority (51 percent) of the Democrats say that their party organization has grown weaker over the past decade, as compared with only 8 percent of the Republicans.[9] Similarly, in Texas and Georgia, Democrats were much less likely than Republicans to see organizational improvement; in Texas, the figures were 34 percent and 85 percent, respectively, while in Georgia the figures were 33 percent and 66 percent, respectively.[10] These patterns were repeated in all the other states in the region as well, and in the region as a whole the corresponding numbers of Democrats and Republicans seeing organizational improvement were 34 percent and 77 percent respectively. At the other end of the scale, 40 percent of the Democrats say their organizations have gotten worse over the past decade, as compared with only 11 percent of the Republicans.

We stop far short of sounding the death knell of the southern Democratic Party, of course. It still enjoys a base of support and a perceived legitimacy (far superior to that of the Republican Party in the 1890s at the birth of the Democratic Solid South) that enable it to win at many electoral levels and in many areas of the region, often on a consistent basis. But in contrast to the period before the mid-1960s, its victories are less numerous and more toughly contested.

In short, then, there has been significant change in the South's political system. This change has not been, and is not likely to be, circular, simply leading to the reestablishment of the old order under a new party label, however. At the same time, there are clear elements of continuity with the past. For example, many of the same issues—most notably, racially charged social and political issues—that were historically important in the region continue to play significant roles in the contemporary southern political system. Thus we can expect change to continue but change often affected by persistent and familiar elements of a political system that still has some roots in the past. A continuing irony is that many of the elements of southern politics that have contributed to dramatic change also contribute in other ways to the persistence of long-standing political patterns. For example, the symbolic conservatism that has redounded to the electoral benefit of the Republican Party, thereby helping to fuel the rise of interparty competition in the region, may also militate against the reform of structures and practices (such as off-year elections) that retard an even more rapid rise of interparty competition.[11] This intriguing blend of dramatic electoral and partisan change and vestiges of past practices and patterns is likely to mark the South's electoral and partisan politics for some time to come.

Notes

Introduction: Changing Electoral and Party Politics in the South

1. V. O. Key, Jr., *Southern Politics in State and Nation* (New York: Alfred A. Knopf, 1949); Numan V. Bartley and Hugh D. Graham, *Southern Politics and the Second Reconstruction* (Baltimore: Johns Hopkins University Press, 1975), chap. 1; Jasper B. Shannon, *Toward a New Politics in the South* (Knoxville: University of Tennessee Press, 1949); Earl Black and Merle Black, *Politics and Society in the South* (Cambridge, Mass.: Harvard University Press, 1987), esp. 3–12.

2. These changes are addressed, for example, in William C. Havard, "The South: A Shifting Perspective," in *The Changing Politics of the South*, ed. William C. Havard (Baton Rouge: Louisiana State University Press, 1972), 3–36; Alexander P. Lamis, *The Two-Party South* (New York: Oxford University Press, 1988); Bartley and Graham, *Southern Politics and the Second Reconstruction;* James F. Lea, ed., *Contemporary Southern Politics* (Baton Rouge: Louisiana State University Press, 1988); Black and Black, *Politics and Society in the South;* Robert H. Swansbrough and David M. Brodsky, eds., *The South's New Politics: Realignment and Dealignment* (Columbia: University of South Carolina Press, 1988), esp. chap. 1; Robert P. Steed, Laurence W. Moreland, and Tod A. Baker, eds., *The Disappearing South? Studies in Regional Change and Continuity* (Tuscaloosa: University of Alabama Press, 1990); and Charles D. Hadley and Lewis Bowman, eds., *Southern State Party Organizations and Activists* (Westport, Conn.: Praeger, 1995).

3. See, for example, Paul Allen Beck, "Partisan Dealignment in the Post-War South," *American Political Science Review* 71 (1977): 477–496; Harold W. Stanley and David S. Castle, "Partisan Changes in the South: Making Sense of Scholarly Dissonance," in *The South's New Politics: Realignment and Dealignment*, ed. Robert H. Swansbrough and David M. Brodsky (Columbia: University of South Carolina Press, 1988); and David M. Brodsky, "The Dynamics of Recent Southern Politics," in *The South's New Politics: Realignment and Dealignment*, ed. Robert H. Swansbrough and David M. Brodsky (Columbia: University of South Carolina Press, 1988).

4. William J. Crotty, "Introduction: The Study of Southern Party Elites," in *Political Parties in the Southern States: Party Activists in Partisan Coalitions*, ed. Tod A. Baker,

Charles D. Hadley, Robert P. Steed, and Laurence W. Moreland (New York: Praeger, 1990), 1–17; and Hadley and Bowman, *Southern Party Organizations and Activists*.

5. Earl Black and Merle Black, *The Vital South: How Presidents are Elected* (Cambridge, Mass.: Harvard University Press, 1992).

6. Black and Black, *The Vital South*, 5.

7. Robert P. Steed, "Southern Electoral Politics as Prelude to the 1992 Elections," in *The 1992 Presidential Election in the South: Current Patterns of Southern Party and Electoral Politics,* ed. Robert P. Steed, Laurence W. Moreland, and Tod A. Baker (Westport, Conn.: Praeger, 1994), 3–7; and Harold W. Stanley, "The South and the 1992 Presidential Election," in *The 1992 Presidential Election in the South: Current Patterns of Southern Party and Electoral Politics,* ed. Robert P. Steed, Laurence W. Moreland, and Tod A. Baker (Westport, Conn.: Praeger, 1994), 197–210.

8. See Charles S. Bullock III, "Creeping Realignment in the South," in *The South's New Politics: Realignment and Dealignment,* ed. Robert H. Swansbrough and David M. Brodsky (Columbia: University of South Carolina Press, 1988), 220–237.

9. See, for example, Charles S. Bullock III, "The South in Congress: Power and Policy," in *Contemporary Southern Politics,* ed. James F. Lea (Baton Rouge: Louisiana State University Press, 1988), 177–193; and Harold W. Stanley, "The Reagan Legacy and Party Politics in the South," in *The 1988 Presidential Election in the South: Continuity Amidst Change in Southern Party Politics,* ed. Laurence W. Moreland, Robert P. Steed, and Tod A. Baker (New York: Praeger, 1991), 21–33.

10. Stanley, "The South and the 1992 Presidential Election."

11. *Congressional Quarterly Weekly Report* 52 (1994): 3230–3231; *Charleston Post and Courier,* November 10, 1994.

12. See, among others, Samuel J. Eldersveld, *Political Parties: A Behavioral Analysis* (Chicago: Rand McNally, 1964), esp. chap. 12; V. O. Key, Jr., *Politics, Parties, and Pressure Groups,* 5th ed. (New York: Thomas Y. Crowell, 1964); Everett Carll Ladd, Jr., *American Political Parties: Social Change and Political Response* (New York: W. W. Norton, 1970); James L. Sundquist, *Dynamics of the Party System: Alignment and Realignment of Political Parties in the United States* (Washington, D.C.: Brookings Institution Press, 1973); Everett Carll Ladd, Jr., and Charles D. Hadley, *Transformations of the American Party System: Political Coalitions from the New Deal to the 1970s* (New York: W. W. Norton, 1975); William J. Crotty, *Political Reform and the American Experiment* (New York: Thomas Y. Crowell, 1977); Robert Harmel and Kenneth Janda, *Parties and Their Environments: Limits to Reform?* (New York: Longman, 1982); William J. Crotty, *Party Reform* (New York: Longman, 1983); David E. Price, *Bringing Back the Parties* (Washington, D.C.: Congressional Quarterly Press, 1984); Paul Allen Beck and Frank J. Sorauf, *Party Politics in America* (New York: HarperCollins, 1992); and John E. Bibby, *Politics, Parties, and Elections in America,* 2d ed. (Chicago: Nelson-Hall, 1992).

13. See, for example, Bartley and Graham, *Southern Politics and the Second Reconstruction;* Black and Black, *Politics and Society in the South;* Lamis, *The Two-Party South;* Swansbrough and Brodsky, *The South's New Politics: Realignment and Dealignment;* and Robert P. Steed, "Party Reform, the Nationalization of American Politics, and Party Change in the South," in *Political Parties in the Southern States: Party Activists in Partisan Coalitions,* ed. Tod A. Baker, Charles D. Hadley, Robert P. Steed, and Laurence W. Moreland (New York: Praeger, 1990), 21–39.

1. Voting Rights in the South After *Shaw* and *Miller:* The End of Racial Fairness?

The authors thank Angela Peppe, M. A., J. D., and Aaron Resnick for their assistance on the chapter. This text is based on the authors' book *Voting Rights and Democracy: The Law and Politics of Districting* (Chicago: Nelson-Hall, 1996).

1. Section 1 of that amendment (ratified in 1870) declared, "The right of citizens of the United States to vote shall not be denied or abridged by the United States or by any state on account of race, color, or previous condition of servitude."

2. This amendment reads, in part, "The right of citizens of the United States to vote shall not be denied or abridged by the United States or by any State on account of sex."

3. *Smith v. Allwright*, 321 U.S. 649 (1944).

4. See, generally, Steven F. Lawson, *Black Ballots* (New York: Columbia University Press, 1976); Steven F. Lawson, *In Pursuit of Power* (New York: Columbia University Press, 1985); and Richard K. Scher, *Politics in the New South: Republicanism, Race, and Leadership in the Twentieth Century* (New York: Paragon House, 1992), especially pt. 3.

5. Quoted in Scher, *Politics in the New South*, 197–198.

6. The questions are deliberately posed as polar opposites to make a point. In fact, of course, the interests of minority and majority groups frequently overlap, and crossover voting is common. On the other hand, there are instances, especially when the minority and majority communities offer different candidates of choice, in which interests diverge, polarized voting occurs, and the minority voice finds its voice swamped under the tide of the majority.

7. *Gomillion v. Lightfoot*, 364 U.S. 339 (1960).

8. *Colegrove v. Green*, 328 U.S. 549 (1946).

9. It did so in *Baker v. Carr*, 369 U.S. 186 (1962).

10. Quoted in Gerald Gunther, *Constitutional Law*, 10th ed., University Casebook Series (Mineola, N.Y.: Foundation Press, 1980), 711.

11. See Lawson, *Black Ballots;* Richard Scher and James Button, "Voting Rights: Implementation and Impact," in *Implementation of Civil Rights Policy*, ed. Charles S. Bullock III and Charles M. Lamb (Monterey, Calif.: Brooks/Cole Publishing, 1984), 20–54; and Scher, *Politics in the New South*, for helpful overviews and detailed bibliographies on these developments.

12. *Plessy v. Ferguson*, 163 U.S. 537 (1896).

13. See, for example, Scher and Button, "Voting Rights"; *The Voting Rights Act*, ed. Lorn Foster (New York: Praeger, 1985); and Bernard Grofman and Chandler Davidson, *Controversies in Minority Voting* (Washington, D.C.: Brookings Institution Press, 1992), for overviews and additional citations.

14. See Chandler Davidson and Bernard Grofman, *Quiet Revolution in the South* (Princeton: Princeton University Press, 1994).

15. See Scher and Button, "Voting Rights," 25–27; and Laughlin McDonald, "The Quiet Revolution in Voting Rights," *Vanderbilt Law Review* 42 (1989): 1262. McDonald's piece is an especially thorough and helpful analysis of the Voting Rights Act.

16. *South Carolina v. Katzenbach*, 383 U.S. 301 (1966).

17. Scher and Button, "Voting Rights," 26.

18. Section 2 reads as follows: "(a) No voting qualification or prerequisite to vot-

ing standard, practice, or procedure shall be imposed or applied by any State or political subdivision in a manner which results in a denial or abridgment of the right of any citizen of the United States to vote on account of race or color. . . . (b) A violation of subsection (a) is established if, based on the totality of circumstances, it is shown that the political processes leading to nomination or election in the State or political subdivision are not equally open to participation by members of a class of citizens protected by subsection (a) in that its members have less opportunity than other members of the electorate to participate in the political process and to elect representatives of their choice. The extent to which members of a protected class have been elected to office in the State or political subdivision is one circumstance which may be considered: *Provided,* That nothing in this section establishes a right to have members of a protected class elected in numbers equal to their population."

19. For an especially helpful overview, see the voting rights symposium in *Stetson Law Review,* 21 (1992).

20. The Senate report accompanying the 1982 VRA Amendments attempted to clarify what constituted the "totality of circumstances." They included: "the extent of any history of official discrimination in the state or political subdivision that touched the right of the members of the minority group to register, to vote, or otherwise to participate in the democratic process; the extent to which voting in the elections of the state or political subdivision is racially polarized; the extent to which the state or political subdivision has used unusually large election districts, majority vote requirements, anti-single-shot provisions, or other voting practices or procedures that may enhance the opportunity for discrimination against the minority group; if there is a candidate slating process, whether the members of the minority group have been denied access to that process; the extent to which members of the minority group in the state or political subdivision bear the effects of discrimination in such areas as education, employment and health, which hinder their ability to participate in the political process; whether political campaigns have been characterized by overt or subtle racial appeals; the extent to which members of the minority group have been elected to public office in the jurisdiction." The report listed two additional factors that "in some cases" have been useful in establishing violations of minority voting rights: "whether there is a significant lack of responsiveness on the part of elected officials to the particularized needs of the members of the minority group [;] whether the policy underlying the state or political subdivision's use of such voting qualification, prerequisite to voting, or standard, practice or procedure is tenuous." Quoted in *Thornburg V. Gingles,* 478 U.S. 30, 36–37 (1986).

21. *Thornburg v. Gingles* (1986).

22. Helpful overviews can be found in Bernard Grofman, Lisa Handley, and Richard G. Niemi, *Minority Representation and the Quest for Voting Equality* (New York: Cambridge University Press, 1992).

23. There is a long literature, well known to political scientists and voting rights lawyers, about the possible dilutive effects of multimember legislative districts on minority residents. In brief, the argument runs that in multimember or at-large election systems, the minority vote is essentially swamped by the majority vote unless the minority vote is very large (and the majority vote correspondingly small) or there is a substantial crossover vote, so that significant numbers of majority voters

also vote for the minority candidate of choice. To the extent that voting is racially polarized, this latter condition will not occur. Some references include Leonard Cole, "Electing Blacks to Municipal Office: Structural and Social Determinants," *Urban Affairs Quarterly* 10 (1974): 17–39; Albert Karnig, "Black Representation on City Councils," *Urban Affairs Quarterly* 12 (1976): 223–242; Susan MacManus, "City Council Election Procedures and Minority Representation: Are They Related?" *Social Science Quarterly* 59 (1978): 153–161; Chandler Davidson and George Korbel, "At-Large Elections and Minority-Group Representation: A Re-examination of Historical and Contemporary Evidence," *Journal of Politics* 43 (1981): 982–1005; Richard Engstrom and Michael McDonald, "The Election of Blacks to City Councils," *American Political Science Review* 75 (1981): 344–354; Albert Karnig and Susan Welch, "Electoral Structure and Black Representation on City Councils," *Social Science Quarterly* 63 (1982): 99–114; Jeffrey S. Zax, "Election Methods and Black and Hispanic City Council Membership, *Social Science Quarterly* 71 (1990): 339–355; Charles S. Bullock III and Susan A. MacManus, "Testing Assumptions of the Totality-of-the-Circumstances Test," *American Politics Quarterly* 21 (1993): 290–306; and, in book-length form, Grofman and Davidson, *Controversies in Minority Voting*. See also, for an overview, James W. Button and Richard K. Scher, "The Election and Impact of Black Officials in the South," in *Public Policy and Social Institutions,* ed. Harrell C. Rodgers, Jr. (Greenwich: JAI Press, 1984), 183–218. A helpful overview, with citations, can also be found in *Thornburg v. Gingles* (1986) at 42ff.

24. The specific language of the three-pronged *Gingles* test (as it has become known) is as follows: "First, the minority group must be able to demonstrate that it is sufficiently large and geographically compact to constitute a majority in a single-member district. If it is not, as would be the case in a substantially integrated district, the *multimember form* of the district cannot be responsible for minority voters' inability to elect its candidates. Second, the minority group must be able to show that it is politically cohesive. If the minority group is not politically cohesive, it cannot be said that the selection of a multimember electoral structure thwarts minority group interests. Third, the minority must be able to demonstrate that the white majority votes sufficiently as a bloc to enable it—in the absence of special circumstances such as the minority candidate running unopposed . . . —usually to defeat the minority's preferred candidate" (*Gingles* [1986] at 50–51).

25. Immense problems are associated with the determination of how many minority voters or what percentage of the minority voting age population (VAP) needs to be included in order to optimize the likelihood that the district will "work," that is, will elect the minority group's candidate(s) of choice. It is fair to say that a great deal of effort and time in debate and litigation over competing district plans—at all levels—is devoted to wrangling by experts over the statistical and methodological issues involved in calculating the correct "working size" of the district. For an overview of the conceptual and methodological issues and difficulty, see Kimball Brace et al., "Minority Voting Equality: The 65 Percent Rule in Theory and Practice," *Law and Social Policy* 10 (1988): 48, and Bernard Grofman, "The Use of Ecological Regression to Estimate Racial Bloc Voting," *University of San Francisco Law Review* 27 (1993): 593–625.

26. There is a debate about the validity of this position. The counterargument is that blacks for long periods of time have voted and have perhaps even decided the

outcomes of elections—only to find that the candidate elected continued to ignore their needs and claims. On the other hand, there is some reason to think that "influence" districts can actually work to the extent that they allow minority residents to be a force in policy and decision making, even though "their" candidate was not elected. See Katherine I. Butler, "Denial or Abridgement of the Right to Vote: What Does it Mean," in Foster, ed., *The Voting Rights Act,* 44–62; and J. Morgan Kousser, "Beyond *Gingles:* Influence Districts and the Pragmatic Tradition in Voting Rights Law," *University of San Francisco Law Review* 27 (1993): 584–589, on this point. A parallel line of reasoning, in a context involving political fairness/partisanship—specifically the manner in which voters for losing candidates continue to be adequately represented in legislative halls—rather than racial fairness, can be found in another key voting rights decision, *Bandemer v. Davis* (1986).

27. Kousser, "Beyond *Gingles*" (1993), argues that the failure of the Court in *Gingles* to provide a "bright line" standard but to decide each case on its factual merits makes both legal and policy sense. It is our view, however, that the failure of the Court to address some or all of the fundamental issues outlined here created immense problems for architects of districting plans during the 1991–1992 cycle and prevented resolution of key issues raised both by proponents and by critics of the racial fairness standard.

28. The text of the Fourteenth Amendment reads in part, "No State shall make or enforce any law which shall abridge the privileges or immunities of citizens of the United States; nor shall any State deprive any person of life, liberty, or property, without due process of law; nor deny to any person within its jurisdiction the equal protection of the laws."

29. At this point we are well reminded of Justice Douglas's famous observation in *Wright v. Rockefeller,* "Government has no business in designing electoral districts along racial lines" (376 U.S. 52 [1964] at 66); and Justice Burger's outraged dissent in *United Jewish Organizations of Williamsburg v. Carey:* "The drawing of political boundary lines with the sole, explicit purpose of reaching a predetermined racial result simply cannot be squared with the Constitution" (430 U.S. 144 [1977] at 181).

30. Lani Guinier was formerly professor of law at the University of Pennsylvania. In 1993 President Clinton nominated her for assistant U.S. attorney general for civil rights. Her nomination was withdrawn, however, because of political fallout generated by some of her writings on voting rights. Much of what she had written was not considered unusual or especially controversial in academic political science and legal circles. Conservative politicians, however, effectively used the media to make her into an antimajoritarian demon, and her nomination was withdrawn. Her most important writings include "Keeping the Faith: Black Voters in the Post-Reagan Era," *Harvard Civil Rights–Civil Liberties Law Review* 24 (1989): 393–435; "The Triumph of Tokenism: The Voting Rights Act and the Theory of Black Electoral Success," *Michigan Law Review* 90 (1991): 1077–1154; and "Voting Rights and Democratic Theory: Where Do We Go from Here?" in Bernard Grofman and Chandler Davidson, eds., *Controversies in Minority Voting: A Twenty-Five Year Perspective on the Voting Rights Act of 1965* (Washington, D.C.: Brookings Institution Press, 1992), 283–292. Guinier prepared a book-length text incorporating her views in *The Tyranny of the Majority* (New York: Basic Books, 1994).

31. See Kousser, "Beyond *Gingles,*" 562.

32. It should be remembered, too, that unusual and politically interesting coalitions of minority groups and Republicans were assembled during the districting process. Many—but not all—black and Hispanic groups thought it was in their interest to promote districts that "worked" for them. Republicans also saw that "packing" minorities, especially African-Americans, into access and influence districts left heavily white districts that might well work for them.

33. "Suits Challenging Redrawn Districts That Help Blacks," *New York Times*, February 14, 1994, 1-A.

34. *Shaw v. Reno*, 113 S. Ct. 2816 (1993).

35. See the *New York Times*, June 29, 1993, p. A1, and June 30, 1993, p. A8, for useful analyses of the decision and its consequences.

36. *United Jewish Organizations v. Carey*, 430 U.S. 144 (1977). Readers will recall that *UJO* held that favoring minority voters did not necessarily constitute a constitutional violation against the majority community.

37. *Shaw v. Reno* (1993) at 2825.

38. *Shaw v. Reno* (1993) at 2825, quoting *Brown v. Board of Education*, 347 U.S. 483 (1954).

39. *Shaw v. Reno* (1993) at 2827.

40. The first three are specifically mentioned in *Shaw;* the fourth is strongly implied (*Shaw* [1993] at 2827).

41. This statement rests on a lengthy and complex bibliography; space prevents our full attention to it here. On compactness, readers are especially referred to Richard G. Niemi et al., "Measuring Compactness and the Role of a Compactness Standard in a Test for Partisan and Racial Gerrymandering," *Journal of Politics* 52 (1990): 1155–1181. Contiguity has been stretched by courts almost to absurd limits; bridges and even ferryboats have been given approval, although opposite corners at the intersection of streets have not been regarded as contiguous. See Office of Attorney General Bob Butterworth, *Memorandum of Law: 1992 Florida Reapportionment and Redistricting*, 34–35. Communities of interest are intuitively obvious and useful heuristic devices but often in practice prove difficult to demarcate precisely. And it is no secret that preservation of political boundaries, in districting, has historically often been overlooked in order to serve other purposes—such as upholding the population equity standard.

42. The *Shaw* case is not finished. It was reheard in federal district court in North Carolina; the court upheld the constitutionality of District 12. The case, *Shaw v. Hunt*, commonly called *Shaw II*, is on appeal to the U.S. Supreme Court. *Shaw v. Hunt*, No. 92–202-CIV-5-BR, 861 F. Supp. 408 (1994), 1994 U.S. Dist. Lexis 11102. A final decision is not expected until late in the 1995–1996 term. *Shaw v. Hunt*, 115 S. Ct. 2639 (1995).

43. *Hays v. Louisiana 839 F. Supp. 1188 (W. D. La. 1993)*.

44. *Miller v. Johnson*, 115 S. Ct. 2475 (1995).

45. The U.S. Supreme Court refused to hear Hays on the grounds that none of the plaintiffs lived in the district in question. *United States v. Hays*, 115 S. Ct. 2431 (1995).

46. *Hays* (1993).

47. *Hays* (1993) at 1199.

48. *Hays* (1993) at 1195.

49. *Hays* (1993) at 1216.

50. *Hays* (1993) at 1204–1211.

51. *Hays* (1993) at 1204–1211.

52. *Hays* (1993) at 1202.

53. *Hays* (1993) at 1198.

54. *Hays* (1993) at 1194.

55. *Hays* (1993) at 1205.

56. *Hays* (1993) at 1194.

57. Louisiana is a covered jurisdiction under section 5.

58. This argument is based on the "totality of circumstances" test in section 2, under which racial minorities can assert that their voting rights have been violated and can seek relief.

59. *Hays* (1993) at 1205.

60. *Hays* (1993) at 1207–1209.

61. *Hays* (1993) at 1209.

62. At the very beginning of the *Hays* decision, the judges wrote, "In its simplest form, this case poses the question, 'Does the state have the right to create a racial majority-minority congressional district by racial gerrymandering?' In simplest form, the answer—largely supplied by the United States Supreme Court's opinion in *Shaw v. Reno* . . . , is 'Yes, but only if the state does it right.' . . . we conclude that the Legislature did not 'do it right'" (*Hays* [1993] at 1188).

63. *Miller v. Johnson*, 115. S. Ct. 2475 (1995).

64. *Miller* (1995) at 2484.

65. *Miller* (1995) at 2484.

66. This became Congressional District 11, the so-called "Sherman's March" district.

67. *Miller* (1995) at 2483, 2485, 2488.

68. *Miller* (1995) at 2487.

69. *Miller* (1995) at 2486.

70. *Miller* (1995) at 2486.

71. *Miller* (1995) at 2490.

72. *Miller* (1995) at 2490–2491.

73. *Miller* (1995) at 2491–2493.

74. *Miller* (1995) at 2492.

75. *Miller* (1995) at 2492.

76. *Miller* (1995) at 2490.

77. *Miller* (1995) at 2487.

78. *Miller* (1995) at 2483, 2485, 2488.

79. *Miller* (1995) at 2488.

80. *Miller* (1995) at 2488.

81. *Miller* (1995) at 2488.

82. *Miller* (1995) at 2490.

83. *Miller* (1995) at 2490.

84. *Miller* (1995) at 2486.

85. *Miller* (1995) at 2486.

86. *Miller* (1995) at 2486

87. *Miller* (1995) at 2481.

88. *South Carolina v. Katzenbach*, 383 U.S. 301 (1966).

89. *Miller* (1995) at 2494.

90. A less charitable view can be found in Selwyn Carter, "Willful Retreat from Justice," *Southern Changes* 17 (1995): 1–3.

91. In a pointed dissent to *Miller*, Justice Ginsburg felt that because of the direction in which the decision moved, and because of the key questions it left unanswered, federal courts would become more, not less, involved in what are fundamentally state and local districting matters. See *Miller* (1995) at 2497ff.

92. There is no indication in *Miller* or *Shaw* that the preeminent position occupied by the equal population standard has in any way been modified.

93. *Miller* (1995) at 2491.

94. *Miller* (1995) at 2494.

95. *Miller* (1995) at 2488.

96. *Miller* (1995) at 2487.

97. The reason is that a vote dilution case may well rest on the effectiveness of the minority vote in aggregate. It strikes at the very heart of racial fairness, namely, whether minority voters can compete effectively and equally with the majority to elect candidates of choice. A claim of vote dilution could be based on "cracking" of a legitimate minority community by slicing it into pieces as new district lines are drawn. *Miller* (1995), at 7, suggests that this approach is not legitimate and may be grounds for legal action.

98. *Miller* (1995) at 2492.

99. *Miller* (1995) at 2486.

100. *Kirwan v. Podberesky*, 115 S. Ct. 2001 (1995).

101. Following the *Miller* decision, the Georgia legislature met for some twenty days and spent more than $500,000 attempting to redistrict its congressional seats. It failed to do so and gave over the whole enterprise to federal courts. In this instance, political realities, legal complexities, and raw partisanship failed to coalesce into a working alliance. Whether or not this same harsh experience will be felt in other southern states remains to be seen. See Kevin Sack, "Legislators Letting Court Remap Georgia Voting Districts," *New York Times*, September 13, 1995 (source: America Online).

2. Voter Turnout and Candidate Participation: Effects of Affirmative Action Districting

1. Kimball Brace, Bernard Grofman, and Lisa Handley, "Does Redistricting Aimed to Help Blacks Necessarily Help Republicans?" *Journal of Politics* 49 (1987): 169–185.

2. Charles S. Bullock III, "Redistricting and Changes in the Partisan and Racial Composition of Southern Legislators," *State and Local Government Review* 19 (1987): 62–67; Charles S. Bullock III and Ronald Keith Gaddie, "Changing from Multi-Member to Single-Member Districts: Partisan, Racial, and Gender Impacts," *State and Local Government Review* 25 (1993): 153–162.

3. Charles S. Bullock III and Ronald Keith Gaddie, "Contestation, Turnover, and Turnout in Multi-Member and Single-Member Districts" (paper presented at the

annual meeting of the American Political Science Association, Washington, D.C., September, 1993).

4. Gary C. Jacobson and Samuel Kernell, *Strategy and Choice in Congressional Elections* (New Haven, Conn.: Yale University Press, 1981); David T. Canon, *Actors, Athletes, and Astronauts: Political Amateurs in the United States Congress* (Chicago: University of Chicago Press, 1990).

5. James M. Vanderleeuw, "A City in Transition: The Impact of Changing Racial Composition on Voting Behavior," *Social Science Quarterly* 71 (1990): 326–338.

6. James Loewen, "Preliminary Report on Racial Bloc Voting, Political Mobilization, and Redistricting Plans in New York City," included in the submission under section 5 of the Voting Rights Act for Preclearance of 1992 Redistricting Plan for New York State Senate and New York State Assembly, May 5, 1992.

7. Loewen notes that, in New York City, confusion over which precinct a voter lives in can reduce turnout.

8. Maurice Duverger, *Political Parties* (New York: Wiley, 1954).

9. William H. Standing and James A. Robinson, "Inter-Party Competition and Primary Contesting: The Case of Indiana," *American Political Science Review* 52 (1958): 1066–1077.

10. Vanderleeuw, "A City in Transition"; David T. Canon, Matthew M. Schousen, and Patrick J. Sellers, "The Supply-Side of Congressional Redistricting: Race and Strategic Politicians, 1972–1992" (paper presented at the annual meeting of the Midwest Political Science Association, Chicago, April 1993).

11. See James M. Vanderleeuw and Glen H. Utter, "Voter Roll-Off and the Electoral Context: A Test of Two Theses," *Social Science Quarterly* 74 (1993): 664–673.

12. Eric W. Austin, Jerome M. Clubb, William H. Flanigan, Peter Granda, and Nancy Zingale, "Electoral Participation in the United States, 1968–1986," *Legislative Studies Quarterly* 16 (1991): 145–164; Bullock and Gaddie, "Changing from Multi-Member to Single-Member Districts."

13. V. O. Key, Jr., *Southern Politics in State and Nation* (New York: Alfred A. Knopf, 1949).

14. Peggy Heilig and Robert J. Mundt, *Your Voice at City Hall* (Albany, N.Y.: SUNY Press, 1984).

15. Charles S. Bullock III, Ronald Keith Gaddie, and John C. Kuzenski, "The Candidacy of David Duke as a Stimulus to Black Voting," in *David Duke and the Rebirth of Race in Southern Politics*, ed. John C. Kuzenski, Charles S. Bullock III, and Ronald Keith Gaddie (Nashville: Vanderbilt University Press, 1995).

16. Paul R. Abramson and William Claggett, "Racial Differences in Self-Reported and Validated Turnout in the 1988 Presidential Election," *Journal of Politics* 53 (1991): 186–197; Jonathan Nagler, "The Effect of Registration Law and Education on U.S. Voter Turnout," *American Political Science Review* 85 (1991): 1393–1406.

17. Raymond E. Wolfinger and Steven J. Rosenstone, *Who Votes?* (New Haven: Yale University Press, 1980).

18. Malcolm Jewell and David Breaux, "The Effect of Incumbency in State Legislative Elections," *Legislative Studies Quarterly* 13 (1988): 495–514; Jewell and Breaux, "Southern Primary and Electoral Competition and Incumbent Success," *Legislative Studies Quarterly* 16 (1991): 129–143.

19. Charles D. Hadley, "The Impact of the Louisiana Open Elections System Re-

form," *State Government* 58 (1986): 152–157; Thomas A. Kazee, "The Impact of Electoral Reform: 'Open Elections' and the Louisiana Party System," *Publius* 13 (1985): 132–139.

20. Jim Leggett, "'Black Max' May Lead to Polarization in State of Louisiana," *Alexandria Town Talk* (October 18, 1991), D-8.

21. Susan A. MacManus and Ronald Keith Gaddie, "Reapportionment in Florida: The Stakes Keep Getting Higher," in *Reapportionment and Representation in Florida: An Historical Collection*, ed. Susan A. MacManus (Tampa: Intrabay Innovation Institute, 1991).

22. Leggett, "'Black Max' May Lead to Polarization in State of Louisiana."

23. Bullock, Gaddie, and Kuzenski, "The Candidacy of David Duke as a Stimulus to Black Voting."

24. Examination of the variance inflation factors and regression of each predictor on all other independent variables produced no evidence that collinearity might be a problem.

25. Bullock and Gaddie, "Changing from Multi-Member to Single-Member Districts"; Bullock and Gaddie, "Contestation, Turnover, and Turnout."

26. Bullock, Gaddie, and Kuzenski, "The Candidacy of David Duke as a Stimulus to Black Voting."

27. Wolfinger and Rosenstone, *Who Votes?*

28. Louisiana Government Studies, *The Louisiana Legislature, 1992–1996* (Baton Rouge: Louisiana Government Studies, 1992).

29. Bullock and Gaddie, "Contestation, Turnover, and Turnout in Multi-member and Single-member Districts."

30. Bullock, Gaddie, and Kuzenski, "The Candidacy of David Duke as a Stimulus to Black Voting."

31. Vanderleeuw and Utter, "Voter Roll-off and the Electoral Context."

32. Key, *Southern Politics.*

3. The Impact of Election Timing on Republican Trickle-Down in the South

1. As of 1995, the GOP controls the governorship in Alabama, Mississippi, South Carolina, Tennessee, Texas, and Virginia.

2. Kevin Phillips, *The Emerging Republican Majority* (Garden City, N.Y.: Anchor Books, 1969).

3. Stephen A. Salmore and Barbara G. Salmore, "The Transformation of State Electoral Politics," in *The State of the States*, ed. Carl E. Van Horn (Washington, D.C.: Congressional Quarterly Press, 1993): 57–58.

4. A statistical analysis of the popular vote on the 1954 Tennessee state constitutional amendment moving the state's elections out of presidential election years similarly indicates no partisan impact in that no statistical relationship was found between electoral support for the Democratic candidate for governor and for the amendment at the county level.

5. The Council of State consists of the subgubernatorial statewide elected executive branch officers.

6. Malcolm Jewell and David M. Olson, *American State Political Parties and Elections* (Homewood, Ill.: Dorsey Press, 1982).

7. Angus Campbell, "Surge and Decline: A Study of Electoral Change," in *Elections and the Political Order*, ed. Angus Campbell et al. (New York: Wiley, 1966); James Campbell, "The Revised Theory of Surge and Decline," *American Journal of Political Science* 31 (1987): 965–979.

8. V. O. Key, Jr., *American State Politics: An Introduction* (New York: Alfred A. Knopf, 1956), 42.

9. Austin Ranney, "Parties in State Politics," in *Politics in the American States,* ed. Herbert Jacob and Kenneth Vines (Boston: Little, Brown, 1976).

10. Russell Benjamin, "Gubernatorial Elections: The Coattail Connection?" (paper presented at the annual meeting of the Southern Political Science Association, Savannah, Ga., November 1993).

11. Harold W. Stanley, "Southern Partisan Change: Dealignment, Realignment, or Both?" *Journal of Politics* 50 (1988): 64–88.

12. Louisiana's general primary electoral system diminishes the likelihood of contested two-party races. However, the second primary race in 1987 for lieutenant governor did face off Democratic and Republican candidates and is included in the analysis.

13. I thank an anonymous source at one of the national political parties for use of the data.

14. I thank John Haskell of Drake University and Greg Hager and David Sheaves of the Institute for Research in the Social Sciences at the University of North Carolina at Chapel Hill for their assistance with this project.

15. Arkansas, which had two-year terms for statewide offices until the 1986 election cycle, also had down-ticket races that fell in 1980 and 1984. In addition, Florida had a special election for treasurer in the presidential year of 1988 that is included in the analysis.

16. John Wildgen, "Voting Behavior in Gubernatorial Elections," in *Louisiana Politics: Festival in a Labyrinth,* ed. James Bolner (Baton Rouge: Louisiana State University Press), 319–343.

17. Focusing on the determination of coefficient measure allows comparisons across models of the degree to which variation of the independent variable explains variation of the dependent variable, allowing the analysis to move beyond the more basic question of whether or not the relationships between the independent and dependent variables are significant. While not an issue in this particular analysis, the adjusted R^2 improves upon the standard R^2 because it takes into account the number of independent variables included in the model.

18. Alexander P. Lamis, *The Two-Party South* (New York: Oxford University Press, 1988); Jay Barth, "'Opportunity Ladders' in the Contemporary South: Differences in the Quality of the 'Products' Offered by the Two Parties" (paper presented at the annual meeting of the Southern Political Science Association, Savannah, Ga., November 1993).

19. Jay Barth, "Dual Partisanship in the South: Anachronism or a Real Barrier to Republican Success in the Region?" *Midsouth Political Science Review* 13 (1992): 487–500.

20. Campbell, "Surge and Decline: A Study of Electoral Change."

21. Campbell, "The Revised Theory of Surge and Decline."

22. Merle Black and Earl Black, "Democratic Gubernatorial Runoff Primaries in the Modern South" (paper presented at the annual meeting of the American Political Science Association, Chicago, Ill., September 1987).

23. Charles S. Bullock III and Loch K. Johnson, *Runoff Elections in the United States* (Chapel Hill: University of North Carolina Press, 1992): 160.

24. Most southern states did continue to place some term limits (usually two terms) on the governors as states began to allow gubernatorial succession to occur during this century. However, typically no limits were placed on subgubernatorial statewide officeholders.

4. Changes in the Composition of Political Activists, 1952–1992

1. For information concerning the results of political participation research, see: Lester W. Milbrath and M. L. Goel, *Political Participation*, 2d ed. (Chicago: Rand McNally, 1977); Sidney Verba and Norman H. Nie, *Participation in America* (New York: Harper and Row, 1972); Sidney Verba, Norman H. Nie, and Jae-on Kim, *Participation and Social Equality* (Chicago: University of Chicago Press, 1978); Raymond E. Wolfinger and Steven J. Rosenstone, *Who Votes?* (New Haven: Yale University Press, 1980); M. Margaret Conway, *Political Participation in the United States* (Washington, D.C.: Congressional Quarterly Press, 1991); Steven J. Rosenstone and John Mark Hansen, *Mobilization, Participation, and Democracy in America* (New York: Macmillan, 1993); and Henry E. Brady, Sidney Verba, and Kay Lehman Schlozman, "Beyond SES: A Resource Model of Political Participation," *American Political Science Review* 89 (1995): 271–294. For recent research in the area of participation bias, see: Stephen Earl Bennett and David Resnick, "Implications of Nonvoting for Democracy in the United States," *American Journal of Political Science* 34 (1990): 771–803; Jan E. Leighley and Jonathan Nagler, "Individual and Systemic Influences on Turnout: Who Votes? 1984," *Journal of Politics* 54 (1992): 718–740; Jan E. Leighley and Jonathan Nagler, "Socioeconomic Bias in Turnout, 1964–1988: The Voters Remain the Same," *American Political Science Review* 86 (1992) 725–736; Rosenstone and Hansen, *Mobilization, Participation, and Democracy;* and Sidney Verba, Kay Lehman Schlozman, Henry Brady, and Norman H. Nie, "Citizen Activity: Who Participates? What Do They Say?" *American Political Science Review* 87 (1993): 303–318.

2. See, for example, V. O. Key, Jr., *Southern Politics in State and Nation* (New York: Alfred A. Knopf, 1949); and Donald R. Matthews and James W. Prothro, *Negroes and the New Southern Politics* (New York: Harcourt, Brace and World, 1966).

3. Key, *Southern Politics,* chap. 24.

4. Key, *Southern Politics,* 502–504.

5. *Statistical Abstract of the United States* (Washington, D.C.: U.S. Department of Commerce, Bureau of the Census, 1993).

6. For information concerning the changes in political participation levels in the South, see David J. Garrow, *Protest at Selma* (New Haven, Conn.: Yale University Press, 1978); and Harold W. Stanley, *Voter Mobilization and the Politics of Race: The South and Universal Suffrage, 1952–1984* (New York: Praeger, 1987).

7. Verba and Nie, *Participation in America,* 1972.

8. See, for example, Verba and Nie, *Participation in America;* Wolfinger and Rosenstone, *Who Votes?;* Rosenstone and Hansen, *Mobilization, Participation, and Democracy;* Key, *Southern Politics;* Alexander P. Lamis, *The Two-Party South* (New York: Oxford University Press, 1988); and Earl Black and Merle Black, *Politics and Society in the South* (Cambridge, Mass.: Harvard University Press, 1987).

9. Kristi Andersen, "Working Women and Political Participation, 1952–1972," *American Journal of Political Science* 19 (1975): 439–453; Susan Welch, "Women as Political Animals? A Test of Some Explanations for Male-Female Political Participation Differences," *American Journal of Political Science* 21 (1977): 711–730; Eileen L. McDonagh, "To Work or Not to Work: The Differential Impact of Achieved and Derived Status upon the Political Participation of Women, 1956–1976," *American Journal of Political Science* 26 (1982): 280–297; Kristi Andersen and Elizabeth A. Cook, "Women, Work, and Political Attitudes," *American Journal of Political Science* 29 (1985): 606–625; and Kay Lehman Schlozman, Nancy Burns, Sidney Verba, and Jesse Donahue, "Gender and Citizen Participation: Is There a Different Voice?" *American Journal of Political Science* 39 (1995): 267–293.

10. Gerald M. Pomper, *Voters' Choice* (New York: Harper and Row, 1975).

11. See Stephen D. Shaffer, "The Policy Biases of Political Activists," *American Politics Quarterly* 8 (1980): 15–33, for a national study looking at participation bias with regard to a wider range of issues.

12. These data were obtained through the Inter-University Consortium for Political and Social Research. The original collectors of the data, the ICPSR, and the relevant funding agencies bear no responsibility for the use or interpretation of these data.

13. It is important to note that this measure involves reported, not validated, vote. Validated vote measures are not available for each of the presidential election studies.

14. The 1952 study does not include the data needed to construct the campaigning measure.

15. Leighley and Nagler, in "Socioeconomic Bias in Turnout," argue that income rather than education should be used to measure social class in studying participation bias. They base this conclusion on the argument that income is more closely tied to the provision of government services than is education. We have, however, chosen to use education because it is the easier variable to measure in a comparable fashion across time. Education is also more strongly related to participation (Wolfinger and Rosenstone, *Who Votes?*). We did investigate the participation bias with regard to income (dividing respondents into high and low income categories based upon the sample median) and found results quite similar to those reported here for education.

16. Previous researchers (Verba, Schlozman, Brady, and Nie, "Citizen Activity"; Wolfinger and Rosenstone, *Who Votes?;* Rosenstone and Hansen, *Mobilization, Participation, and Democracy;* Leighley and Nagler, "Individual and Systemic Influences on Turnout"; Leighley and Nagler, "Socioeconomic Bias in Turnout") have developed and used a variety of bias measures. We have explored the use of several of these measures with the data under analysis here and concluded that they do not produce conclusions substantially different from the bias measure we employ.

17. Social desirability is a potential problem in measuring opinions about racial

issues. To minimize the possibility of this problem, we examined each of the racial issue items included in the analysis to ensure that (1) the number of missing data cases was small, (2) there was sufficient variation in the responses given to the item, and (3) a statistically significant (at the .05 level) relationship existed between respondents' race and responses given to the item.

18. Some of the social service items were asked of only half the respondents in the 1972 study. Thus in examining social service issue opinions, attention is limited for that year to "Form 1" respondents.

19. The 1952 study does not contain items that can be used to construct either a racial or social service opinion scale.

20. The appendix (table 4.A2) contains the results used in these calculations.

5. Age and Partisanship, 1952–1992

1. For excellent bibliographies of the age and partisanship literature, see Paul R. Abramson, "Generations and Political Change in the United States," *Political Sociology* 4 (1989): 235–280, and the December 1992 issue of *Political Behavior*.

2. Paul R. Abramson, "Generations and Political Change"; Paul R. Abramson, *Generational Change in American Politics* (Lexington, Mass.: D. C. Heath, 1975); Paul R. Abramson, "Generational Change and the Decline of Party Identification in America, 1952–1974," *American Political Science Review* 70 (1976): 469–478; Paul R. Abramson, "Developing Party Identification: A Further Examination of Life-Cycle, Generational, and Period Effects," *American Journal of Political Science* 23 (1979): 78–96; Philip E. Converse, *The Dynamics of Party Support* (Beverly Hills, Calif.: Sage, 1976); Philip E. Converse, "Rejoinder to Abramson," *American Journal of Political Science* 23 (1979): 97–100; Helmut Norpoth and Jerrold G. Rusk, "Partisan Dealignment in the American Electorate," *American Political Science Review* 76 (1982): 522–537.

3. Paul Allen Beck, "A Socialization Theory of Partisan Realignment," in *The Politics of Future Citizens,* ed. Richard G. Niemi (San Francisco: Jossey-Bass, 1974); Paul Allen Beck, "Partisan Dealignment in the Post-War South," *American Political Science Review* 77 (1977): 477–496; Paul Allen Beck, "Incomplete Realignment: The Reagan Legacy for Parties and Elections," in *The Reagan Legacy: Promise and Performance,* ed. Charles O. Jones (Chatham, N.J.: Chatham House, 1989), 145–171; Helmut Norpoth, "Under Way and Here to Stay: Party Realignment in the 1980s?" *Public Opinion Quarterly* 51 (1987): 376–391; John R. Petrocik, "Realignment: New Party Coalitions and the Nationalization of the South," *Journal of Politics* 49 (1987): 348–375; Abramson, "Generations and Political Change"; Warren Miller, "Party Identification and Political Belief Systems: Changes in Partisanship in the United States, 1980–84," *Electoral Studies* 5 (1986): 101–121; Warren Miller, "Generational Changes and Party Identification," *Political Behavior* 14 (1992): 333–352.

4. Raymond Wolfinger and Robert B. Arseneau, "Partisan Change in the South, 1952–1976," in *Political Parties: Development and Decay,* ed. Louis Maisel and Joseph Cooper (Beverly Hills: Sage, 1978); Raymond Wolfinger and Michael G. Hagen, "Republican Prospects, Southern Comfort," *Public Opinion* 8 (1985): 8–13; Earl Black and Merle Black, *Politics and Society in the South* (Cambridge, Mass.: Harvard Univer-

sity Press, 1987); Norpoth, "Under Way and Here to Stay"; Miller, "Party Identification"; and Miller, "Generational Changes."

5. Abramson, "Generational Changes"; Abramson, "Developing Party Identification," 80, n. 5, and 85–86, fig. 1; Miller, "Generational Changes," 337.

6. Miller, "Generational Changes," 335; Converse, *Dynamics;* Norpoth and Rusk, "Partisan Dealignment"; Abramson, "Generations and Political Change," 247, 251–252.

7. Miller, "Generational Changes," 341.

8. W. Phillips Shively, "Information Costs and the Partisan Cycle" (paper presented at the annual meeting of the American Political Science Association, Washington, D.C., September 1977), 16–20; William Claggett, "Partisan Acquisition Versus Partisan Intensity: Life-Cycle, Generation, and Period Effects, 1952–1976," *American Journal of Political Science* 25 (1981): 202; Warren Miller, "Party Identification, Realignment, and Party Voting: Back to the Basics," *American Political Science Review* 85 (1991): 557–568; and Miller, "Generational Changes," 352, n. 3.

9. Richard Nadeau and Harold W. Stanley, "Presidential Voting Defection in the South, 1952–1988" (paper presented at the annual meeting of the Southern Political Science Association, Atlanta, Ga., November 1992).

10. Miller, "Party Identification, Realignment"; and Bruce E. Keith, David B. Magleby, Candice J. Nelson, Elizabeth Orr, Mark C. Westlye, and Raymond E. Wolfinger, *The Myth of the Independent Voter* (Berkeley: University of California Press, 1992).

11. Miller, "Generational Changes."

12. Miller, "Generational Changes," 338.

13. Harold W. Stanley, *Voter Mobilization and the Politics of Race: The South and Universal Suffrage, 1952–1984* (New York: Praeger, 1987).

14. Converse, *Dynamics;* Norpoth and Rusk, "Partisan Dealignment"; and Abramson, "Generations and Political Change."

15. Miller, "Party Identification, Realignment," 559, 564.

16. In this chapter we define the South as the eleven states of the former Confederacy and the non-South as the remaining states and the District of Columbia. We define natives of a region as those who report growing up in the region. We employ the National Election Studies surveys between 1952 and 1990, excluding those for 1954 and 1962 because of the lack of variables denoting where the respondent grew up. One could quibble that "native nonsouthern whites" combines different regions that should be kept separate. We do not pursue this refinement here.

17. Philip E. Converse, "Change in the American Electorate," in *The Human Meaning of Social Change,* ed. Angus Campbell and Philip E. Converse (New York: Russell Sage, 1972), 263–338; Beck, "Partisan Dealignment"; Black and Black, *Politics and Society in the South,* 15–19; and Thad W. Brown, *Migration and Politics: The Impact of Population Mobility on American Voting Behavior* (Chapel Hill: University of North Carolina Press, 1988).

18. Miller, "Generational Changes"; Norval D. Glenn, "Sources of the Shift to Political Independence: Some Evidence from a Cohort Analysis," *Social Science Quarterly* 72 (1972): 494–519; Norval D. Glenn, *Cohort Analysis* (Beverly Hills, Calif.: Sage, 1977), 499; Norval D. Glenn and Ted Hefner, "Further Evidence on Aging and Party Identification," *Public Opinion Quarterly* 36 (1972): 31–47.

19. Unfortunately, restricting our analysis to natives cannot remedy the problem posed by contrasts with earlier years in which a regional native population includes those who have since migrated out of a region. In this limited sense, we cannot follow strictly the closed-population requirement.

20. If we calculate that the party balance for native southern whites is sixty percentage points (percentage Democratic minus the percentage Republican), and that the party balance for migrant whites is zero, then the simple growth of the proportion of migrant whites mentioned in the text would lead to a change in the party balance from fifty-six in 1952 to forty-eight in 1964. (For kindred comments about the impact of southern whites who moved into the non-South, see Converse, "Change," 314–315.)

21. Converse, *Dynamics*, 154.

22. Converse, "Change," 311.

23. Black and Black, *Politics and Society;* Miller, "Party Identification, Realignment"; and Alexander P. Lamis, *The Two-Party South* (New York: Oxford University Press, 1988).

24. Miller, "Generational Changes," 341.

25. Converse, *Dynamics;* and Abramson, "Generations and Political Change."

26. Beck, "Incomplete Realignment."

27. Abramson, "Generations and Political Change"; and Miller, "Generational Changes."

28. Abramson, "Developing Party Identification," 85.

29. Raymond Wolfinger and Robert B. Arseneau, "Partisan Change in the South, 1952–1972" (paper presented at the annual meeting of the American Political Science Association, Chicago, September 1974), 10; and Beck, "Partisan Dealignment," 484.

30. The 1962 NES survey did not include questions that would permit native southern whites to be identified. But if we take note of the overall partisanship of southern whites in 1962 (73 percent) and interpolate from 1960 and 1964 to suppose that nonnative southern whites form 20 percent of the sample, even if only 60 percent of the nonnative southern whites were partisans (a relatively low percentage for the period), there would still be a decline from 1952 to 1958 among native southern whites in the level of partisanship.

31. Donald R. Matthews and James W. Prothro, *Negroes and the New Southern Politics* (New York: Harcourt, Brace and World, 1966). Moreover, the parent-youth survey in the spring of 1965, immediately prior to the summer of 1965, marking the end of the steady-state period (Converse, *Dynamics*, 107–108), revealed the partisanship level of native southern white parents ($n = 161$) to be roughly seven or eight percentage points below the level of the same age cohort for 1952–1958 (Tom W. Rice, "The Partisanship of Native Southern Whites, 1965–1982" [paper presented at the Citadel Symposium on Southern Politics, Charleston, S. C., March 1992], table 1).

32. Sampling considerations suggest that the four-percentage-point drop may have been even larger for two reasons: the young seem to have been undersampled among native southern whites in the 1960 and 1964 NES surveys (32 percent of native southern whites in 1952–1958 but 25 percent in 1960–1964; 32 percent among native nonsouthern whites in both periods), and in 1964 the Deep South, a

region in which erstwhile Democratic whites responded favorably to the Republican Goldwater, was undersampled. From 1952 to 1960 the Deep South averaged 28.5 percent of the southern sample; in 1964, 18 percent. If the Deep South subsample had constituted 28.5 percent in 1964, the overall partisan level would have dropped another 1.5 percentage points.

33. The later percentages of independents for native whites in the South (and non-South) were 1966: 26 (29), 1968–1970: 38 (30), 1972–1980: 34 (38), 1982–1990: 36 (34), and 1992: 39 (39).

34. Richard Nadeau and Harold W. Stanley, "Class Polarization in Partisanship Among Native Southern Whites, 1952–1990," *American Journal of Political Science* 37 (1993): 900–918.

35. Philip E. Converse, Warren Miller, and Donald Stokes, "Stability and Change in 1960: A Reinstating Election," *American Political Science Review* 55 (1961): 269–280; Bernard Cosman, *Five States for Goldwater: Continuity and Change in Southern Presidential Voting Patterns* (University: University of Alabama Press, 1966); Nadeau and Stanley, "Presidential Voting Defection."

36. Stanley, *Voter Mobilization*, 159.

37. Beck, "Partisan Dealignment"; Paul Allen Beck and Paul Lopatto, "The End of Southern Distinctiveness," in *Contemporary Southern Political Attitudes and Behavior*, ed. Laurence W. Moreland, Tod A. Baker, and Robert P. Steed (New York: Praeger, 1982), 160–182; Wolfinger and Arseneau, "Partisan Change in the South, 1952–1976"; Wolfinger and Hagen, "Republican Prospects"; and Black and Black, *Politics and Society*, 20–22.

38. Converse, *Dynamics*.

39. Converse, *Dynamics;* Norpoth and Rusk, "Partisan Dealignment"; Abramson, "Generations and Political Change"; and Miller, "Generational Changes."

40. Compare Norpoth and Rusk, "Partisan Dealignment"; and Converse, "Change in the American Electorate."

41. Warren Miller, "The Electorate's View of the Parties," in *The Parties Respond*, ed. Sandy Maisel (Boulder, Colo.: Westview Press, 1990), 97–115.

42. Norpoth, "Under Way and Here to Stay"; Abramson, "Generations and Political Change"; and Miller, "Generational Changes."

43. Warren Miller, "The Puzzle Transformed: Explaining Declining Turnout," *Political Behavior* 14 (1992): 1–43; and Miller, "Generational Changes and Party Identification."

44. Norpoth, "Under Way and Here to Stay."

45. Michael Corbett, *American Public Opinion: Trends, Processes, and Patterns* (New York: Longman, 1991); and Norpoth, "Under Way and Here to Stay," 385.

46. John G. Geer, "The Electorate's Partisan Evaluations: Evidence of a Continuing Democratic Edge," *Public Opinion Quarterly* 55 (1991): 218–231.

47. Everett Carll Ladd, "Age, Generation, and Party ID," *Public Perspective* 3 (1992): 15–16.

48. Converse, *Dynamics*, 112.

49. Miller, "Generational Changes," 349.

50. Edward G. Carmines and James A. Stimson, *Issue Evolution: Race and the Transformation of American Politics* (Princeton: Princeton University Press, 1989).

51. Beck, *A Socialization Theory;* Beck, "Partisan Dealignment"; Miller, "The Electorate's View"; and Miller, "Generational Changes."

52. Wolfinger and Hagen, "Republican Prospects."

53. Norpoth, "Under Way and Here to Stay."

54. Miller, "Party Identification, Realignment."

6. Out of the Phone Booths: Republican Primaries in the Deep South

1. Robert P. Steed, Laurence W. Moreland, and Tod A. Baker, eds., *The 1984 Presidential Election in the South: Patterns of Southern Party Politics* (New York: Praeger, 1986); Alexander P. Lamis, *The Two-Party South* (New York: Oxford University Press, 1988).

2. Earl Black and Merle Black, *Politics and Society in the South* (Cambridge, Mass.: Harvard University Press, 1987).

3. This transformation was anticipated as early as midcentury by V. O. Key, Jr., *Southern Politics in State and Nation* (New York: Alfred A. Knopf, 1949), and Alexander Heard, *A Two-Party South?* (Chapel Hill: University of North Carolina Press, 1952).

4. C. Vann Woodward, *Origins of the New South, 1877–1913* (Baton Rouge: Louisiana State University Press, 1951), 372. Cited in Black and Black, *Politics and Society in the South,* 5.

5. Key, *Southern Politics in State and Nation,* 441.

6. Heard, *A Two-Party South?* 105–107.

7. Ibid., 106.

8. From interviews conducted by the author with Republican officials in various southern states, 1986 to present.

9. David E. Sturrock, "The Elephant as Tortoise? The Continued Rise of Two-Party Competition in the Down-Ticket South" (paper presented at the Eighth Citadel Symposium on Southern Politics, Charleston, S. C., March 1992).

10. This participation continued to expand in 1994, when Republican primary turnout in the seven states holding gubernatorial elections rose by 24.9 percent over 1990 levels, while Democratic voting declined 9.1 percent over the same period. Accordingly, the Republican share of the two-party primary vote in these states rose from 28.5 percent in 1990 to 35.3 percent in 1994. Especially large Republican gains (69 percent or more) occurred in Alabama, Georgia, and Tennessee, although GOP turnout also dropped notably (46 percent and 35 percent, respectively) in Arkansas and Texas. These variations indicate that cycle-to-cycle differences in the number, visibility, and resources of primary candidates can exert a dramatic influence on primary turnout that is independent of (and even contrary to) longer-term demographic or political trends.

11. Heard, *A Two-Party South?* 247–248.

12. Black and Black, *Politics and Society in the South,* 308–316; Lamis, *The Two-Party South,* 212–215.

13. Ironically, election laws in these "open" primary states stipulate that a sec-

ond, or runoff, primary (held if no candidate receives an outright majority in the initial primary) must be "closed," that is, limited to those voters who participated in the party's first primary. Happily, this complication can be ignored for the purposes of this study.

14. The large number of "decrease" counties reported for Mississippi in table 6.5 reflects the unusual circumstances of that state's 1979 Republican primary. Gubernatorial candidate Leon Bramlett hoped that his service as Democratic state chairman in the 1960s, and his close association with such leading Democrats as former U.S. senator James Eastland and former governor John Bell Williams, would draw conservative Democrats into the Republican primary. Although Bramlett lost a close race to the considerably more moderate Gil Carmichael, a county-by-county analysis suggests he did have some success in raising Republican primary turnouts above their normally negligible levels, particularly in the Delta. Judging by subsequent turnout patterns, it appears that most of these voters viewed the Republican primary as a one-time-only adventure. This episode offers further evidence that Republican primary voting habits are new enough, or tentative enough, to be significantly affected by factors peculiar to a given candidate or campaign. (Also see note 16.)

15. It can be argued that population increase will also be associated with county-level growth in *Democratic* primary voting. However, a brief, unsystematic review of these data suggests that this relationship is much weaker than the population–Republican primary correlations reported in table 6.8.

16. The 1994 metropole turnout shares were Alabama, 36.9 percent; Arkansas, 20.6 percent; and Georgia, 55.4 percent. These numbers indicate that the relative influence of metro Birmingham and metro Atlanta in Republican primaries is continuing the decline first evident in 1990. In Arkansas, however, metro Little Rock's share has proven to be highly unstable (1978, 17.3 percent; 1990, 40.0 percent; 1994, 20.6 percent). The 1990 metro turnout was inflated by the gubernatorial bid of U.S. congressman Tommy Robinson. Thanks to his earlier tenure as Pulaski County sheriff, Robinson was both widely known and highly controversial in the Little Rock area, and many of his admirers and detractors apparently made one-time visits to the Republican primary to support or oppose him.

7. Dixie Versus the Nonsouthern Megastates in American Presidential Politics

Special thanks are expressed to Cynthia M. Smith, David Elliott, Billie Humke, and Carrie Heyl for assistance and advice on manuscript preparation. Also, I am grateful to my very able graduate assistant, Michelle English, for aid in assembling data.

1. Earl Black and Merle Black, *The Vital South: How Presidents Are Elected* (Cambridge, Mass.: Harvard University Press, 1992).

2. Black and Black could point out correctly that the Clinton campaign forced the Republicans to commit resources to the South that might otherwise have gone for vital midwestern states or Pennsylvania. Furthermore, the last chapter in their

1992 book outlined a strategy whereby a Democrat, perhaps from the South, could at least carry a few southern states. With perhaps even greater foresight than they would have imagined at the time, the Blacks mentioned Arkansas and Tennessee as possibilities. They also suggested a focus on states with serious economic problems. Louisiana as carried by the Clinton-Gore ticket would fit into this scheme.

3. C. B. Holman, "Go West, Young Democrat," *Polity* 22 (1989): 323.

4. Ibid.

5. Ibid.

6. Most studies have classified these few states as the Deep South. Specifically, see Jack Bass and Walter DeVries, *The Transformation of Southern Politics* (New York: Basic Books, 1976); Earl Black and Merle Black, *Politics and Society in the South* (Cambridge, Mass.: Harvard University Press, 1987); Bernard Cosman, *Five States for Goldwater: Continuity and Change in Southern Presidential Voting Patterns* (University: University of Alabama Press, 1966); Donald Matthews and James Prothro, *Negroes and the New Southern Politics* (New York: Harcourt, Brace and World, 1966).

7. Most studies classify the six other states as the Peripheral South. However, this chapter splits the Peripheral South into two categories.

8. E. J. Dionne, Jr., *Why Americans Hate Politics* (New York: Simon and Schuster, 1991); Thomas Byrne Edsall and Mary D. Edsall, *Chain Reaction: The Impact of Race, Rights, and Taxes in American Politics* (New York: W. W. Norton, 1991).

9. Holman, "Go West, Young Democrat."

10. See Black and Black, *The Vital South;* Edward G. Carmines and Harold W. Stanley, "Ideological Realignment in the American South: Where Have All the Conservatives Gone?" in *The Disappearing South? Studies in Regional Change and Continuity,* ed. Robert P. Steed, Laurence W. Moreland, and Tod. A. Baker (Tuscaloosa: University of Alabama Press, 1990).

11. Black and Black, *The Vital South*.

12. Daniel J. Elazar, *American Federalism* (New York: Harper and Row, 1984).

13. The Dukakis campaign had been strategically outfoxed by the Bush campaign in 1988. However, longer-term forces had been working against the Democrats. Edsall and Edsall, *Chain Reaction,* trace the trend back to 1968. The Clinton campaign was eager not to be seen as overly liberal on the key social issues and at the same time did not want to alienate key Democratic groups.

14. The author's file on southern election history found Eisenhower doing well in urban areas. However, his showing was unimpressive in the Black Belt and in some rural areas. A states' rights slate did well with South Carolina Republicans. Eisenhower won majorities among blacks. This trend might reflect the close association of Chief Justice Earl Warren with the school integration decision in *Brown v. Board of Education of Topeka* (1954).

15. Walter Dean Burnham, "The Reagan Heritage," in *The Election of 1988,* ed. Gerald Pomper (Chatham, N.J.: Chatham House, 1989).

16. Black and Black, *The Vital South;* and Holman, "Go West, Young Democrat."

17. Much was made of Richard Nixon's so-called Southern Strategy. In the close election of 1968 he essentially split the South with Wallace. Nixon carried five states. Wallace carried five. The largest southern state of them all, Texas, went to Hubert Humphrey. The Southern Strategy became a central focus for Nixon after he be-

came president. Arguably it paved the way for the Republican Party to become the normal presidential party of the South.

18. It will be recalled that Black and Black saw Democratic opportunities in such states as Arkansas, Louisiana, and Tennessee. See note 2.

19. Holman, "Go West, Young Democrat," 326.

20. See George Rabinowitz and Stuart Elaine McDonald, "The Power of the States in U.S. Presidential Elections," *American Political Science Review* 80 (1986): 65–87.

8. Increasing Liberalism Among Southern Members of Congress, 1970–1990, with an Analysis of the 1994 Congressional Elections

The author acknowledges the assistance of Eric Jepsen, Tim Noble, Louis Wenzel, and Michael Falkenberg, who helped compile the data sets. Several of the themes pursued in this chapter were first examined in Layne Hoppe and Frank Giesber, "Freer Trade between Mexico and the United States: An Analysis of the Contending Forces in the United States" (paper delivered at the annual meeting of the Southwestern Conference on Latin American Studies, Merida, Mexico, 1992).

1. Louis Hartz, *The Liberal Tradition in America* (New York: Harcourt Brace Jovanovich, 1955).

2. Julius Turner, *Party and Constituency: Pressures on Congress*, rev. ed., ed. Edward V. Schneier, Jr. (Baltimore, Md.: Johns Hopkins University Press, 1970).

3. John Kingdon, *Congressmen's Voting Decisions*, 3d ed. (Ann Arbor: University of Michigan Press, 1989).

4. Jerrold Schneider, *Ideological Coalitions in Congress* (Westport, Conn.: Greenwood Press, 1979); William R. Shaffer, *Party and Ideology in the U.S. Congress* (Lanham, Md.: University Press of America, 1980); Keith T. Poole and R. Steven Daniels, "Ideology, Party, and Voting in the U.S. Congress, 1959–1980," *American Political Science Review* 79 (1985): 373–399.

5. For example, David W. Brady and Charles S. Bullock III, "Coalition Politics in the House of Representatives," in *Congress Reconsidered*, ed. Lawrence C. Dodd and Bruce I. Oppenheimer (Washington, D.C.: Congressional Quarterly Press, 1981), 186–203.

6. James A. Davis, *The Logic of Causal Order* (Beverly Hills: Sage, 1985), cited in William Buchanan, *Understanding Political Variables*, 4th ed. (New York: Macmillan, 1988), 210.

7. Laurence W. Moreland, Robert P. Steed, and Tod A. Baker, "Ideology, Issues, and Realignment Among Southern Party Activists," in *The South's New Politics: Realignment and Dealignment*, ed. Robert H. Swansbrough and David M. Brodsky (Columbia: University of South Carolina Press, 1988), 268–281. A study that finds some evidence of member behavioral change is Kenny J. Whitby and Franklin D. Gilliam, Jr., "A Longitudinal Analysis of Competing Explanations for the Transformation of Southern Congressional Politics," *Journal of Politics* 53 (1991): 504–518.

8. Linda Fowler, "How Interest Groups Select Issues for Rating Voting Records of Members of the U.S. Congress," *Legislative Studies Quarterly* 7 (1982): 401–413. For some cautions on weaknesses of interest group ratings, see James M. Snyder, Jr.,

"Artificial Extremism in Interest Group Ratings," *Legislative Studies Quarterly* 17 (1992): 319–345.

9. William R. Shaffer, "Rating the Performance of the ADA in Congress," *Western Political Quarterly* 42 (1989): 33–51.

10. Eric R. A. N. Smith, Richard Herrera, and Cheryl L. Herrera, "The Measurement Characteristics of Congressional Roll-Call Indexes," *Legislative Studies Quarterly* 15 (1990): 283–295.

11. Richard Herrera, "The Understanding of Ideological Labels by Political Elites: A Research Note," *Western Political Quarterly* 45 (1992): 1021–1035.

12. V. O. Key, Jr., *Southern Politics in State and Nation* (New York: Alfred A. Knopf, 1949).

13. Earl Black and Merle Black, *Politics and Society in the South* (Cambridge, Mass.: Harvard University Press, 1987).

14. Barbara Decker and John Stanley, "Party Decomposition and Region: The House of Representatives, 1945–1970," *Western Political Quarterly* 27 (1974): 249–264.

15. Charles S. Bullock III, "Congressional Roll-Call Voting in a Two-Party South," *Social Science Quarterly* 66 (1985): 789–804.

16. V. Jerome Stephens, "Southern Republican Congressmen: A New Breed or a Chip Off the Old Democratic Bloc[?]" (paper delivered at the Third Citadel Symposium on Southern Politics, Charleston, S.C., March 1982); Earl Black and Merle Black, *The Vital South: How Presidents Are Elected* (Cambridge, Mass.: Harvard University Press, 1992); Robert L. Boucher, Jr., and Albert D. Cover, "The Changing Nature of the 'Solid South' in the United States Senate" (paper presented at the annual meeting of the Midwest Political Science Association, Chicago, April 1994).

17. Charles L. Prysby, "Contemporary Southern Electoral Politics: Convergence with National Patterns" (paper presented at the Fourth Citadel Symposium on Southern Politics, Charleston, S.C., March 1984).

18. Charles L. Prysby, "Congressional Elections in the American South: Changing Patterns of Electoral Competition, 1974–1988" (paper presented at the annual meeting of the Southern Political Science Association, Memphis, Tenn., November 1989); Robert S. Erikson and Gerald C. Wright, "Voters, Candidates, and Issues in Congressional Elections," in *Congress Reconsidered*, ed. Lawrence C. Dodd and Bruce I. Oppenheimer (Washington, D.C.: Congressional Quarterly Press, 1993), 91–114.

19. Michael W. Combs, John R. Hibbing, and Susan Welch, "Black Constituents and Congressional Roll-Call Votes," *Western Political Quarterly* 37 (1984): 424–434; Kenny J. Whitby, "Effects of the Interaction Between Race and Urbanization on Votes of Southern Congressmen," *Legislative Studies Quarterly* 10 (1985): 505–517.

20. Bernard Grofman, Robert Griffin, and Amihai Glazer, "The Effect of Black Population on Electing Democrats and Liberals to the House of Representatives," *Legislative Studies Quarterly* 17 (1992): 365–379.

21. Richard Fleisher, "Explaining the Change in Roll-Call Voting Behavior of Southern Democrats," *Journal of Politics* 55 (1993): 327–341. Fleisher does not have district-level survey data on voters' attitudes that could explain why some districts are more liberal; instead he relies on a surrogate measure, the percentage of the vote cast in a district for liberal Democrat Walter Mondale in 1984, adjusted for the percentage of black voters in the district.

22. David Rohde, "Something's Happening Here; What It Is Ain't Exactly Clear," in *Home Style and Washington Work: Studies in Congressional Politics*, ed. Morris P. Fiorina and David W. Rohde (Ann Arbor: University of Michigan Press, 1989), 137–163.

23. William R. Shaffer, "Southern Democratic Congressional Ideology: A Cohort Analysis" (paper presented at the Fifth Citadel Symposium on Southern Politics, Charleston, S.C., March 1986).

24. Kevin B. Grier and Michael Munger, "Comparing Interest Group PAC Contributions to House and Senate Incumbents, 1980–1986," *Journal of Politics* 55 (1993): 615–643.

25. Frank J. Sorauf, *Inside Campaign Finance: Myths and Realities* (New Haven, Conn.: Yale University Press, 1992).

26. Keith T. Poole, Thomas Romer, and Howard Rosenthal, "The Revealed Preferences of Political Action Committees," *American Economic Review* 77 (1987): 298–302.

27. Theodore J. Eismeier and Philip H. Pollock III, "Strategy and Choice in Congressional Elections: The Role of Political Action Committees," *American Journal of Political Science* 30 (1986): 197–213.

28. Margaret Ann Latus, "Assessing Ideological PACs: From Outrage to Understanding," in *Money and Politics in the United States*, ed. Michael J. Malbin (Chatham, N.J.: Chatham House, 1994), 142–171.

29. Some good summary data on PAC congressional contributions can be found in Norman J. Ornstein, Thomas E. Mann, and Michael J. Malbin, *Vital Statistics on Congress, 1993–1994* (Washington, D.C.: Congressional Quarterly Press, 1994).

30. See Richard K. Scher, *Politics in the New South: Republicanism, Race, and Leadership in the Twentieth Century* (New York: Paragon House, 1992), for a review of various definitions.

31. The scores for each member, representative or senator, were simply combined into a single data base for each year. See "Ideology and the Two Houses of Congress" below for support for this decision.

32. This variable was coded only for the 1986 (Senate) and 1992 data bases; there were no reporting requirements prior to 1974, of course, and no group rating scores were available in the *Almanac of American Politics* (1982), the data source for 1980 scores.

33. It should be pointed out that, the number of senators being small overall, these scores are based on very small n.

34. These numbers are based on this chapter's definition of the South and on party affiliations of the members at the time the election returns were complete. There continue to be changes in affiliation that have been taken into account in the 1995 data used in this postscript. Some useful reports on the changes relevant here include Rhodes Cook, "Dixie Voters Look Away: South Shifts to the GOP," *Congressional Quarterly Weekly Report* 52 (1994): 3230–3232; Dave Kaplan, "Southern Democrats a Dying Breed," *Congressional Quarterly Weekly Report* 52 (1994): 3356; Rhodes Cook, "Democratic Congressional Base Shredded by November Vote," *Congressional Quarterly Weekly Report* 52 (1994): 3517–3518.

35. The analysis in this section is based on a data set created by the author, using ADA ratings for the 103rd Congress contained in an ADA press release, "ADA Voting Record Reveals Congress Divided, Stymied by Partisanship: 104th Congress to

be Most Extreme in Recent Memory," December 11, 1994; on House and Senate election returns reported in the *Washington Post*, "Election 1994," November 10, 1994, pp. A31 and A37; and on unpublished ADA scores for the first one hundred days of the 104th Congress, released to the author by the ADA.

36. Kaplan, "Southern Democrats a Dying Breed"; Rhodes Cook, "Losses in Swing Districts Doomed Democrats," *Congressional Quarterly Weekly Report* 52 (1994): 3354–3355, 3357. For an interesting analysis of the 1992 elections, see Kevin A. Hill, "Does the Creation of Majority Black Districts Aid Republicans? An Analysis of the 1992 Congressional Elections in Eight Southern States," *Journal of Politics* 57 (1995) 384–401.

37. There remain a number of internal ideological differences between southern and nonsouthern members of Congress; see, for example, Stanley P. Berard, "Realignment and Congressional Change: Southern Democrats, 1979–1990" (paper presented at the annual meeting of the Midwest Political Science Association, Chicago, April 1994).

38. David Rohde, *Parties and Leaders in the Postreform House* (Chicago: University of Chicago Press, 1991).

9. Representation and Party in the Virginia General Assembly Since the Civil Rights and Reapportionment Revolutions

1. Data for all years except 1994 come from various editions of the *Statistical Abstract of the United States*. The 1994 results were provided by the National Conference of State Legislatures. Two aspects in the long-term trend in the party makeup of state legislatures are worth noting. First, it is only too clear how costly the second Nixon administration—more exactly, I suppose, Watergate—was for the Republican Party. In 1970, outside the South, Republicans held 1,951 of 4,135 state house seats, or 47 percent of the total. By 1976, they held only 1,628, or 38 percent. From 1966 to 1970, outside the South, Republicans held a 50.1 percent majority of state senate seats; six years later, they held only 39 percent of them. The second point is related. The Republican tide supposedly set in motion by the Reagan presidency did little for that party's representation in state legislatures outside the South. By and large, Republican seats in both upper and lower chambers were little higher at the end of the Reagan presidency than in 1978.

2. This general discussion of Virginia politics, like the more specific consideration of party competition in the General Assembly, owes a huge debt to my colleague Larry Sabato. He has labored long, hard, and successfully to make politics in Virginia (and in the nation) comprehensible to scholars, activists, and interested citizens and to provide a ready source of data analysis, particularly in his frequent *University of Virginia News Letters* and in the five editions he has prepared of *Virginia Votes*, published at four-year intervals by the Weldon Cooper Center for Public Service at the University of Virginia (the late Ralph Eisenberg produced an earlier edition spanning the period 1924 to 1968). Each edition provides not only city and county returns for all federal and statewide elections but also well-informed commentary and analysis of trends and issues in the elections covered. Beginning with

the 1979–1982 volume, Sabato has regularly included discussion and data pertaining to General Assembly elections as well.

3. And occasionally hundreds of thousands of dollars. Sabato's unpublished "Highlights of the 1993 General Election of Governor" reports (p. 88) that in 1993 the Democratic speaker of the house spent $235,604 and the Democratic floor leader $193,655 in their quest for reelection. The former won with 70 percent of the vote, the latter with 59 percent.

4. For an early and discerning treatment, see Ralph Eisenberg, "Legislative Apportionment: How Representative is Virginia's Present System?" *University of Virginia News Letter*, April 1961.

5. The discussion of House and Senate redistricting procedures and politics through the mid-1970s draws heavily on Robert Jack Austin, "The Redistricting Process After One Man–One Vote: The Case of Virginia" (Ph.D. diss., University of Virginia, 1976).

6. See John G. Schuiteman and John G. Selph, "The 1981/82 Reapportionment of the Virginia House of Delegates," *University of Virginia News Letter,* June 1983.

7. This summary figure conceals considerable variation from one election to another in the importance of open-seat gains relative to those involving the defeat of incumbents. Thus in 1989, the Republican gain of four seats in the House was achieved by the net addition of three open seats and the net of one defeated Democratic incumbent. In the 1991 House elections, the GOP had a net gain of one open seat and one seat captured by the defeat of a Democratic incumbent. In 1993, Republicans defeated three Democratic incumbents while losing none of their own and held all open seats vacated by Republicans while capturing three vacated by Democrats.

8. A black female running as an Independent defeated a white male Democratic incumbent in 1985. In 1989 in southwestern Virginia, an Independent running a write-in campaign defeated an incumbent Democrat whose father as a Virginia circuit judge had imposed a huge and highly unpopular fine for contempt of court on the United Mine Workers Union. Both affiliated with the Democratic caucus in the House and ran and won reelection as Democrats.

9. The data on open seats for both the house and the senate report only those filled in general elections. Usually but not invariably, an open seat created in the interim and filled by special election is retained by the party that originally held it.

10. Electoral Competition and Southern State Legislatures: The Dynamics of Change

Thanks are due to Keith E. Hamm and John Alford for their many practical suggestions and contributions of expertise in the execution of this project.

1. Harold W. Stanley, "Southern Partisan Change: Dealignment, Realignment, or Both?" *Journal of Politics* 50 (1988): 64–88.

2. Charles S. Bullock III, "Regional Realignment from an Officeholding Perspective," *Journal of Politics* 50 (1988): 553–574.

3. Ibid., 570.

4. Robert Harmel and Keith E. Hamm, "Development of a Party Role in a No-

Party Legislature," *Western Political Quarterly* 39 (1986): 79–92; Ronald Hedlund and Keith E. Hamm, "Stacking State Legislative Committees: Does the Majority Party Always Control?" (paper presented at the annual meeting of the Western Political Science Association, Pasadena, Calif., March 1993).

5. Malcolm E. Jewell and David Breaux, "The Effects of Districting Patterns on Two-Party Competition for Legislative Seats in the South" (paper presented at the annual meeting of the Southern Political Science Association, Tampa, Fla., November 1991); Malcolm E. Jewell and David Breaux, "Patterns of Electoral Competition in Southern State Legislative Elections" (paper presented at the annual meeting of the Southern Political Science Association, Atlanta, Ga., November 1990); Malcolm Jewell and David Breaux, "The Effect of Incumbency on State Legislative Elections," *Legislative Studies Quarterly* 13 (1988): 495–514. Bullock, "Regional Realignment from an Officeholding Perspective"; Charles S. Bullock III and Ronald Keith Gaddie, "Changing from Multi-Member Districts to Single-Member Districts" (paper presented at the annual meeting of the Midwest Political Science Association, Chicago, Ill., April 1991). Charles S. Bullock III and Ronald Keith Gaddie, "Partisan Challenges in Multi-Member Districts and Single-Member Districts" (paper presented at the annual meeting of the Southern Political Science Association, Tampa, Fla., November 1991). Michael W. Giles and Anita Pritchard, "Campaign Expenditures and Legislative Elections in Florida," *Legislative Studies Quarterly* 19 (1985): 71–88. Euel Elliott, Ronald Keith Gaddie, and Gerhard S. Gryski, "The Dynamics of Republican Legislative Strength in the South: A Bicameral Perspective" (paper presented at the annual meeting of the Southern Political Science Association, Memphis, Tenn., November 1989). Laura R. Winsky, "The Role of District, State, and National Factors in State Legislative Elections" (paper presented at the Conference on State Legislatures, Lexington, Ky., May 1990). Joseph A. Aistrup, "Republican Contestation of U.S. State Senate Elections in the South," *Legislative Studies Quarterly* 15 (1990): 227–245. William E. Cassie and Robert Kirby Goidel, "Open Versus Closed Primaries in Southern States: Conventional Wisdom, Registration Laws, and Split-Level Realignment" (paper presented at the annual meeting of the Southern Political Science Association, Tampa, Fla., November 1991). Joel A. Thompson and William E. Cassie, "Milking the Cow: Campaign Contributions to State Legislative Candidates in North Carolina" (paper presented at the annual meeting of the North Carolina Political Science Association, Salisbury, N.C., March 1990). James W. Corey, "Florida State 1990 Legislative Elections" (paper presented at the annual meeting of the American Political Science Association, Washington, D.C., August 29–September 1, 1991). R. Bruce Anderson and Keith E. Hamm, "Is the South Still Different? Competition and State Legislative Elections in the South, 1968–1990" (paper presented at the Eighth Citadel Symposium on Southern Politics, Charleston, S.C., March 1992).

6. Laura R. Winsky, "The Role of District, State, and National Factors in State Legislative Elections" (paper presented at the Conference on State Legislatures, Lexington, Ky., May 1990). Laura R. Winsky, "The Effects of District and National Factors on State Legislative Elections in the South and Non-South" (paper presented at the annual meeting of the Southern Political Science Association, Atlanta, Ga., November 1990). Cassie and Goidel, "Open Versus Closed Primaries in Southern States."

7. Thomas M. Holbrook and Emily van Dunk, "Electoral Competition in the American States," *American Political Science Review* 87 (1994): 955–962.

8. Paul T. David, *Party Strength in the United States, 1872–1970* (Charlottesville: University of Virginia Press, 1972); Austin Ranney, "Parties in State Politics," in *Politics in the American States*, ed. Herbert Jacob and Kenneth Vines (Boston: Little, Brown, 1976).

9. Samuel C. Patterson and Gregory A. Caldiera, "The Etiology of Party Competition," *American Political Science Review* 78 (1984): 691–707. Charles J. Barrilleaux, "A Dynamic Model of Partisan Competition in the American States," *American Journal of Political Science* 30 (1986): 822–850; and perhaps most succinctly found in Jeffrey M. Stonecash's "Inter-Party Competition, Political Dialogue, and Public Policy: A Critical Review," *Policy Studies Journal* 16 (1987): 243–262.

10. Louisiana has been dropped for reasons of incompatibility in the election set. The runoff scenario in Louisiana is not party based and therefore does not "fit" within the reasonable theoretical confines of a study of party competition.

11. Keith E. Hamm and R. Bruce Anderson, "Contours and Patterns of Contestation and Competition in State Legislative Elections" (paper presented at the annual meeting of the Southern Political Science Association, Savannah, Ga., November 1993).

12. Malcolm Jewell, *Representation in State Legislatures* (Lexington: University Press of Kentucky, 1982).

13. For example, Joseph A. Aistrup's "Republican Contestation of U.S. State Senate Elections in the South," *Legislative Studies Quarterly* 15 (1990): 227–245.

14. To generate the over-time variables, a simple counter variable was used, with one increment for each election in the array. The n of the counter depended on the n of elections by year. Thus, Mississippi differs from Arkansas in the n of the counter, as Mississippi has a four-year election cycle. The counter allowed time to be used as a variable in the correlations: each variable (contestation, competition, and others) was computed for each year $(1 \ldots k)$ and correlated with the counter variable $(1 \ldots k)$ over the range of elections. In fact, this procedure measures not time per se (which might give the impression that for Mississippi repeated elections had been inserted in years where no election had occurred) but rather the impact of a series of elections occurring *in* time (and in sequence).

15. In a hypothetical case, party X wins forty victories in a one-hundred-seat chamber. This result means that their victory percentage, overall, is 40 percent. Of these forty victories, five won in races in which competing party Y claimed at least 40 percent of the vote; the percentage of relative victories with competitive challengers (see text) is, then, 12.5 percent.

16. I am not arguing that these changes in competition are necessarily *causative* (in terms of type of victory) at this time; I am simply exploring some of the correlative possibilities.

17. Or their elections held during this time frame, excluding special elections.

18. William E. Cassie, "More May Not Always Be Better: Republican Recruiting Strategies in Southern Legislative Elections," *American Review of Politics* 15 (1994): 141–156.

19. Table 10.5 does, however, show an increased number of Republican seats in the South during the period of this study.

20. Holbrook and van Dunk, "Electoral Competition in the American States."

21. Richard G. Niemi, Simon Jackman, and Laura Winsky, "Competitiveness in Multi-Member Districts," *Legislative Studies Quarterly* 16 (1991): 91–110.

Conclusion: Southern Party and Electoral Politics in the 1990s: Change or Continuity?

1. For example, Black and Black present data showing, for the population at large, that white migrants to the South are more liberal on race-related matters than native white southerners; see Earl Black and Merle Black, *Politics and Society in the South* (Cambridge, Mass.: Harvard University Press, 1987), chap. 9. Looking more specifically at in-migrants who are active in the Democratic Party, Steed, Moreland, and Baker analyze data showing in-migrants to be more liberal than native white southerners on a wide range of issues in the mid-1980s; see Robert P. Steed, Laurence W. Moreland, and Tod A. Baker, "Searching for the Mind of the South in the Second Reconstruction," in *The Disappearing South? Studies in Regional Change and Continuity,* ed. Robert P. Steed, Laurence W. Moreland, and Tod A. Baker (Tuscaloosa: University of Alabama Press, 1990), chap. 8.

2. For a discussion of the ideological and issue position homogeneity among Republican activists, see Laurence W. Moreland, Robert P. Steed, and Tod A. Baker, "Ideology, Issues, and Realignment Among Southern Party Activists," in *The South's New Politics: Realignment and Dealignment,* ed. Robert H. Swansbrough and David M. Brodsky (Columbia: University of South Carolina Press, 1988); and Laurence W. Moreland, "The Ideological and Issue Bases of Southern Parties," in *Political Parties in the Southern States: Party Activists in Partisan Coalitions,* ed. Tod A. Baker, Charles D. Hadley, Robert P. Steed, and Laurence W. Moreland (New York: Praeger, 1990).

3. See, for example, Robert P. Steed and John McGlennon, "A 1988 Postscript: Continuing Coalitional Diversity," in *Political Parties in the Southern States: Party Activists in Partisan Coalitions,* ed. Tod A. Baker, Charles D. Hadley, Robert P. Steed, and Laurence W. Moreland (New York: Praeger, 1990); and Tod A. Baker, Robert P. Steed, and Laurence W. Moreland, "Preachers and Politics: Jesse Jackson, Pat Robertson, and the 1988 Presidential Nomination Campaign in South Carolina," in *The Bible and the Ballot Box: Religion and Politics in the 1988 Election,* ed. James L. Guth and John C. Green (Boulder, Colo.: Westview Press, 1991).

4. See, for example, Black and Black, *Politics and Society in the South,* esp. chaps. 8, 10–11.

5. See the state-by-state analyses in *The 1984 Presidential Election in the South: Patterns of Southern Party Politics,* ed. Robert P. Steed, Laurence W. Moreland, and Tod A. Baker (New York: Praeger, 1986); and *The 1988 Presidential Election in the South: Continuity Amidst Change in Southern Party Politics,* ed. Laurence W. Moreland, Robert P. Steed, and Tod A. Baker (New York: Praeger, 1991).

6. David Breaux, Stephen D. Shaffer, and Patrick Cotter, "Mass-Elite Linkage in the Contemporary South: Results from the NSF Grassroots Party Activists Project" (paper presented at the annual meeting of the Southern Political Science Association, Atlanta, Ga., November 1992).

7. Edward G. Carmines and Harold W. Stanley, "Ideological Realignment in the

American South: Where Have All the Conservatives Gone?" in *The Disappearing South? Studies in Regional Change and Continuity*, ed. Robert P. Steed, Laurence W. Moreland, and Tod A. Baker (Tuscaloosa: University of Alabama Press, 1990), chap. 2.

8. See, for example, Black and Black, *Politics and Society in the South*, chaps. 11–12; Alexander P. Lamis, *The Two-Party South* (New York: Oxford University Press, 1988), chaps. 2–3; and Richard K. Scher, *Politics in the New South: Republicanism, Race, and Leadership in the Twentieth Century* (New York: Paragon House, 1992), esp. chap. 5.

9. Robert P. Steed, Laurence W. Moreland, and Tod A. Baker, "South Carolina: Toward a Two-Party System," in *Southern State Party Organizations and Activists*, ed. Charles D. Hadley and Lewis Bowman (Westport, Conn.: Praeger, 1995), 195.

10. Frank B. Feigert and Nancy L. McWilliams, "Texas: Yeller Dogs and Yuppies," in *Southern State Party Organizations and Activists*, ed. Charles D. Hadley and Lewis Bowman (Westport, Conn.: Praeger, 1995), 84–85; and Brad Lockerbie and John A. Clark, "Georgia: Two-Party Political Reality?" in *Southern State Party Organizations and Activists*, ed. Charles D. Hadley and Lewis Bowman (Westport, Conn.: Praeger, 1995), 141. Scher also addresses Democratic organizational decline; see Scher, *Politics in the New South*, 175–176.

11. Black and Black make a persuasive argument that this sort of conservatism among the majority of white southerners, rooted in a traditionalistic political culture and buttressed by a general sense of satisfaction with their state, their region, and their current way of life, suggests a "quiescent, acquiescent, and content mass base" in which "the tasks of political liberalism, let alone radicalism—criticism, reform, calls to prophetic justice—face formidable obstacles." See Black and Black, *Politics and Society in the South*, 229, 231.

Select Bibliography

Abramson, Paul R. *Generational Change in American Politics*. Lexington, Mass.: D. C. Heath, 1975.

——. "Generational Change and the Decline of Party Identification in America, 1952–1974." *American Political Science Review* 70 (1976): 469–478.

——. "Developing Party Identification: A Further Examination of Life-Cycle, Generational, and Period Effects." *American Journal of Political Science* 23 (1979): 78–96.

——. "Generations and Political Change in the United States." *Political Sociology* 4 (1989): 235–280.

Abramson, Paul R., and William Claggett. "Racial Differences in Self-Reported and Validated Turnout in the 1988 Presidential Election." *Journal of Politics* 53 (1991): 186–197.

Aistrup, Joseph A. "Republican Contestation of U.S. State Senate Elections in the South." *Legislative Studies Quarterly* 15 (1990): 227–245.

Andersen, Kristi. "Working Women and Political Participation, 1952–1972." *American Journal of Political Science* 19 (1975): 439–453.

Andersen, Kristi, and Elizabeth A. Cook. "Women, Work, and Political Attitudes." *American Journal of Political Science* 29 (1985): 606–625.

Baker, Tod A., Robert P. Steed, and Laurence W. Moreland. "Preachers and Politics: Jesse Jackson, Pat Robertson, and the 1988 Presidential Nomination Campaign in South Carolina." In *The Bible and the Ballot Box: Religion and Politics in the 1988 Election*, edited by James L. Guth and John C. Green. Boulder, Colo.: Westview Press, 1991.

Barone, Michael. *Our Country: The Shaping of America from Roosevelt to Reagan*. New York: Free Press, 1966.

Barrilleaux, Charles J. "A Dynamic Model of Partisan Competition in the American States." *American Journal of Political Science* 30 (1986): 822–840.

Barth, Jay. "Dual Partisanship in the South: Anachronism or a Real Barrier to Republican Success in the Region?" *Midsouth Political Science Review* 13 (1992): 487–500.

Bartley, Numan V., and Hugh D. Graham. *Southern Politics and the Second Reconstruction*. Baltimore: Johns Hopkins University Press, 1975.

Bass, Jack, and Walter DeVries. *The Transformation of Southern Politics*. New York: Basic Books, 1976.

Beck, Paul Allen. "A Socialization Theory of Partisan Realignment." In *The Politics of Future Citizens*, edited by Richard G. Niemi. San Francisco: Jossey-Bass, 1974.

———. "Partisan Dealignment in the Post-War South." *American Political Science Review* 71 (1977): 477–496.

———. "Incomplete Realignment: The Reagan Legacy for Parties and Elections." In *The Reagan Legacy: Promise and Performance,* edited by Charles O. Jones. Chatham, N.J.: Chatham House, 1989.

Beck, Paul Allen, and Paul Lopatto. "The End of Southern Distinctiveness." In *Contemporary Southern Political Attitudes and Behavior,* edited by Laurence W. Moreland, Tod A. Baker, and Robert P. Steed. New York: Praeger, 1982.

Beck, Paul Allen, and Frank J. Sorauf. *Party Politics in America*. New York: HarperCollins, 1992.

Bennett, Stephen Earl, and David Resnick. "Implications of Nonvoting for Democracy in the United States." *American Journal of Political Science* 34 (1990): 771–803.

Bibby, John E. *Politics, Parties, and Elections in America*. 2d ed. Chicago: Nelson-Hall, 1992.

Black, Earl, and Merle Black. *Politics and Society in the South*. Cambridge, Mass.: Harvard University Press, 1987.

———. *The Vital South: How Presidents Are Elected*. Cambridge, Mass.: Harvard University Press, 1992.

Brace, Kimball, Bernard Grofman, and Lisa Handley. "Does Redistricting Aimed to Help Blacks Necessarily Help Republicans?" *Journal of Politics* 49 (1987): 169–185.

Brady, David W., and Charles S. Bullock III. "Coalition Politics in the House of Representatives." In *Congress Reconsidered,* edited by Lawrence C. Dodd and Bruce I. Oppenheimer. Washington, D.C.: Congressional Quarterly Press, 1981.

Brady, Henry E., Sidney Verba, and Kay Lehman Schlozman. "Beyond SES: A Resource Model of Political Participation." *American Political Science Review* 89 (1995): 271–294.

Brodsky, David M. "The Dynamics of Recent Southern Politics." In *The South's New Politics: Realignment and Dealignment,* edited by Robert H. Swansbrough and David M. Brodsky. Columbia: University of South Carolina Press, 1988.

Brown, Thad W. *Migration and Politics: The Impact of Population Mobility on American Voting Behavior*. Chapel Hill: University of North Carolina Press, 1988.

Bullock, Charles S., III. "Congressional Roll-Call Voting in a Two-Party South." *Social Science Quarterly* 66 (1985): 789–804.

———. "Redistricting and Changes in the Partisan and Racial Composition of Southern Legislators." *State and Local Government Review* 19 (1987): 62–67.

———. "Creeping Realignment in the South." In *The South's New Politics: Realignment and Dealignment,* edited by Robert H. Swansbrough and David M. Brodsky. Columbia: University of South Carolina Press, 1988.

———. "Regional Realignment from an Officeholding Perspective." *Journal of Politics* 50 (1988): 553–574.

——. "The South in Congress: Power and Policy." In *Contemporary Southern Politics*, edited by James F. Lea. Baton Rouge: Louisiana State University Press, 1988.

Bullock, Charles S., III, and Ronald K. Gaddie. "Changing from Multi-Member to Single-Member Districts: Partisan, Racial, and Gender Impacts." *State and Local Government Review* 25 (1993): 153–162.

Bullock, Charles S., III, and Loch Johnson. *Runoff Elections in the United States*. Chapel Hill: University of North Carolina Press, 1992.

Bullock, Charles S., III, and Susan A. MacManus. "Testing Assumptions of the Totality-Of-The-Circumstances Test." *American Politics Quarterly* 21 (1993): 290–306.

Burnham, Walter Dean. "The Reagan Heritage." In *The Election of 1988*, edited by Gerald Pomper. Chatham, N.J.: Chatham House, 1989.

——. "The Legacy of George Bush: Travails of an Understudy." In *The Election of 1992*, edited by Gerald Pomper. Chatham, N.J.: Chatham House, 1993.

Button, James W., and Richard K. Scher. "The Election and Impact of Black Officials in the South." In *Public Policy and Social Institutions*, edited by Harrell C. Rodgers, Jr. Greenwich, Conn.: JAI Press, 1984.

Campbell, Angus. "Surge and Decline: A Study of Electoral Change." In *Elections and the Political Order*, edited by Angus Campbell, et al. New York: Wiley, 1966.

Campbell, James. "The Revised Theory of Surge and Decline." *American Journal of Political Science* 31 (1987): 965–979.

Canon, David T. *Actors, Athletes, and Astronauts: Political Amateurs in the United States Congress*. Chicago: University of Chicago Press, 1990.

Carmines, Edward G., and Harold W. Stanley. "Ideological Realignment in the American South: Where Have All the Conservatives Gone?" In *The Disappearing South? Studies in Regional Change and Continuity*, edited by Robert P. Steed, Laurence W. Moreland, and Tod A. Baker. Tuscaloosa: University of Alabama Press, 1990.

Carmines, Edward G., and James A. Stimson. *Issue Evolution: Race and the Transformation of American Politics*. Princeton: Princeton University Press, 1989.

Cassie, William E. "More May Not Always Be Better: Republican Recruiting Strategies in Southern Legislative Elections." *American Review of Politics* 15 (1994): 141–156.

Claggett, William. "Partisan Acquisition Versus Partisan Intensity: Life-Cycle, Generation, and Period Effects, 1952–1976." *American Journal of Political Science* 25 (1981): 193–214.

Cole, Leonard. "Electing Blacks to Municipal Office: Structural and Social Determinants." *Urban Affairs Quarterly* 10 (1974): 17–39.

Combs, Michael W., John R. Hibbing, and Susan Welch. "Black Constituents and Congressional Roll-Call Votes." *Western Political Quarterly* 37 (1984): 424–434.

Converse, Philip E. "Change in the American Electorate." In *The Human Meaning of Social Change*, edited by Angus Campbell and Philip E. Converse. New York: Russell Sage, 1972.

——. *The Dynamics of Party Support*. Beverly Hills, Calif.: Sage, 1976.

——. "Rejoinder to Abramson." *American Journal of Political Science* 23 (1979): 97–100.

Converse, Philip E., Warren Miller, and Donald Stokes. "Stability and Change in 1960: A Reinstating Election." *American Political Science Review* 55 (1961): 269–280.

Conway, M. Margaret. *Political Participation in the United States*. Washington, D.C.: Congressional Quarterly Press, 1991.

Corbett, Michael. *American Public Opinion: Trends, Processes, and Patterns*. New York: Longman, 1991.

Cosman, Bernard. *Five States for Goldwater: Continuity and Change in Southern Presidential Voting Patterns*. University: University of Alabama Press, 1966.

Crotty, William J. *Political Reform and the American Experiment*. New York: Thomas Y. Crowell, 1977.

———. *Party Reform*. New York: Longman, 1983.

———. "Introduction: The Study of Southern Party Elites." In *Political Parties in the Southern States: Party Activists in Partisan Coalitions*, edited by Tod A. Baker, Charles D. Hadley, Robert P. Steed, and Laurence W. Moreland. New York: Praeger, 1990.

David, Paul T. *Party Strength in the United States, 1872–1970*. Charlottesville: University of Virginia Press, 1972.

Davidson, Chandler, and Bernard Grofman. *Quiet Revolution in the South*. Princeton: Princeton University Press, 1994.

Davidson, Chandler, and George Korbel. "At-Large Elections and Minority-Group Representation: A Re-examination of Historical and Contemporary Evidence." *Journal of Politics* 43 (1981): 982–1005.

Decker, Barbara, and John Stanley. "Party Decomposition and Region: The House of Representatives, 1945–1970." *Western Political Quarterly* 27 (1974): 249–264.

Dionne, E. J., Jr. *Why Americans Hate Politics*. New York: Simon and Schuster, 1991.

"Dixie Voters Look Away: South Shifts to the GOP." *Congressional Quarterly Weekly Report* 44 (1994): 3230–3231.

Duverger, Maurice. *Political Parties*. New York: Wiley, 1954.

Edsall, Thomas Byrne, and Mary D. Edsall. *Chain Reaction: The Impact of Race, Rights, and Taxes in American Politics*. New York: W. W. Norton, 1991.

Eismeier, Theodore J., and Philip H. Pollock III. "Strategy and Choice in Congressional Elections: The Role of Political Action Committees." *American Journal of Political Science* 30 (1986): 197–213.

Elazar, Daniel J. *American Federalism*. New York: Harper and Row, 1984.

Eldersveld, Samuel J. *Political Parties: A Behavioral Analysis*. Chicago: Rand McNally, 1964.

Engstrom, Richard, and Michael McDonald. "The Election of Blacks to City Councils." *American Political Science Review* 75 (1981): 344–354.

Erikson, Robert S., and Gerald C. Wright. "Voters, Candidates, and Issues in Congressional Elections." In *Congress Reconsidered*, edited by Lawrence C. Dodd and Bruce I. Oppenheimer. Washington, D.C.: Congressional Quarterly Press, 1993.

Feigert, Frank B., and Nancy L. McWilliams. "Texas: Yeller Dogs and Yuppies." In *Southern State Party Organizations and Activists*, edited by Charles D. Hadley and Lewis Bowman. Westport, Conn.: Praeger, 1995.

Fleisher, Richard. "Explaining the Change in Roll-Call Voting Behavior of Southern Democrats." *Journal of Politics* 55 (1993): 327–341.

Foster, Lorn, ed. *The Voting Rights Act*. New York: Praeger, 1985.

Fowler, Linda. "How Interest Groups Select Issues for Rating Voting Records of Members of the U.S. Congress." *Legislative Studies Quarterly* 7 (1982): 401–413.

Garrow, David J. *Protest at Selma*. New Haven, Conn.: Yale University Press, 1978.

Geer, John G. "The Electorate's Partisan Evaluations: Evidence of a Continuing Democratic Edge." *Public Opinion Quarterly* 55 (1991): 218–231.

Giles, Michael W., and Anita Pritchard. "Campaign Expenditures and Legislative Elections in Florida." *Legislative Studies Quarterly* 10 (1985): 71–88.

Glenn, Norval D. "Sources of the Shift to Political Independence: Some Evidence from a Cohort Analysis." *Social Science Quarterly* 72 (1972): 494–519.

———. *Cohort Analysis*. Beverly Hills, Calif.: Sage, 1977.

Glenn, Norval D., and Ted Hefner. "Further Evidence on Aging and Party Identification." *Public Opinion Quarterly* 36 (1972): 31–47.

Grier, Kevin B., and Michael Munger. "Comparing Interest Group PAC Contributions to House and Senate Incumbents, 1980–1986." *Journal of Politics* 55 (1993): 615–643.

Grofman, Bernard, and Chandler Davidson. *Controversies in Minority Voting: A Twenty-Five-Year Perspective on the Voting Rights Act of 1965*. Washington, D.C.: Brookings Institution Press, 1992.

Grofman, Bernard, Robert Griffin, and Amihai Glazer. "The Effect of Black Population on Electing Democrats and Liberals to the House of Representatives." *Legislative Studies Quarterly* 17 (1992): 365–379.

Grofman, Bernard, Lisa Handley, and Richard G. Niemi. *Minority Representation and the Quest for Voting Equality*. New York: Cambridge University Press, 1992.

Guinier, Lani. *The Tyranny of the Majority*. New York: Basic Books, 1994.

Hadley, Charles D. "The Impact of the Louisiana Open Elections System Reform." *State Government* 58 (1986): 152–157.

Hadley, Charles D., and Lewis Bowman, eds. *Southern State Party Organizations and Activists*. Westport, Conn.: Praeger, 1995.

Harmel, Robert, and Keith E. Hamm. "Development of a Party Role in a No-Party Legislature." *Western Political Quarterly* 39 (1986): 79–92.

Harmel, Robert, and Kenneth Janda. *Parties and Their Environments: Limits to Reform?* New York: Longman, 1982.

Hartz, Louis. *The Liberal Tradition in America*. New York: Harcourt Brace Jovanovich, 1955.

Havard, William C. "The South: A Shifting Perspective." In *The Changing Politics of the South*, edited by William C. Havard. Baton Rouge: Louisiana State University Press, 1972.

Heard, Alexander. *A Two-Party South?* Chapel Hill: University of North Carolina Press, 1952.

Heilig, Peggy, and Robert J. Mundt. *Your Voice at City Hall*. Albany, N.Y.: SUNY Press, 1984.

Herrera, Richard. "The Understanding of Ideological Labels by Political Elites: A Research Note." *Western Political Quarterly* 45 (1992): 1021–1035.

Hill, Kevin A. "Does the Creation of Majority Black Districts Aid Republicans? An Analysis of the 1992 Congressional Elections in Eight Southern States." *Journal of Politics* 57 (1995): 384–401.

Holbrook, Thomas M., and Emily van Dunk. "Electoral Competition in the American States." *American Political Science Review* 87 (1994): 955–962.

Jacobson, Gary C., and Samuel Kernell. *Strategy and Choice in Congressional Elections*. New Haven, Conn.: Yale University Press, 1981.

Jewell, Malcolm. *Representation in State Legislatures*. Lexington: University Press of Kentucky, 1982.

Jewell, Malcolm, and David Breaux. "The Effect of Incumbency on State Legislative Elections." *Legislative Studies Quarterly* 13 (1988): 495–514.

———. "Southern Primary and Electoral Competition and Incumbent Success." *Legislative Studies Quarterly* 16 (1991): 129–143.

Jewell, Malcolm, and David M. Olson. *American State Political Parties and Elections*. Homewood, Ill.: Dorsey Press, 1982.

Karnig, Albert. "Black Representation on City Councils." *Urban Affairs Quarterly* 12 (1976): 223–242.

Karnig, Albert, and Susan Welch. "Electoral Structure and Black Representation on City Councils." *Social Science Quarterly* 63 (1982): 99–114.

Kazee, Thomas A. "The Impact of Electoral Reform: 'Open Elections' and the Louisiana Party System." *Publius* 13 (1985): 132–139.

Keith, Bruce E., David B. Magleby, Candice J. Nelson, Elizabeth Orr, Mark C. Westlye, and Raymond E. Wolfinger. *The Myth of the Independent Voter*. Berkeley: University of California Press, 1992.

Key, V. O., Jr. *American State Politics: An Introduction*. New York: Alfred A. Knopf, 1956.

———. *Politics, Parties, and Pressure Groups*. 5th ed. New York: Thomas Y. Crowell. 1964.

———. *Southern Politics in State and Nation*. New York: Alfred A. Knopf, 1949.

Kingdon, John. *Congressmen's Voting Decisions*. Ann Arbor: University of Michigan Press, 1989.

Kuzenski, John C., Charles S. Bullock III, and Ronald Keith Gaddie, eds. *David Duke and the Rebirth of Race in Southern Politics*. Nashville: Vanderbilt University Press, 1995.

Ladd, Everett Carll, Jr. *American Political Parties: Social Change and Political Response*. New York: W. W. Norton, 1970.

———. "Age, Generation, and Party ID." *Public Perspective* 3 (1992): 15–16.

Ladd, Everett Carll, Jr., and Charles D. Hadley. *Transformations of the American Party System: Political Coalitions from the New Deal to the 1970s*. New York: W. W. Norton, 1975.

Lamis, Alexander P. *The Two-Party South*. New York: Oxford University Press, 1988.

Latus, Margaret Ann. "Assessing Ideological PACs: From Outrage to Understanding." In *Money and Politics in the United States*, edited by Michael J. Malbin. Chatham, N.J.: Chatham House, 1994.

Lawson, Steven F. *Black Ballots*. New York: Columbia University Press, 1976.

———. *In Pursuit of Power*. New York: Columbia University Press, 1985.

Lea, James F., ed. *Contemporary Southern Politics*. Baton Rouge: Louisiana State University Press, 1988.

Leighley, Jan E., and Jonathan Nagler. "Individual and Systemic Influences on Turnout: Who Votes? 1984." *Journal of Politics* 54 (1992): 718–740.

———. "Socioeconomic Bias in Turnout, 1964–1988: The Voters Remain the Same." *American Political Science Review* 86 (1992): 725–736.

Lockerbie, Brad, and John A. Clark. "Georgia: Two-Party Political Reality?" In *Southern State Party Organizations and Activists,* edited by Charles D. Hadley and Lewis Bowman. Westport, Conn.: Praeger, 1995.

McDonagh, Eileen L. "To Work or Not to Work: The Differential Impact of Achieved and Derived Status upon the Political Participation of Women, 1956–1976." *American Journal of Political Science* 26 (1982): 280–297.

MacManus, Susan. "City Council Election Procedures and Minority Representation: Are They Related?" *Social Science Quarterly* 59 (1978): 153–161.

———, ed. *Reapportionment and Representation in Florida: An Historical Collection.* Tampa, Fla.: Intrabay Innovation Institute, 1991.

Matthews, Donald R., and James W. Prothro. *Negroes and the New Southern Politics.* New York: Harcourt, Brace and World, 1966.

Milbrath, Lester W., and M. L. Goel. *Political Participation.* 2d ed. Chicago: Rand McNally, 1977.

Miller, Warren. "Party Identification and Political Belief Systems: Changes in Partisanship in the United States, 1980–84." *Electoral Studies* 5 (1986): 101–121.

———. "The Electorate's View of the Parties." In *The Parties Respond,* edited by Sandy Maisel. Boulder, Colo.: Westview Press, 1990.

———. "Party Identification, Realignment, and Party Voting: Back to the Basics." *American Political Science Review* 85 (1991): 557–568.

———. "Generational Changes and Party Identification." *Political Behavior* 14 (1992): 333–352.

———. "The Puzzle Transformed: Explaining Declining Turnout." *Political Behavior* 14 (1992): 1–43.

Moreland, Laurence W., Robert P. Steed, and Tod A. Baker. "Ideology, Issues, and Realignment Among Southern Party Activists." In *The South's New Politics: Realignment and Dealignment,* edited by Robert H. Swansbrough and David M. Brodsky. Columbia: University of South Carolina Press, 1988.

———, eds. *The 1988 Presidential Election in the South: Continuity Amidst Change in Southern Party Politics.* New York: Praeger, 1991.

Nadeau, Richard, and Harold W. Stanley. "Class Polarization in Partisanship Among Native Southern Whites, 1952–1990." *American Journal of Political Science* 37 (1993): 900–918.

Nagler, Jonathan. "The Effect of Registration Law and Education on U.S. Voter Turnout." *American Political Science Review* 85 (1991): 1393–1406.

Niemi, Richard G., et al. "Measuring Compactness and the Role of a Compactness Standard in a Test for Partisan and Racial Gerrymandering." *Journal of Politics* 52 (1990): 1155–1181.

Norpoth, Helmut. "Under Way and Here to Stay: Party Realignment in the 1980s?" *Public Opinion Quarterly* 51 (1987): 376–391.

Norpoth, Helmut, and Jerrold G. Rusk. "Partisan Dealignment in the American Electorate." *American Political Science Review* 76 (1982): 522–537.

Ornstein, Norman J., Thomas E. Mann, and Michael J. Malbin. *Vital Statistics on Congress, 1993–1994.* Washington, D.C.: Congressional Quarterly Press, 1994.

Patterson, Samuel C., and Gregory A. Caldiera. "The Etiology of Party Competition." *American Political Science Review* 78 (1984): 691–707.

Petrocik, John R. "Realignment: New Party Coalitions and the Nationalization of the South." *Journal of Politics* 49 (1987): 348–375.

Phillips, Kevin. *The Emerging Republican Majority*. Garden City, N.Y.: Anchor Books, 1969.

Pomper, Gerald M. *Voters' Choice*. New York: Harper and Row, 1975.

Poole, Keith T., and R. Steven Daniels. "Ideology, Party, and Voting in the U.S. Congress, 1959–1980." *American Political Science Review* 79 (1985): 373–399.

Poole, Keith T., Thomas Romer, and Howard Rosenthal. "The Revealed Preferences of Political Action Committees." *American Economic Review* 77 (1987): 298–302.

Price, David E. *Bringing Back the Parties*. Washington, D.C.: Congressional Quarterly Press, 1984.

Rabinowitz, George, and Stuart Elaine McDonald. "The Power of the States in U.S. Presidential Elections." *American Political Science Review* 80 (1986): 65–87.

Ranney, Austin. "Parties in State Politics." In *Politics in the American States*, edited by Herbert Jacob and Kenneth Vines. Boston: Little, Brown, 1976.

Rohde, David. "Something's Happening Here; What It Is Ain't Exactly Clear." In *Home Style and Washington Work: Studies in Congressional Politics*, edited by Morris P. Fiorina and David W. Rohde. Ann Arbor: University of Michigan Press, 1989.

———. *Parties and Leaders in the Postreform House*. Chicago: University of Chicago Press, 1991.

Rosenstone, Steven J., and John Mark Hansen. *Mobilization, Participation, and Democracy in America*. New York: Macmillan, 1993.

Salmore, Stephen A., and Barbara G. Salmore. "The Transformation of State Electoral Politics." In *The State of the States*, edited by Carl E. Van Horn. Washington, D.C.: Congressional Quarterly Press, 1993.

Scher, Richard K. *Politics in the New South: Republicanism, Race, and Leadership in the Twentieth Century*. New York: Paragon House, 1992.

Scher, Richard K., and James Button. "Voting Rights: Implementation and Impact." In *Implementation of Civil Rights Policy*, edited by Charles S. Bullock III and Charles M. Lamb. Monterey, Calif.: Brooks/Cole Publishing, 1984.

Schlozman, Kay Lehman, Nancy Burns, Sidney Verba, and Jesse Donahue. "Gender and Citizen Participation: Is There a Different Voice?" *American Journal of Political Science* 39 (1995): 267–293.

Schneider, Jerrold. *Ideological Coalitions in Congress*. Westport, Conn.: Greenwood Press, 1979.

Shaffer, Stephen D. "The Policy Biases of Political Activists." *American Politics Quarterly* 8 (1980): 15–33.

Shaffer, William R. *Party and Ideology in the U.S. Congress*. Lanham, Md.: University Press of America, 1980.

———. "Rating the Performance of the ADA in Congress." *Western Political Quarterly* 42 (1989): 33–51.

Shannon, Jasper Berry. *Toward a New Politics in the South*. Knoxville: University of Tennessee Press, 1949.

Smith, Eric R. A. N., Richard Herrera, and Cheryl L. Herrera. "The Measurement

Characteristics of Congressional Roll-Call Indexes." *Legislative Studies Quarterly* 15 (1990): 283–295.

Sorauf, Frank J. *Inside Campaign Finance: Myths and Realities*. New Haven, Conn.: Yale University Press, 1992.

Standing, William H., and James A. Robinson. "Inter-Party Competition and Primary Contesting: The Case of Indiana." *American Political Science Review* 52 (1958): 1066–1077.

Stanley, Harold W. *Voter Mobilization and the Politics of Race: The South and Universal Suffrage, 1952–1984*. New York: Praeger, 1987.

———. "Southern Partisan Change: Dealignment, Realignment, or Both?" *Journal of Politics* 50 (1988): 64–88.

———. "The Reagan Legacy and Party Politics in the South." In *The 1988 Presidential Election in the South: Continuity Amidst Change in Southern Party Politics*, edited by Laurence W. Moreland, Robert P. Steed, and Tod A. Baker. New York: Praeger, 1991.

———. "The South and the 1992 Presidential Election." In *The 1992 Presidential Election in the South: Current Patterns of Southern Party and Electoral Politics*, edited by Robert P. Steed, Laurence W. Moreland, and Tod A. Baker. Westport, Conn.: Praeger, 1994.

Stanley, Harold W., and David S. Castle. "Partisan Changes in the South: Making Sense of Scholarly Dissonance." In *The South's New Politics: Realignment and Dealignment*, edited by Robert H. Swansbrough and David M. Brodsky. Columbia: University of South Carolina Press, 1988.

Steed, Robert P. "Party Reform, the Nationalization of American Politics, and Party Change in the South." In *Political Parties in the Southern States: Party Activists in Partisan Coalitions*, edited by Tod A. Baker, Charles D. Hadley, Robert P. Steed, and Laurence W. Moreland. New York: Praeger, 1990.

———. "Southern Electoral Politics as Prelude to the 1992 Elections." In *The 1992 Presidential Election in the South: Current Patterns of Southern Party and Electoral Politics*, edited by Robert P. Steed, Laurence W. Moreland, and Tod A. Baker. Westport, Conn.: Praeger, 1994.

Steed, Robert P., and John McGlennon. "A 1988 Postscript: Continuing Coalitional Diversity." In *Political Parties in the Southern States: Party Activists in Partisan Coalitions*, edited by Tod A. Baker, Charles D. Hadley, Robert P. Steed, and Laurence W. Moreland. New York: Praeger, 1990.

Steed, Robert P., Laurence W. Moreland, and Tod. A Baker. "South Carolina: Toward a Two-Party System." In *Southern States Party Organizations and Activists*, edited by Charles D. Hadley and Lewis Bowman. Westport, Conn.: Praeger, 1995.

———, eds. *The 1984 Presidential Election in the South: Patterns of Southern Party Politics*. New York: Praeger, 1986.

———, eds. *The Disappearing South? Studies in Regional Change and Continuity*. Tuscaloosa: University of Alabama Press, 1990.

———, eds. "Searching for the Mind of the South in the Second Reconstruction. In *The Disappearing South? Studies in Regional Change and Continuity*, edited by Robert P. Steed, Laurence W. Moreland, and Tod A. Baker. Tuscaloosa: University of Alabama Press, 1990.

———, eds. *The 1992 Presidential Election in the South: Current Patterns of Party and Electoral Politics*. Westport, Conn.: Praeger, 1994.

Stonecash, Jeffrey M. "Inter-Party Competition, Political Dialogue, and Public Policy: A Critical Review." *Policy Studies Journal* 16 (1987): 243–262.

Sundquist, James L. *Dynamics of the Party System: Alignment and Realignment of Political Parties in the United States*. Washington, D.C.: Brookings Institution Press, 1973.

Swansbrough, Robert H., and David M. Brodsky, eds. *The South's New Politics: Realignment and Dealignment*. Columbia: University of South Carolina Press, 1988.

Turner, Julius. *Party and Constituency: Pressures on Congress*. Rev. ed. Edited by Edward V. Schneier, Jr. Baltimore, Md.: Johns Hopkins University Press, 1970.

Vanderleeuw, James M. "A City in Transition: The Impact of Changing Racial Composition on Voting Behavior." *Social Science Quarterly* 71 (1990): 326–338.

Vanderleeuw, James M., and Glen H. Utter. "Voter Roll-Off and the Electoral Context: A Test of Two Theses." *Social Science Quarterly* 74 (1993): 664–673.

Verba, Sidney, and Norman H. Nie. *Participation in America*. New York: Harper and Row, 1972.

Verba, Sidney, Norman H. Nie, and Jae-on Kim. *Participation and Social Equality*. Chicago: University of Chicago Press, 1978.

Verba, Sidney, Kay Lehman Schlozman, Henry Brady, and Norman H. Nie. "Citizen Activity: Who Participates? What Do They Say?" *American Political Science Review* 87 (1993): 303–318.

Welch, Susan. "Women as Political Animals? A Test of Some Explanations for Male-Female Political Participation Differences." *American Journal of Political Science* 21 (1977): 711–730.

Whitby, Kenny J. "Effects of the Interaction Between Race and Urbanization on Votes of Southern Congressmen." *Legislative Studies Quarterly* 10 (1985): 505–517.

Whitby, Kenny J., and Franklin D. Gilliam, Jr. "A Longitudinal Analysis of Competing Explanations for the Transformation of Southern Congressional Politics." *Journal of Politics* 53 (1991): 504–518.

Wildgen, John. "Voting Behavior in Gubernatorial Elections." In *Louisiana Politics: Festival in a Labyrinth*, edited by James Bolner. Baton Rouge: Louisiana State University Press, 1982.

Wolfinger, Raymond. "Partisan Change in the South, 1952–1976." In *Political Parties: Development and Decay*, edited by Louis Maisel and Joseph Cooper. Beverly Hills, Calif.: Sage, 1978.

Wolfinger, Raymond, and Michael G. Hagen. "Republican Prospects, Southern Comfort." *Public Opinion* 8 (1985): 8–13.

Wolfinger, Raymond, and Steven J. Rosenstone. *Who Votes?* New Haven: Yale University Press, 1980.

Contributors

R. BRUCE ANDERSON is a research associate in the Department of Political Science at Rice University. He has been involved in an extensive research project on state legislatures.

TOD A. BAKER is professor of political science at The Citadel. He has served as a codirector of The Citadel Symposium on Southern Politics since 1978. He has coedited nine books and has written professional papers and journal articles in the fields of southern politics and religion and politics.

JAY BARTH is assistant professor of political science at Hendrix College. His research interests include southern politics, elections, and political behavior.

CHARLES S. BULLOCK III is the Richard B. Russell Professor of Political Science at the University of Georgia. He is the author or coeditor of ten books and dozens of professional papers and journal articles; sits on the editorial boards of the *Journal of Politics, Social Science Quarterly,* and the University of Georgia Press; and is a past president of the Southern Political Science Association.

PATRICK R. COTTER is associate professor of political science at the University of Alabama. His past affiliations with the Capstone Poll at the University of Alabama and the National Network of State Polls have focused much of his research on public opinion and political behavior, especially in the South. He is coauthor of two books and has written numerous journal articles.

THOMAS F. EAMON is professor of political science at East Carolina University. He has published and presented conference papers in the areas of black politics, southern politics, and urban politics.

SAMUEL H. FISHER III is assistant professor of political science at the University of South Alabama. He is the director of the USA Polling Group and has conducted extensive research on Alabama and southern politics.

RONALD KEITH GADDIE is assistant professor of political science at the University of Oklahoma. He is the coauthor of two books and the author or coauthor of numerous articles, conference papers, and technical reports.

LAYNE HOPPE is professor of political science at Texas Lutheran University. His research interests include Congress and international economics.

JOHN J. HOTALING is a former state lobbyist for the teachers' union in Florida and currently serves as a political consultant and freelance journalist. He is the head of Associated Writers, Ink.

CLIFTON McCLESKEY is professor of government at the University of Virginia. He is the author or coauthor of a number of books and journal articles on such topics as mental health, judicial review, Hispanic voting behavior, and Texas politics.

JON L. MILLS is professor of law in the College of Law, University of Florida. A former member of the Florida House of Representatives, where he served as Speaker during the late 1980s, he is also director of the Center for Governmental Responsibility in the College of Law.

LAURENCE W. MORELAND is professor of political science at The Citadel. A codirector of The Citadel Symposium on Southern Politics, he has coedited nine books and has written widely for professional journals and professional conference presentations. He is currently planning a book on the 1996 presidential election in the South.

RICHARD NADEAU is assistant professor of political science at the University of Montreal. His areas of specialization are electoral behavior and public opinion.

RICHARD K. SCHER is professor of political science at the University of Florida. He has written many books and journal articles on southern politics, Florida politics, and voting rights.

HAROLD W. STANLEY is associate professor of political science at the University of Rochester. The author of two books and the coeditor of a third, he has also published extensively in professional journals. He has done much research on southern politics and examined the presidential nominating process during a year that he spent as a visiting research professor at the University of Alabama.

ROBERT P. STEED is professor of political science at The Citadel. He is a codirector of The Citadel Symposium on Southern Politics and is the coeditor of nine books. He has written numerous articles, book chapters, and conference papers and is currently coediting a manuscript on local party activists.

DAVID E. STURROCK is assistant professor of political science at the State University of New York, College at Brockport. He has done research and writing on party behavior and electoral change in the South as well as in California, New York, and Ohio.

FELITA T. WILLIAMS is an instructor of political science at Dekalb College. She was formerly an African American Future Faculty Fellow at the University of Alabama.

Index